Indian Mujahideen
The Secret Jihad in South Asia

INDIAN MUJAHIDEEN

THE SECRET JIHAD IN SOUTH ASIA

Brig. (Retd.) Krishankant S.M

NEHA PUBLISHERS & DISTRIBUTORS
DELHI

Publisher
NEHA PUBLISHERS & DISTRIBUTORS
4832/24,Prahlad Lane,S-207 Ansari
Road, Daryaganj, Delhi-110002
Ph.: 43570976, 23278261
Email: nehapubdistributors@gmail.com

Edition: 2015

ISBN: 978-93-80318-65-3

Laser Typesetting
JEE-VEE Graphics, Delhi

Price: 1195/-

Printed
Vikas Computers, Delhi

Preface

The actual meaning of Mujahideen is a struggler. However in practice, it has been identified with such men who are fighting Jihad (in their own way) for self glorified Islamic cause. Now, it is always related to religious and Islamic connection. The word is also used as some sort of title to Islamic names.

Many names of Muslims proudly carry the word Mujahid because the acts of those who fight for the religion are glorified in Islamic scriptures. As it is, Holy Qoran prescribes that those who die in the cause of Islam and become martyrs attain paradise directly to enjoy all comforts such as company of many virgins. Thus, the word Mujahideen has come to stand for a religious fighter although in real sense the word is not connected to religion.

The Indian Mujahedeen (IM) has emerged as a well-organized jihadi terrorist group in India, claiming responsibility for a number of terror attacks perpetrated in various urban centers of India during 2007-2008. Even though the exact moment of IM's formation is not known, the recent arrest of a number of IM operatives has revealed its possible existence and involvement in terror strikes in India as far back as late October 2005.

Since the IM had been formed on an agenda of waging a violent war against Hindu India, no spell of moderate militancy separated the IM's birth from its first act of violence. Within a relatively short time period, however, the IM underwent three distinct phases of ideological expansion: traversing from a narrow India-centric ideology to revenge-seeking and eventually embracing the concerns of Muslims in other countries.

The present book aims at catering to this curiosity of the readers.

—*Editor*

Contents

Preface (*v*)

1. Understanding the Indian Mujahideen 1

2. Terror and the Indian Mujahideen 32

3. Countering the Indian Mujahideen: India's Counter Terrorism Success 64

4. Indian Mujahideen: Terrorist Group and Great Threat to India 90

5. New Global Threat: Transnational Salafis and Jihad 118

6. The Role of Palestinians in the Transnational Jihad Movement 157

7. Political Destabilization in South and Central Asia: The Role of the CIA-ISI Terror Network 197

8. Second Sunrise of Indian Jihad 252

Bibliography 293

Index 295

1

Understanding the Indian Mujahideen

INTRODUCTION

India has been plagued with insurgency and militancy over the last five decades. The long festering insurgency in northeast India is presently at a low ebb. The khalistani militancy was nipped in the bud in the early 1990s, although there have been renewed attempts at a revival. The militancy in the state of Jammu and kashmir (J&k) has been ongoing for the past two decades. These insurgencies, by and large, have remained confined to their own geographical precincts. however, a disturbing phenomenon has occurred over the past few years. Terrorism, by and large motivated by Islamic *Jihad*, has spread to the Indian hinterland. Increasingly, the targets of attack are not restricted to the state symbols and the security forces, as was the feature in the heyday of the northeast and J&k militancies, but have now extended to the innocent and defenceless civilian populace. The terror attacks today target not only the populace in general but also the economic and commercial hubs of the Indian heartland in particular.

This terrorism, on a pan-Indian scale, has been scripted by Pakistan's Inter-services Intelligence (IsI) through its strategic assets – the Lashkar-e-Tayyeba (LeT), Jaish-e-Mohammed (JeM) and harkat-ul-Jihad-al-Islami (HUJI). To increase deniability and introduce a degree of calibration, the 'terror masters' across the border have now attempted to 'Indianise' terror, by aiding, abetting and nurturing a terrorist organisation called the 'Indian Mujahideen' (IM).

Terror, as India is witnessing today, made its first appearance in the Mumbai serial blasts of 1993, which claimed more than 300 lives. These terror blasts were traced to the Dawood Ibrahim crime syndicate. The October 2005 Delhi blasts, July 2006 Mumbai blasts, March 2007 Varanasi attacks, august 2007 Lumbini Park (hyderabad) blasts – all left a trail of horror, death and fear as never before. These were quickly followed by blasts in Jaipur, Bengaluru, ahmedabad and Delhi in 2008. The distinct feature of these attacks, apart from being intensely ruthless and callous, was the fact that responsibility for them was taken by a group called "Indian Mujahideen".

Who are the Indian Mujahideen? Is it al Qaeda inspired? Or is it an outrider of the LeT, the HUJI or the IsI? Is it another name for the students Islamic Movement of India (SIMI) or a breakaway segment of SIMI? The IM has mutated into a radical extremist organisation, with a pan-Indian spread. Its emergence and radical stand has brought to the fore questions left to be answered by the security and intelligence agencies.

The IM has arrived on the Indian scene casting a deep shadow of Islamic terror, threatening to subsume and consume unsuspecting, poor and desperate sections of the Indian society. The threat that this group poses to the very fabric of the secular and democratic structure of this nation, begs an insight into this new terror signature called the Indian Mujahideen.

ORIGIN AND BRIEF HISTORY

The Pakistani military and IsI have been aiding and abetting terror in India for a long time. The IsI and other fanatic religious groups have been fanning communal hatred by exploiting perceived 'victimisation' or 'marginalisation' of the Muslim population, adding fuel to the fire whenever riots ravage the country. They have been giving different nuances to various ideologies like the wahhabi and Deobandi schools of thought, to give legitimacy to their version of terror in the name of Islam. Drawing their own interpretations of various edicts as enshrined in the *Quran*, there has been an exponential spread of 'radical' teaching in the mushrooming *madrasas*. But it is not only the unsuspecting, helpless and poor sections of the society that have been indoctrinated and manipulated into waging *Jihad* as a legitimate tool of war against non-believers. A study of the *modus operandi* of the IM has shown the role of educated, techno-savvy people in masterminding and executing terror attacks. One such tool that was exploited is the students Islamic Movement of India (SIMI), which gave birth to the IM.

Students Islamic Movement of India (SIMI) Connections SIMI was founded with 250 members on 15 April 1977, by Mohammed ahmedullah siddiqui, as the students' wing of the Jamaat-e-Islami hind (JIh).

JIH was the first organised Islamic reformist movement in India formed in Lahore on 26 august 1941, under the leadership of sayyid abul ala Mawdudi. However, the alliance between the JIH and SIMI lasted only till 1981, when radical student members of SIMI protested against Yasser arafat's visit to India, while the senior JIH leaders saw him as a champion. The rift in ideologies led JIH to abandon SIMI and float a new students' wing, the students Islamic Organisation, while SIMI continued as a separate hardline Islamic organisation.

After breaking away from JIH, SIMI underwent radicalisation, influenced by a number of events, including the Islamic revolution in Iran. SIMI's fanatical position was dictated entirely by geo-political events taking place in the world, which were interpreted as direct attacks on Islam and Muslims. Events, both domestic and international, which led to a shift in SIMI's philosophy were:

- The soviet invasion of Afghanistan and toppling of the shah of Iran by ayatollah khomeini.
- The imposition of harsh *Shariah* laws in Pakistan by General Zia-ul-haq in 1980.
- The demolition of the Babri Masjid in ayodhya in December 1992.
- The militancy in the kashmir Valley since 1989.

SIMI was first banned on 27 September 2001, in the wake of the 9/11 attacks in the United states. The second ban came on 08

February 2008. However, a special tribunal formed under section 4 of the Unlawful activities Act 1967, lifted the ban on SIMI on 05 August 2008, finding insufficient cause for declaring the organisation unlawful. The ban was subsequently reinstated by the Government of India on 25 august 2008, after a supreme Court judgement on the same.

Following the ban on SIMI in 2001, hundreds of SIMI activists were apprehended from various parts of the country. The ban prompted a number of SIMI members to adopt a radical stand and they met regularly to propagate their cause. These meetings saw the emergence of safdar nagori as a chief exponent of the radical militant ideology. Mohammed Islam, previously the chief coordinator of SIMI, however, stood opposed on a moderate stand. These ideological differences resulted in a rift in SIMI. One faction advocated the cause of *Jihad* while the other adopted a softer stand. These differences came to a head in the aftermath of the Godhra riots in 2002. Spurred on by the Godhra carnage, the hardline faction broke away to start a militant wing. This divide, abetted by the ISI, LeT and HUJI, eventually led to the creation of a new militant offshoot organisation of SIMI called the Indian Mujahideen. It was co-founded by riyaz shahbandri and abdul subhan Qureshi. The IM, at this point in time, consisted of students, most of them kashmiris, studying in Deobandi *madrasas* in south Gujarat, andhra Pradesh, karnataka and Maharashtra. Approximately 200 of its members reportedly went to Pakistan for arms and explosives training. It is now believed that the 2008 blasts in India were the handiwork of some of these members, who returned to India after receiving training. In fact, in 2006, 30 students went missing from *madrasas* in Gujarat and it is believed that they were sent to Pakistan to receive training on various aspects of inflicting terror. Three years hence, this group is still at large. On 18 September 2006, four students were arrested from the Tadkeshwar *madrasa* at surat, who revealed the active involvement of LeT operatives in recruiting local *madrasa* students and sending them to Pakistan via Bangladesh for training in terror camps and to avenge the Godhra riots. Following these events, SIMI's, and now the IM's, radicalisation was complete, winning the support of a number of Deobandi Muslims in India, who perceived or were indoctrinated into thinking of themselves as 'victims' of both Hindus and the Indian state. The Indian Mujahideen was, thus, born, tasked by its masters to spread *jihadi* tendencies in India, through homegrown militants, aided, abetted and calibrated from across the borders.

MAJOR INCIDENTS AND CASUALTIES

The first terror attacks for which the IM claimed responsibility were the 23 November 2007 serial blasts in the district court premises of Lucknow, Varanasi and Faizabad in Uttar Pradesh. An e-mail claiming responsibly for the blasts was sent five minutes prior to the blasts to TV news channels from the e-mail address, 'id-guru-alhind@yahoo.fr'. The bombs were planted in tiffin boxes and mounted on bicycles, and contained ammonium nitrate and rDX. The investigation corroborated the role of HUJI-B (Bangladesh) as a key player. Evidence shows that the IM was, at this time, playing second fiddle to HuJI-B, and came to the forefront in keeping with its handlers' – the ISI – diktat to become a self-sustaining terror outfit and 'Indianise' *jihadi* terror. However, the serial blasts across India in 2008 quickly established the IM as a prominent terror outfit.

The year 2007 was utilised by the IM to carry out training camps inside India, in the jungles of kerala, karnataka and Maharashtra. Approximately 100 IM members were trained in the use of Improvised explosive Devices (IeDs). The arrest of safdar nagori in March 2008 was the fuse that set off a wave of IeD bombings across India. In fact, a number of cadres who had earlier gone to Pakistan, had come back in the early months of 2008. The IM claimed responsibility for the attacks in Jaipur (13 May 2008), Bengaluru (15 July 2008), ahmedabad serial blasts (26 July 2008), planting of bombs (which were eventually detected and defused) in surat (28 July to 31 July 2008) and the Delhi serial blasts (13 September 2008). The IM did not claim responsibility for the Mumbai 2006 train blasts, in which, increasingly, the IM hand is being revealed. Also, there have been reports of local support provided by the IM to the LeT assault on Mumbai on 26 November 2008.

Analysis of Terror Incidents

Mumbai 7/11 Train Blasts: This is one of the few attacks in the past few years that the IM did not lay claim to. In fact, days after the 11 July 2006 bombing of Mumbai's suburban train system, the Prime Minister went on national television to assert that he was "certain that the terrorist modules responsible for the blasts are instigated from across the border." More recently, in 2009, however, TV audiences were feted to a videotaped police interrogation that was leaked to the media in which Mumbai resident Mohammed sadiq sheikh confessed that he and four other men had carried out the bombings on behalf of an organisation that has since become well known as the IM. Yet, in November 2006, a 10,667-page chargesheet filed by Maharashtra prosecutors, alleged that seven Pakistani LeT operatives, each paired with an Indian partner, had planted the bombs. Sheikh's testimony leaves room for the possibility that the unidentified Pakistan perpetrators were, in fact, five Indians and more disturbing, that the Indians now being tried for planting the bombs may have had a peripheral role in the attacks or none at all. "Although both the Government of India and Mumbai Police appear convinced that an unassailable case has been built up, serious questions remain on both the integrity and content of the evidence." The question marks over the role of the LeT or the IM or both remain, with Mohdammed sheikh being discharged in May 2009 for his alleged role in the July 2006 Mumbai train blasts, after the Mumbai anti-Terrorism squad (aTs) stated that "there was no prima-facie evidence to prove his involvement but added that he was deeply involved."

In fact, in September 2008, doubts over the real perpetrators had started when the Mumbai Police crime branch arrested five IM operatives and held them responsible for the ahmedabad, Delhi, Mumbai 7/11 and all other blasts since 2005. Sheikh's release indicates the finesse with which IM terrorists operate, in that they leave very few (identifiable) signatures behind. Contradictory claims being made by police officials on different occasions cast serious doubts on investigations and whether the police is getting hold of the right people and is in possession of any evidence to convict or even charge them.

Blasts Outside Uttar Pradesh courts (23 November 2007): a series of near-simultaneous explosions ripped through court complexes in Lucknow, Faizabad and Varanasi, killing 14 and injuring nearly 50 people. An outfit calling itself the Al-Hind Mujahideen claimed responsibility in an e-mail to media houses. The blasts were purportedly carried out in retaliation to the assault by some lawyers on three JeM militants in a Lucknow court. It is now established that these blasts were carried out by a module of IM operatives, led by Mohammed saif, who was arrested from Batla house in new Delhi in September 2008. This module ably supported the HUJI-B in carrying out these blasts.

Jaipur Serial Blasts: On 13 May 2008, nine blasts rocked the Pink City within a span of 20 minutes, starting at 7.25 pm. The tenth bomb was found and defused. This was the first time that the city of Jaipur was subjected to terrorist attacks. Nine bombs in seven locations exploded between 7.25 to 7.45 pm. The blasts were synchronised to inflict maximum casualties. The first two blasts occurred at Manak Chowk and as the crowd ran towards Johri Bazar, another two blasts at the national handloom Centre blocked the exit point, pushing the panicked crowd towards Tripolia Bazaar and Chandpol area, where subsequent blasts caused severe casualties. One of the blasts occurred in the vicinity of hawa Mahal, a popular tourist attraction, while two others occurred outside Hindu temples at sanganeri Gate and Chandpole. The bombs were of low intensity, but by meticulously placing them in highly crowded areas, the terrorists ensured a high death toll. Most of the bombs were planted on locally purchased bicycles in tiffin boxes, containing ammonium nitrate, tightly packed with metal pellets, shrapnel and ball bearings. The bombs were shaped to blast the pellets and shrapnel in a 60 degree arc, for maximum damage, with minimum explosives.

The Indian operational commander of HUJI-B, Mohammed Jalaluddin, arrested in Lucknow in 2007, had revealed during investigations that Jaipur was the prime target in the sights of HUJI-B. Police found credible evidence linking the Jaipur terror suspects to Bangladeshi militants. During interrogations, the bicycle sellers confirmed that the suspected terrorists who bought bicycles spoke Bengali. Two days after the blasts, the IM claimed responsibility for the attacks by sending an e-mail (containing a video) to a private TV channel. The e-mail address used was 'guru_alhindi_ jaipur@yahoo.co.uk'. The video showed a bicycle (serial number 129489) containing a parcel. Police officials confirmed that the bicycle used in Choti Choupad blast had the same serial number. Through the e-mail, the IM sought to caution the nation and threatened to "demolish the faith of the infidels of India". The e-mail was later traced by the police to a Ghaziabad cyber café.

The blasts followed patterns similar to the bomb blasts in hyderabad and Varanasi.

Police and intelligence sources suspect a collaborative effort of HUJI-B, LeT, SIMI and IM. The tactics of attaching bombs onto bicycles bears a resemblance to the November 2007 bombings in Uttar Pradesh by HUJI-B. The responsibility claimed by the IM for the blasts establishes the nexus between HuJI-B and the Indian outfit. In the first week of August 2008, the police made arrests and detained seven persons for questioning. One of the shopkeepers questioned had allegedly sold nine bicycles to a single individual, two days before the blasts took place.

Bengaluru Serial Blasts: On 25 July 2008, a series of nine low intensity bombs went off between 1.20 to 2.35 pm. The bombs were believed to have been planted around hosur and Mysore road, three days prior to the blasts. One unexploded bomb was found on 26 July 2008 and was defused by the bomb disposal squad. The bombs were rudimentary devices, composed of ammonium nitrate and urea, but for the first time, a high-tech micro chip was used that was programmed to go off at a set date and time. Mobile phones were used to trigger the bombs.

The blasts were oriented for maximum psychological impact and the motive was to target and terrorise the IT capital of India. On 29 July 2008, the Bengaluru Police ATS arrested sameer sadiq, a SIMI activist from Bengaluru. On 30 July 2008, the Intelligence Bureau (IB) named rasool khan Parti and Mohammed Sufiya Ahmed Patangiya, both currently residing in Karachi, as the masterminds behind the terror attack.

Ahmedabad Serial Blasts: On 26 July 2008, 18 blasts shook ahmedabad. Most of the blasts took place in commercial areas, where people had gathered for evening shopping, a few in city buses, and two bombs went off near hospitals. Three live bombs were also recovered.

The effect of the blasts was sensational and created panic and fear amongst the people. These went off within an hour at 13 locations. The blasts started off at Jawahar Chowk at 7.45 pm and exploded in different areas of the city. The last two were high intensity blasts, with explosives laden in cars parked near the LG Government hospital and Civil hospital. One blast was averted at the LG Government hospital, in which bombs located in a car, failed to explode.

The IM activists who planned the ahmedabad blasts rented a nondescript house in Vatva area of ahmedabad in the second week of May 2008. It was rented by Zahid shaikh, a native of ahmedabad, who was given the responsibility to set up base. The house was used as the headquarters, where Mufti abu Bashir and Mohammad Qayamuddin, the executors of the blasts, Tauqueer, the group leader, and others stayed to plan and execute the explosions. The house was also used to conduct the necessary reconnaissance to identify potential blast sites and recruit local youth. The operatives vacated the house on 25 July 2008, one day before the blasts were executed.

Investigations revealed that about 40 Muslim boys, of whom 23 were from Gujarat, underwent training in May 2008 from HUJI operatives in Central Gujarat. This training camp is believed to be the final precursor to the ahmedabad blasts. The clockwork precision in the execution of the serial blasts and the statements rendered by the arrested persons also highlight the involvement of the ISI. Most of the bombs were planted on bicycles in tiffin boxes containing low grade explosives, and kept in blue polythene bags similar to the ones used in the Jaipur blasts. The bombs in LG and Civil hospitals were placed in automobiles packed with gas cylinders to cause maximum casualties. all the bombs were placed with timer devices and microprocessors and ammonium nitrate as the explosive device.

Five minutes prior to the blasts, various news channels received a 14page terror e-mail titled "The rise of Jihad" from the IM. The e-mail address used was 'alarbi_gujurat@yahoo.com'. It stated that "ahmedabad will see death in 5 minutes from now. stop it if you can". among other things, the e-mail also claimed that the organisation was taking revenge for the killing of Muslims in the 2002 Gujarat riots. The e-mail was later traced to the IP address of an american national, kenneth haywood, residing at sanpada, navi Mumbai. The unsecured wi-Fi network of the individual was believed to have been hacked to send the e-mail. Hours after the blast, abdul halim, Maulvi of the radical ahl-e-hadith Tanzeem in ahmedabad was apprehended. Three persons, namely, abdul kadir, hasil Mohammed and hussain Ibrahim, were also arrested from ahmedabad. The involvement of at least 50 local youths in the execution of the terror strike is suspected. The police carried out its biggest operation against terror on 16 august 2008, in which nine SIMI activists were arrested in connection with the 26 July 2008 serial blasts.

Surat (Recovery of Live Bombs): The surat police recovered 29 bombs from various parts of the city between 28 July and 31 July 2008. The materials used in the blasts were similar to those used in ahmedabad, except that integrated circuits were used for the preparation of the surat bombs. Investigations revealed that faulty circuits and detonators had rendered the blasts ineffective. The ahmedabad Police crime branch carried out the investigation of the case. About 10 suspects were apprehended for involvement in the case. The apprehended revealed the names of Tanveer Pathan, Zahir Qayamuddin kapadia and sajid Mansuri as the persons responsible for planting the bombs in surat on the directions of abdul subhan Qureshi alias Tauqueer. all the 29 bombs were planted by Tanvir, Zahir and sajid. These bombs were carried in stolen wagonr cars and planted on 24/25 July 2008. On 26 July 2008, Tanvir with Zahir, took two cars and parked them at Puna General hospital and at a doctor's residence in the Varachha area of Surat.

Delhi Serial Blasts: On 13 September 2008, the national capital was rocked by five bomb blasts in high security areas, including Barakhambha road, near India Gate, Connaught Place, Greater kailash and Gaffar Market (karol Bagh). Most of the bombs were placed inside dustbins and contained ammonium nitrate. Four bombs were recovered later and diffused.

The IM claimed responsibility for the blasts in an e-mail titled "Message of Death", which was sent to TV channels. The e-mail claimed that the attack was intended to remind Delhi of the Babri Masjid demolition, stating that it had accomplished "Op BaD", that is, terror strikes in Bengaluru, ahmedabad and Delhi. It also stated that it demonstrated the Indian Mujahideen's capability to strike in Bengaluru, ahmedabad and Delhi, and to strike at will even in high security zones. The e-mail was later traced to the wi-Fi network of kamran Power Control Pvt Ltd in Chembur, Mumbai.

The suspect list of the Delhi serial blasts comprised 13 people. Out of these suspects, two were killed on 19 September 2008, when the Delhi police raided L-18, Batla house, in Jamia nagar. Two other persons were subsequently apprehended on 19 September 2008 and three more on 21 September 2008. A Delhi Police officer, Mohan Chand Sharma, was also killed in the crossfire at Batla House. The Delhi Police claims that at least some members of the Delhi module, led by atif ameen, were also responsible for the hyderabad, Jaipur and ahmedabad serial blasts. a suspect by the name of Zeeshan, in his interrogation, claimed that atif had a good network of confederates in Mumbai and karnataka. He had sent some members to procure explosives used in the Delhi blasts from one sharukh in Manipal, karnataka. atif was also believed to have been preparing sajid (killed in the Batla house encounter) for *fidayeen* attacks.

The Uttar Pradesh ATS arrested one hakim abdul karim, a resident of azmagarh, and a student of biotechnology in Integral University, Lucknow, in January 2009. He is believed to have procured ball bearings for the Delhi blasts from azamgarh on the direction of atif, who wanted to avoid linkages with the Jaipur blasts, for which 20,000 ball bearings were purchased by hakim from Chandni Chowk in Delhi.

Mehrauli Blast: Three people were killed and a few others injured, when two motorcycle-borne youth accidentally dropped a tiffin box packed with crude explosives at a flower market in

Mehrauli on 29 September 2008, just 10 days after the Batla house encounter and the apprehension of the Delhi blasts' IM module. This incident showed that despite the arrests, some members of the module or another similar module were well placed in Delhi to execute attacks at short notice, hence, pointing to the deep spread of the IM or affiliated outfits. The investigation is in progress, to assess leads into the funding and technical support behind these blasts. It is suspected that the perpetrators comprise a nexus of IM, SIMI, LeT, HUJI and ISI. The extent of the nexus and the role of the IM in other serial blasts, including the Varanasi court blasts in November 2007, are also under the scanner.

Mumbai Attacks (26 November 2008): while the involvement of the LeT in the 26/11 assault is without doubt, it is difficult to believe that an assault of this scale and magnitude could have been possible without local support. In an e-mail to local news stations, an organisation calling itself the "Deccan Mujahideen" claimed responsibility for the Mumbai strike during the initial phases of the attack. While the IM's role in the attack is yet to be officially confirmed, at least two of the terrorists, whose conversations were intercepted during the course of the assault, indicated that they were linked to terrorists of the Islamist persuasion in India. One of the terrorists phoned a news station, demanding that *jihadis* be released from prison in exchange for the hostages. "We want all *mujahideen* held in India to be released and only after that we will release the people", a man named sahadullah told a media outlet. "Please release all the *mujahideen* and Muslims in India should not be troubled."

The e-mail sent by the IM to media houses immediately after the Delhi blasts on 13 September 2008 had also threatened deadly attacks in Mumbai. "You threatened to murder them and your mischief went to such an extent that you even dared to abuse and insult Maulana Mahmood-ul-hasan Qasmi and misbehaved with the Muslim women and children there.... If this is the degree to which your arrogance has reached, and if you think that by these stunts you can scare us, then let the Indian Mujahideen warn all the people of Mumbai that whatever deadly attacks you will face in future, the only responsible elements for it will be the Mumbai

ATS and their guardians: Vilasrao Deshmukh and rr Patil." The message warned ATS officials, "You are already on our hit-list and this time very very seriously." This could be another indicator of some local terrorist elements or their supporters being aware of an impending attack. ajmal amir kasab has also revealed during his interrogation that the strike on Mumbai was scheduled for September 2008, but called off at the last minute.

The recent arrest in the United states of David Coleman headley a.k.a Daood Gilani and Tahaawur hussain rana, american and Canadian nationals respectively, both of Pakistani origin, has further brought to light the role of local sleeper cells in the assault on Mumbai on 26 November 2008. Technical intercepts available with the Federal Bureau of Investigation (FBI) have revealed that some IM members of the Delhi module had contacted headley, in an attempt to flee the country, after the Delhi blasts in September 2008. This indicates their prior interaction with headley, who ran an agency facilitating immigration from Tardeo, Mumbai. Their repeated visits to India and Pakistan seem to have established a pattern of carrying out reconnaissance for the LeT of prospective targets and the same is suspected in the case of the Mumbai attacks as well. Coupled with their contact with local youth in several Indian cities, this scenario further reveals their linkages and the utilisation of Indian youth in providing logistical support for LeT attacks. This support base could well have constituted IM members as well. Therefore, the headley-rana cell further crystallises the bonding between the LeT and IM in carrying out attacks on Indian soil. It is imperative to identify and neutralise several such 'sleeper cells' still active in India.

Thus, it is evident that Pakistani *jihadi* organisations have established in the IM, a rich source of local support modules, who can do the spade work (scouting and identifying vulnerable locations) for executing terror attacks in major Indian cities well in advance and provide logistics support (stocking and ferrying munitions, prepare hideouts) to actual executers from across the border, who would converge at the striking location only on the eve of launching an attack. a similar pattern has emerged in the aforementioned blasts, where some members of the local modules helped in arranging safe hideouts and masqueraded as street vendors at the blast sites for 15 days to more than a month ahead of carrying out the blasts. This helped them to obtain intimate knowledge about the locations and routine police deployments. The difference next time could be a collaboration with better or foreign trained terrorists and the use of different methods to carry out strikes.

Goals/Objectives

Drawing from the radical Deobandi philosophy, the leaders of the IM have adopted an external and militant posture on what they believe to be various issues of concern to the Muslim community. The stated goal of the IM is to 'liberate India' from the influence of Western materialistic culture and further its conversion into an Islamic society.

Minutes before the bombs went off in the three trial court complexes in Uttar Pradesh on 23 November 2007, the IM issued the first (of a series of) 'Manifesto' explaining its actions. It referred to "the pathetic conditions of Muslims in India that idol worshippers can kill our brothers, sisters and outrage the dignity of our sisters at any time and place."

But the manifesto went on to make a far broader point, characterising the IM's bombing campaign as "a war for civilisation." Its authors stated that the organisation wanted to "empower society from injustice, corruption, etc, which is prevailing in society nowadays. Only Islam has the power to establish a civilised society and this could be only possible in Islamic rule, which could be achieved by only one path, *Jihad-Fee-Sabilillah*" (which means *Jihad* in Islam).

Leadership

Dr shahid Badar Jalah was SIMI's President and safdar nagori its General secretary, till the organisation was proscribed in September 2001. The Delhi Police arrested Jalah on 28 July 2008 from his office in Zakir Nagar, Delhi, and charged him with sedition and inciting communal disharmony. however, he was acquitted on 11 November 2008. On 27 March 2008, SIMI's General secretary safdar nagori was arrested, along with 12 other cadres at Indore. Following nagori's arrest, the mantle passed into the hands of Mufti abu Bashir, who has since been arrested. The co-founders of the IM are riyaz Ismail shahbandri and abdus subhan Qureshi alias Tauqeer.

The names of suspected leaders as also names of the Delhi groups are given below:

- abdul subhan Qureshi alias Tauqeer, 36 – a software engineer from Mumbai, an expert in bomb-making and an expert hacker (co-founder).
- riyaz Ismail shahbandri (co-founder).
- Mufti abu Bashir, 28 – architect of the transformation from SIMI to Indian Mujahideen.
- Safdar Nagori, 38 – architect of the transformation from SIMI to Indian Mujahideen.
- Qayamuddin Kapadia, 28 – a trader from Vadodara, he started the first-ever mosque of the *Ahle Hadis Tanzeem* in Vadodara a few years ago.
- sajid Mansuri, 25 – a graduate in psychology and formerly a marketing executive.
- Usman agarbattiwala, 25 – a PG diploma holder in human rights from Vadodara.
- Alamzeb afridi, 24 – an unemployed youth from ahmedabad. He purchased bicycles and then planted them in ahmedabad after mounting the explosives on them.
- abdul razik Mansuri, 27 – an embroidery unit owner.
- Mujib shaikh, 25 – a stone polishing artisan.
- Zahid shaikh, 27 – a mobile phone repair shop owner from ahmedabad.
- amil Parwaz – a native of Ujjain, believed to be involved in the court complexes bomb blasts in Uttar Pradesh in November 2007.

The local group at Delhi is thought to include the following people, most of them from azamgarh:

- Mohammad atif (24) alias Bashir – alleged planner and recruiter, killed in the Jamia nagar encounter on 19 September 2008. he is alleged to have planted a bomb at

M-block market in Greater kailash-I (new Delhi) and the Varanasi bombs.

- Mohammad saif – arrested from Batla house in Jamia nagar after the 19 September encounter. he is alleged to have planted a bomb at regal Cinema in Connaught Place (new Delhi).
- Zeeshan – arrested after the Jamia nagar encounter. He is alleged to have planted a bomb at Barakhamba road in Connaught Place.
- Mohammed sajid (16) alias Pankaj – killed during the Jamia nagar encounter. he is alleged to have planted a bomb at Barakhamba road in Connaught Place.
- Junaid – escaped during the Jamia nagar encounter. He is alleged to have planted a bomb at M-block market in Greater kailash-I (new Delhi) and the Varanasi bombs.
- Mohammad shakeel – arrested on 21 September 2008 from Jamia nagar. He is alleged to have planted a bomb at nehru Place in south Delhi.
- Zia-ur-rehman – arrested on 21 September 2008 from Jamia nagar. He is alleged to have planted a bomb at Connaught Place and on a cycle in ahmedabad.
- saqib nisar – arrested on 21 September 2008 from Jamia nagar.
- shahzad alias Pappu – escaped during the Jamia nagar encounter. He is alleged to have planted a bomb at Central Park, Connaught Place.
- alihas Malik – he is alleged to have planted a bomb at Central Park, Connaught Place.
- Mohammad khalif, arif and salman.

APPRAISAL OF KEY IM CADRES AT LARGE

The IM's future strike capabilities are critically dependent on two men who are central to its plans and are still at large. One of them is riyaz Bhatkal, who organised the quasi-industrial production, the ready-to-assemble ammonium nitrate–based 'U' shaped bombs used in the IM's bombing campaign. The second is abdul subhan Qureshi. Riyaz Bhatkal is a Pakistani trained operative, who on returning to India, put together the bomb manufacturing cell of the IM, consisting mostly of small-time businessmen like arrested suspects ahmad Baba abu Bakr, ali Mohammad ahmad, Javed Muhammad ali and syed Mehmood naushad. Iqbal Bhatkal (riyaz's brother) carried out another round of recruitment through clerical networks. among them was Peerbhoy, a software engineer, who helped design and produce the terror e-mails, secured IM manifestos, and who was expected to testify against his one time associate, but later declined.

The other person recruited was kerala's abdul sattar alias saibuddin, and nasir, who formed a key part of the circle of south Indian *jihadists* recruited by the Bhatkal brothers. Both nasir and sattar had fought street battles for kerala politician abdul Madani (now acquitted in the 1998 serial bombings in Coimbatore) against the rashtriya swayamsewak sangh (rss), on behalf of the terrorist group al-Umma. sattar was known to have fabricated pipe bombs in the 1993 Bombay serial blasts. These two men were allegedly involved in a plot to assassinate kerala Chief Minister ek nayanar. sattar and nasir, the police claim, supplied much of the ammonium nitrate used in bombs built by Bhatkal in Gujarat. evidence also exists that the Bhatkal brothers had sent upwards of 40 men for military training in camps in Pakistan. Incidentally, four kerala men training with the Lashkar in north kashmir were shot dead by the Army in Lolab Valley, while attempting to exfiltrate into Pakistan-occupied kashmir (Pok) for arms training. One of those shot was sattar's son-in-law.

The other key man arrested (and now acquitted) was Mohammad sadiq sheikh, who had recruited atif amin (killed in the Jamia encounter in September 2008). Mumbai police investigators believe that as yet unidentified (suspected) Pakistanis, who helped execute the July 2006 suburban train bombings, were not Pakistanis at all, but amin and other members of the azamgarh cell.

Like the Bhatkal brothers, abdul subhan Quereshi, a co-founder of the IM is still at large. The son of working class parents who had migrated to Mumbai, Qureshi, like the Bhatkal brothers, too, had received technical education. he obtained a diploma in industrial electronics in 1995 and went on to work at several private IT firms in Mumbai. At the time of joining SIMI in 2001, he was working on a wipro project to set up an intranet in Bharat Petro Chemicals. Qureshi orchestrated the September 2008 bombings in Delhi and had the critical and complex task of helping local cells of *jihadists* knit together into a single entity. In the ahmedabad attacks, Qureshi mated Bhatkal's bomb making assets with a group of SIMI operatives, raised by computer graphics designer Qayamuddin kapadia, who, in turn, provided safe houses and logistical support for atif amin's (killed in Jamia encounter) assault team. riyaz Bhatkal and Qureshi are credited with making IM a self-sustaining terrorist network in India. "In the wake of the Mumbai bombings of 2006, the Lashkar came under intense pressure from Pakistan President Pervez Musharraf's regime to scale back operations against India. Lakhvi and other Lashkar Commanders prodded Qureshi, Bhatkal and sheikh (arrested and acquitted) to set up a self-sustaining network in India."

Weapons, Communication Systems and Training Camps

In 2007, a number of training camps were held in various forest locations in India, where Pakistani-trained activists imparted training to the IM cadres in manufacturing IeDs from locally available materials, like ammonium nitrate (used in fertilizers) and hydrogen peroxide (h2O2) for mass casualty actions. Though not as powerful as service rDX or plastic explosives, these materials, when used in multiple strikes, could create mayhem and panic.

The IM terrorists appear to possess great expertise in assembling IeDs from locally available low grade explosive materials such as ammonium nitrate and then fabricating them with ball bearings or iron nails. such training may have been provided to select Indian boys in Pakistan, at the behest of the ISI, and they, in turn, would have passed on their skills to other IM terrorists back home. One such facility being run could be that of azam Cheema, a former Chemistry professor at Lahore University, who trains militants of the LeT, JeM, hM (hizbul Mujahideen)and other splinter groups in bomb making, assembling of IeDs and in the use of ammonium nitrate, at his residential laboratory in

Faisalabad. He had to leave his college job at the coercion of the Jammat-ud-Dawa, for which he now works. The trained 'bomb experts' are then sent to different states of India, where explosives are now 'internally available' and need not be smuggled from across the border. District authorities in Pakistan do not take any action, as this activity receives the 'patronage' of high-ranking ISI officials.

The interrogation of Safdar Nagori, arrested on 07 March 2008, has revealed that the IM is now experimenting with peroxide-based improvised explosives, the kind used in the London 7/7 bombings of 2005. The chemical used in manufacturing these bombs is acetone peroxide (the chemical that was used by richard reid, the shoe bomber) and had been found in one of the (7/7) bombers' house in Leeds, england. The frightening reality that someone can build such bombs – weapons of mass casualty attacks – sitting at home, has brought terror to an unimaginable proximity. The IM is expected to use peroxide-based bombs because they are apprehensive that the Government of India would clamp down on its access to readily available explosives and ammonium nitrate fertilizers, as also due to drying up of supplies from its sponsor (ISI). according to riazuddin nasir (captured in November 2007), the IM has at least 15-20 cadres who manufacture bombs at home.

Maj Gen GD Bakshi, "In so far as communication is concerned, this brand of terrorists does not leave behind electronic signatures, use internet or just face to face communications." Training camps of IM have been located in Vagamon, kerala (December 2007), Pavagarh and Vadodara (January 2008).

Ideology

The IM ideology draws from the wahhabi philosophy of the Deobandi school, which practises a rigid, puritanical version of Islam. all the arrested members of the IM and SIMI, so far, have been students of Deobandi *madrasas* from Bharuch, Ujjain, azamgarh and saharanpur. Saudi arabia has sponsored the spread of wahhabism extensively. In the past 50 years, almost 1,500 mosques and about 10,000 *madrasas* worldwide have been funded by organisations in saudi arabia to promote their cause. It has sponsored the training of *imams*, domination of mass media, and the distribution of wahhabi literature and endowments to universities in exchange for influence over the appointment of wahhabi Islamic scholars. Also referred to as "Petro Islam", saudi charities funded the growth of the wahhabi school of thought throughout the world, when oil prices tripled in the 1970s. when the erstwhile soviet Union invaded Afghanistan, saudi arabian charities funded the Afghan Mujahideen to take on the communists. All its fighters, including the Taliban, were nurtured in *madrasas* on the Afghanistan-Pakistan border, teaching wahhabi, sunni, and ahl-e-hadith schools of thought.

In India, shah waliullah (1703-1762) formed the Deoband school and the ahl-e-hadith school of thought. The Deoband *madrasa* was founded in 1867 by Mohammad Abid Husayn in Saharanpur, UP, influenced by Shah waliullah. In 1879, the institution assumed the additional name of Darul-Ulum (abode of Islamic Learning). The Deobandi wahhabis advocate that a Muslim's first loyalty is to his religion and only then to his country. Secondly, Muslims should recognise only the religious frontiers of their *ummah* (community) and not national frontiers. Thirdly, they have a sacred right and obligation to go to any country to wage *Jihad* to protect the Muslims of that country. The Deobandi and ahle-e-hadith schools were revived in India through funding by Saudi charities, when oil prices skyrocketed in the 1970s. Significantly, a majority of terror groups like the JeM, HUJI, LeT, hua and now the IM owe 'allegiance' to the Deobandi *madrasas* and the Mawdudi school of thought.

Thus, the Deobandi school of thought and wahhabism combined to form an extremist version of radical Islam, which advocates the prominence of *Jihad* for Islamisation. Their prime agenda has been the spread of radical Islam in India, south asia and southeast Asia, where the majority of the world's Muslims live. The Deobandi interpretation of Islamic teachings is also widely practised in Pakistan. It shares the Taliban's restrictive view of women and regards the minority Shias as non-Muslim. Most of the Taliban leadership is known to have attended Deobandi-influenced seminaries in Pakistan. The Deobandi and ahl-e-hadith schools adhere to an absolutely fundamentalist view of Islam, which is influenced by Wahhabi ideology. The Deobandi school has no use for the moderate Barelvi school of thought, which pursues a moderate Sufi version of Islam.

The IM's roots are owed to the Jamaat-e-Islami, the organisation which gave birth to SIMI, from which the IM draws many of its cadres. "Jihad-Feesabilillahi" was the title of a 1939 essay by Maulana abul ala Mawdudi. This essay was in possession of Mohammad sadiq sheikh at the time of his arrest for a suspected role in the Mumbai train blasts. sheikh had picked up this material from a hyderabad seminary named after Mawdudi. It is believed by investigators that sheikh was recruited into the IM by Mujahid salim – the son of the controversial cleric, Maulana abdul Ilahi Mawdudi.

The pursuit of political power, rather than a hotchpotch of beliefs, prayers and rituals was integral to the practice of the religion. "Islam", he insisted, "is a revolutionary ideology which seeks to alter the social order of the entire world and rebuild it in conformity with its own tenets and ideals." It was imperative for Muslims to "seize the authority of state, for an evil system takes root and flourishes under the patronage of an evil government and a pious cultural order can never be established, until the authority of government is wrested from the wicked." Indeed, Mawdudi insisted that the word 'Muslims' referred not to a religious community but a politically bound "international revolutionary party."

"The party of Muslims," Mawdudi concluded, "will inevitably extend the invitation to citizens of other countries to embrace the faith which holds out the promise of true salvation and genuine welfare. At the same time, if the Muslim party commands enough resources, it will eliminate un-Islamic governments and establish the power of Islamic governance in their place." Mawdudi's position was closely tied to questions of communal politics and its impact on identity formation, as also to questions of power in pluralistic societies and to nationalism. This world view, nasr writes, was "informed by the acute despair that gripped the community (Muslim) in the early decades of the 20th century." Mawdudi saw the arya samaji religious revivalism as an existential threat, a proof of the inherent animosity of Hindus towards Islam.

Mawdidi's ideas fired the imagination of Islamist ideologues like Sayyed Qutb and hassan al-Banna, the ideological progenitors of al Qaeda. The Mawdudi essay found in possession of sadiq sheikh at the of his arrest for the 7/11 blasts, is a pointer to the driving ideological force behind the IM. Prior to his arrest, sheikh enjoyed great respect from, and companionship with, the co-founders of the IM, Qureshi and shah Bandri, as well as with several figures linked to the Mumbai train bombings, including Feroze Deshmukh and ehtesham siddiqui.

SIMI statement in 1996 declared that democracy and secularism had failed to protect Muslims (post-1992 Babri Masjid demolition) and, hence, its sole option was to struggle for an Islamic Caliphate. During its last convention in September 2001 (before being banned), SIMI praised Osama as a "true *Mujahid*". In the wake of the Godhra riots, Hafiz Saeed, the LeT founder had stated that "the Hindu is a mean enemy and the proper way to deal with him is the one adopted by our forefathers, who thrashed them by force." since 2003, when Lashkar-trained hyderabad resident asad Yazdani assassinated haren Pandya, the new Indian *jihadists* – the IM – have been following this advice of Hafiz to the hilt.

The intelligence community believes that the serial blasts in Bengaluru and allahabad were executed by a network of wahhabi fundamentalists, masquerading as the Indian Mujahideen. "This terror network started by organising blasts at holy places of rival Barelvi Muslims like the dargah of khwaja Moinuddin Chisti in ajmer, rajasthan… thousands of publications have been brought out by them to convince Muslims to follow the path of 'true Islam'. Members of several front organisations also visit homes to convince people to abandon non-Islamic rituals….These activities have been vehemently opposed by the Barelvis, who also brought out publications countering the Wahhabi ideology, which is believed to provide a theological justification for terror… last straw was the blast at ajmer sharif…. It provoked widespread reaction among the Barelvis against wahhabi fanaticism, which had backed the SIMI." A senior intelligence official has opined, "Fearing their isolation, the Wahhabi elements are now trying to project themselves as people fighting against injustice to Muslims as a whole. The decision to organise serial blasts in ahmedabad, including four in narendra Modi's constituency, was clearly aimed at getting the sympathy of the Muslim masses." The intelligence officer added, "There is a big vacuum in the Muslim leadership and the wahhabis are planning to fill the gap with their violent deeds."

INTERNATIONAL LINKAGES AND FINANCIAL SUPPORT

Interaction with intelligence agencies has revealed the following:

- The banned SIMI, and now the IM, has been receiving generous financial assistance from the world assembly of Muslim Youth (waMY), riyadh, and also maintains close links with the International Islamic Federation of students' Organisation (IFsO) in kuwait. It also has links with the Chicago-based Consultative Committee of Indian Muslims.
- Groups of SIMI sympathisers exist in several Gulf countries. Jamayatul ansar, an organisation of SIMI activists comprising expatriate Indian Muslims, operates in Saudi arabia.
- Several Islamic fundamentalist organisations like the Tamil nadu Muslim Munnetra kazhagam (TMMk), kerala-based national Democratic Front (nDF) and Islamic Youth Centre (IYC) are believed to be providing covert support.
- The outlawed organisation receives funds, training and motivation from the Pakistani ISI. "The bureau is convinced that the IM has been trained by the ISI, which was why the blasts (Bengaluru and ahmedabad) could be executed with professional precision."

The Formalisation of the IM into a Militant Outfit: The formalisation of the IM into a militant outfit was conceived at a meeting of SIMI, LeT and HUJI in kotli, Pok, on 03 May 2008. The terror masterminds of LeT and HUJI had a one-point agenda – an Indian feel to the concept of *Jihad*. It is confirmed by intelligence sources that the Jaipur, Bengaluru and ahmedabad blasts were planned jointly in the presence of LeT and HUJI leaders at the kotli meeting. The decision to trigger serial blasts across India within a short span of time was also taken during this meeting.

ISI Links: Safdar Nagori denied having direct links with the ISI. he did, however, concede to having receiving support from LeT and HUJI. Nagori had also visited the kashmir awareness Bureau in 1996-97, where he met Maulvi abbhas ansari, the executive member of the hurriyat Conference; Mirwaiz Umar Farooq and Yasin Malik of the Jammu and kashmir Liberation Front (JkLF). he had also attended the Iftar party given by Pakistani ambassador riaz khokhar, along with saif nachan and abdul subhan Qureshi alias Tauqeer, in new Delhi. This was the beginning of direct ISI involvement with SIMI.

JeI Links: SIMI/IM members share close ties with the Jamaat-e-Islami (JeI) units in Pakistan, nepal and Bangladesh. They also have a close working relationship with the Islami Chhatra shibir (ICs), the students wing of the Jel in Bangladesh.

Kashmir Links: According to official reports, it is believed that SIMI/IM cadres and kashmiri terrorists were brought together by the ISI through Jel (Pak).

HuJI-B Links: SIMI/IM maintain close links with HUJI-B. There have been reports of HUJI-B recruiting Bangladeshis in India, who have managed to secure ration cards, driving licences and voter identity cards.

LeT Links: The interrogation report of sarfraz nawaz of IM, arrested in Bengaluru, has revealed that the Bengaluru bombings were carried out under the direct command of the LeT. The LeT recruited one IM operative named nazeer, who was a key planner in the IM strike in Bengaluru. however, it was only after the arrest of Muscat entrepreneur ali abdul aziz al-hooti by the Oman Police in January 2009, that investigators in both countries were able to begin unravelling the complex network that existed between the IM bombings in southern India and the LeT assault on Mumbai of 26/11, and a series of planned bombings in west Asia. al-hooti was a key LeT pointsman in Oman. He funnelled funds to LeT and IM operatives in India through Sarfaraz Nawaz of the IM and Mohammad Jaffen of the LeT. Significantly, Alhooti had visited

Mumbai between 10 and 17 November 2008, as revealed by the Maharashtra Police. earlier, in 2007, al-hooti had arranged to ship a LeT operative Fahim ansari from Dubai to an LeT camp in Pakistan. Fahim ansari, arrested by the Uttar Pradesh Police for his alleged role in the rampur Central reserve Police Force (CrPF) camp attack case, is now being tried on charges of having generated a videotape of Mumbai hotels, stations and hospitals, which was used to train the LeT 26/11 assault team. Sarfaraz nawaz of IM, who was working in Muscat, was put in touch with al-hooti through *jihadist* friends in a mosque. It is known that nawaz had joined SIMI in 1996 and was elected to its central committee five years later. His close associates included Safdar Nagori, Yahya kama kutty and abdul shiby, all key architects of the IM.

The debate over the presence or lack of "local support" to the terrorists who attacked Mumbai on 26 November 2008 has been put to rest by the city police's chargesheet made public in February 2009. The chargesheet is categorical that there was indeed local support from within India for the *jihadi* posse that left karachi. "Indeed, the Pakistan and LeT-backed training facilities that some of the Indian Mujahideen-allied terrorists arrested over the past year have spoken of, do suggest the 'external' and 'internal' sources of *Jihad* are not hermetically insulated. The degree of inter-operability and mutual dependence may not be absolute but is not non-existent either. rather than living in denial, the government needs to recognise this."

Al Qaeda/Qaedism and IM: The common strain in ideology among the LeT, HUJI, JeM, IM and al Qaeda has prompted many experts to ponder whether SIMI/IM was the next target of al Qaeda/Qaedism. India's former national security advisor Mk narayanan has stated, "Today, the al Qaeda mindset, even more than the al Qaeda network, provides the most pervasive threat to asian and international stability."

Deductions

Vague Leadership Structure: not much is yet known about who controls the levers within the IM. Although security agencies have identified abdul subhan Qureshi and the Bhatkal brothers as having played crucial leadership roles in the planning and execution of the blasts in the past two years, it seems that the IM is still managed by mentors from the ISI and LeT.

After all, it is these outfits, which have raised and nurtured it. Instructions to carry out blasts, the timing and target sites, are probably dictated by these mentors from across the border, leaving the execution and precise locations, strike dates, etc to the leadership, led by people like Qureshi and Bhatkal.

Proxy: The IM has emerged as another tool in the hands of subversive elements within Pakistan and their *jihadi* brotherhood to torment India. It provides a degree of 'Indianess' or a 'home-grown' terror tag and helps mask Pakistan's complicity in the attacks. sponsors of terror could, therefore, continue to calibrate attacks against India, utilising its various tools such as Pakistani/ kashmiri terrorists and now the home-grown ones, including the IM.

Kerala Youth in Kashmir: LeT recruiters seem to have succeeded in leading a sizeable number of youth into the *jihadi* fold from south India, especially kerala. In October 2008, four boys from kerala were killed by the army in Lolab Valley of north kashmir. The subsequent interrogation of three men from South Kashmir, who had trained along with the five Kerala boys and seven Pakistanis in the wani-Dorusa Forest of Lolab in September 2008 confirmed their participation in the camp. The Special Investigation Team (sIT) of kerala Police obtained information that a terror brigade of 185 keralites was selected by the LeT and provided preliminary training at camps in various centres in kannur and ernakulam. Yasin, Fayaz, shakeer alias rahim and Fayiz, who were killed in encounters with the army in kashmir, and abdul Jabbar, who had escaped the scene, constituted the pilot team sent by the kerala terror *gurus* to kashmir. The three kashmiri youth from shopian revealed, "The Malayalis joined the camp in the second week of September. shakeer alias rahim was their leader. he could speak Urdu."

The five Keralites, who had attended the terror training, wanted to go to Pakistan and get advanced training in weaponry. "Their plan was to go back to kerala after being trained in Pakistan and engage in terrorist and anti-national activities." shabbir ahammed

Tali told the police that 180 more youngsters were waiting in kerala after the preliminary training to join *Jihad*. "One *Ustad* had indoctrinated them," said Tali. The SIT officers had cross-checked this information with Fiaz ahmad and reshi, who said they were also aware of it. The police deduced that the *Ustad* they were referring to was haji Ustad alias Thadiyantavide nazir haji, who is currently absconding. all these people may be IM members, acting for LeT, to coopt Indian citizens into terrorism.

Tactics: Till now, the IM members have succeeded in carrying out blasts by assembling and placing IeDs. The Delhi Police chargesheet of the serial blasts case reveals that atif ameen (killed during the Batla house encounter) wanted to prepare sajid (killed along with atif) for *fidayeen* attacks. This, coupled with the above incident of the youth from kerala attempting to reach Pok for *jihadi* training, akin to the instruction received by Pakistani, kashmiri and other foreign terrorists in the various camps in Pakistan/Pok, could be an attempt to use Indian militants in future *fidayeen* attacks or fire-assaults like Mumbai. This could then provide another layer of deniability for the Pakistani mentors in major terrorist attacks.

Counter-Measures Adopted by the State

In the aftermath of the Mumbai carnage, the government came out with a slew of measures, such as the Unlawful activities (Prevention) amendment act, revamping police and intelligence structures, strengthening coastal security, raising new national security Guards (nsG) hubs, creating a national Investigative agency (nIa), among others. Decades-old schemes such as the national ID Card and Database Project are being rejuvenated. In the recent past, a number of terrorist modules have reportedly been broken up by the police and intelligence agencies all over the country. However, the IM has been successful in establishing a pan-India network with a large number of sleeper cells in the Indian heartland, waiting to be activated as per calibrated requirements.

Recommendations

The following measures may be considered, to curtail the spread of the IM:

- Reforming Madrasa Education: a sizeable number of IM members were well educated and held decent jobs, but were still successfully indoctrinated by hardline Deobandi and wahhabi elements. Leading astray the aggrieved and the poor would be even easier. The Union human resources Development (hrD) Ministry should undertake a study of the kind of education being imparted in the large number of privately-funded (mostly from Gulf countries) *madrasas* mushrooming all over the country, especially in the border areas. The government can then revamp the education system, by implementing more job-oriented and professional education at government-run institutions and also restrict the influence of *madrasas* on Muslim society, especially the hardline ones. Muslims should be encouraged to send their children to open schools and colleges, rather than to single-religion *madrasas*, where they learn in isolation and hence, can sometimes develop a closed and rigid outlook towards society in general. Ghettoisation of the community should be prevented.
- Employment Opportunities: The findings of the Sachar Committee should be comprehensively studied. equal and non-discriminatory job opportunities should be created for all. The private sector should be asked to be more affirmative in this regard, and allegations of discrimination in jobs due to religion or creed should be seriously monitored and addressed by the government. Similarly, by way of agrarian and land reforms in rural areas, the exploitation of poor land labourers should be prevented.
- Political Leadership: a far greater degree of responsibility and leadership should be expected from the Muslim MPs and MLas. They should strive for the upliftment and emancipation of Muslims of their constituencies and be able to instill confidence among them against their perceived fears and vulnerabilities.
- Unbiased Police Action: Police investigations should not be hampered due to political or religious considerations. similarly, the police should not be seen to be acting in a prejudicial manner against the minorities.

- Local Surveillance: a factor which helps the IM cover its tracks well is that many of its members do not have a past record of crime and, hence, evade police scrutiny. A watch should be kept by local police on young boys attending *madrasas* in their respective localities. Students from outside states residing in *madrasas* should be accounted for. Such issues can best be handled by local policemen belonging to the Muslim community, as also by community elders. Incentives should be given for providing information on suspected individuals and activities. More Muslims should be recruited by the intelligence agencies. Community leaders can play an important role in encouraging young men to eschew the path of violence and point out the futility of such means.
- Technical Surveillance: Though prone to misuse, laws which facilitate easy tapping of suspects' communication by intelligence agencies should be passed by the Parliament. The sale of new mobile connections and SIM cards should be strictly regulated and the police should ensure that vendors follow the mandatory procedures. New cell phone connections should be made operational only after a physical verification of the address provided.
- Regulating Use of Commonly-used Explosives: IM members have been able to wreak havoc by fabricating crude explosives with shrapnel. The easy availability of crude chemicals and mixtures such as ammonium nitrate used in fertilizers and gelatin sticks for mining (blasting), should be regulated. The government can designate certain authorised distributors for their sale.
- Close Watch on Criminals and Underworld: More and more interlinkages are developing between terrorist groups, the underworld and criminal elements, due to mutual activities such as drug-trafficking and gun-running. These criminal elements can provide logistics and local support to the terrorists in facilitating their strikes in Indian cities. Therefore, criminals should be tackled seriously and a close watch kept over their activities. Linkages between

politicians and the mafia tend to prevent the police, in certain states, from taking action. This could, in turn, provide safe havens to terrorists.

Stifling Resources: steps should be taken by the intelligence agencies and the Finance Ministry for identifying and blocking the funding/income channels of such groups, which are routed through non-governmental organisations (nGOs) and religious charities, both in India and abroad. A ban, though for the most part a cosmetic step, would display the resolve of the government in tackling the IM.

Conclusion

It is beyond doubt now that terror groups have established a pan-Islamic network, with a large number of sleeper sells in the hinterland, with extreme linkages with J&k, the global terrorists, and the ISI. In the recent past, a number of terrorist modules have been broken up in all metropolitan cities, and hitherto unaffected areas in the country.

Bomb blasts in Jaipur, Bengaluru, and ahmedabad, and a suspected involvement as the support element to the LeT attack in Mumbai on 26/11, are pointers towards the increasing focus of the global *jihadis* in league with the Indian *jihadi* arm, like the IM, on targeting economic prosperity in the Indian hinterland. The audacity with which the terrorists struck the two key Indian cities of Bengaluru and ahmedabad on two consecutive days clearly indicates the level of preparedness and coordination of these attacks without compromising the security of the plan and risk the identification of a large number of perpetrators (minimum of 40-50 persons) in the execution of the plan. A support group of at least 40 IM members is suspected to have assisted the LeT terror attack on Mumbai what is of great concern is that, despite its best efforts, and incentives and monetary rewards to informers, the police has not been able to make much headway in the investigation on the Bengaluru and ahmedabad blast cases. Indian intelligence agencies believe that the IM is a front group, created by the LeT and HUJI, to confuse investigations and cover the tracks of SIMI.

The Delhi Police, however, believes that though the IM is an offshoot of SIMI, it is actually a different group connected to the

LeT. Notwithstanding the accuracy of either of the views, it is beyond doubt that the Indian Mujahideen broke away from SIMI as a hardline faction, and in any case, owes its legacy to it. What is worrisome is that despite a ban on SIMI in 2001, it continued to exist in some form or the other over the past six to seven years or so, before giving birth to the Indian Mujahideen. Another source of worry is that most of the activists recruited so far have been well educated, and quite a few of these belong to Deobandi *madrasas* and are influenced by Mawdudi's hardline views or wahhabi fundamentalism. Intelligence agencies have been patting themselves on the back on having arrested a number of IM activists. But the greater challenge is to get them convicted – the recent acquittal of Mohammad sadiq sheikh is a case in point.

After atif amin of the IM was killed in the Jamia nagar encounter in September 2008, the intelligence agencies were beginning to write the epitaph for the IM until Mumbai 26/11 happened. After the initial furore over the unmistakable LeT hand in the carnage had died down, experts began to realise that this mammoth operation involved colossal administrative support, which would not have been possible without a local hand. Intelligence agencies have begun to seriously investigate the IM and LeT hand in the massive 26/11 fire assault. After all, in the midst of the assault, the IM (by the name of Deccan Mujahideen) did claim a hand in the attack, asking for the release of their members. It must also not be forgotten that Qureshi, Shahbandri, Ansari, Rafiq Sheikh and Riyaz Bhatkal are still at large and these fugitive *jihadists* are working to revive the IM's campaign of terror. Indian police and intelligence agencies have an important role in preventing them from succeeding. At a political level, there is a requirement of strengthening the democratic process of the country against communal forces so that the wahhabis and the Mawdudis wither away.

2

Terror and the Indian Mujahideen

There is something disquieting in what Ashish Khetan has written and said recently on terror in India (in The Hindu and on Tehelka.tv), and centrally within it, the Indian Mujahideen. More so, because it comes from one of the most credible journalist's today, who has done some commendable work over the years. A journalist I personally respect. But there are several reasons which compel this response. And yet, this is not just a response, but also an attempt to elucidate the many complex processes within which 'terror' is located today, and the way the discourse has transformed, and has implications for a people's negotiated relationship with their state.

Over the last one year, through Gulail.com , Ashish Khetan has exposed several cases which have been fabricated against individuals and groups, all of them Muslims. This expose, through the revelation of classified Interrogation Reports in the public realm-using the police's own documents to challenge their own story-has been, till now, the most brilliant and effective way to challenge the cases, which many, suspected to be fabricated from the very start. And this expose was, and remains, a brave and mammoth task requiring extensive contacts, sources, and credibility, as anyone working in the fiercely guarded territories of national security and 'terror' would know.

It is this body of work that constitutes the historical background and legitimating authority of his recent op-ed in The Hindu on terror in India , and forms its silent and silencing basis. And yet, the work itself is neither the point of the article, nor forms the basis of what Mr. Khetan is trying to say, while the article exists primarily in the realm of speculation and an authoritative *khutba* meant for the country's muslims. The larger argument in the opinion piece-the first one in which Mr. Khetan has made sense of his one year long research on terror cases in India-is not based on facts, beyond the jurisdiction of journalistic inquiry, unwarranted, un-necessary, laced with presumptions, and even possibly incorrect. But what makes it dangerous, so much so that the article seemingly overturns the very idea that Mr. Khetan has been challenging in the past, is the way it is implicated, and plays to, an extremely communal politics and narrative within which terror today has been a central rallying point. The ideological framework within which the fabricated terror cases have been expounded-neither supported by facts, nor seeking in any way to serve the struggle for human rights of the citizen-, sits comfortably with particular political agendas today. Let's take it piece by piece.

I am compelled to state that I do not write here as a Muslim. I am neither trying to contest a narrative of terror that has been associated with Muslims, nor am I speaking from the location of a Muslim in whatever else I am trying to say. I write here, today, as a citizen contesting and challenging the infringement of human rights of its citizens by the state-whether minorities or tribals, or any of those peoples, communities, religious groups who have been expendable in the state's slow and gradual weakening of democratic institutions. All in a political game of power and control over peoples and dissent.

Mr. Khetan's central argument is this: the Indian Mujahideen is a reality, a terrible spectre responsible for many of the blasts that have taken place in the last decade, and that Muslims should come to terms with it, develop a political understanding, move out of narrow narratives of victimization, stop defending all and any who have been accused of terrorism, and demand that all should be brought to justice-including the IM who are Muslims. Tactfully arranged within it is a secondary argument: that before the IM was busted in 2008, many innocent Muslims were wrongly prosecuted-as he has shown-and that the police and the judiciary has been complicit in producing and convicting them, making a mockery of the criminal justice system.

The stakes are high. To claim that the IM exists and that it is responsible for the many bomb blasts has huge implications, something that will be discussed later. But it is a claim that cannot be lightly made. What proof is offered behind the claim? None. Only Mr. Khetan's own reading and privileged access to Interrogation Reports(IR), none of which he deigns to share with his readers. Ironically, the only Interrogation Reports that have been revealed are those which have helped prove that the cases against some have been fabricated. It is based on this credibility that Mr Khetan argues that the Interrogation reports reveal a sinister reality of the IM that we as a people, or rather, muslims, have to come to terms with. But there appears to be a misplaced sense of value put on the Interrogation Reports', as well as limited understanding of how they can help prove that the accused in the 7/11 blast, or the others that Mr Khetan has revealed, were innocent.

There are three questions that need to be asked here:

1. Whether such a claim can be made based on IRs
2. Mr Khetan's authority or legitimacy to make such a claim
3. The possible, factual incorrectness of the claim.

The IRs are classified documents and are not meant to be shared publicly. They are prepared by the police for their own use. Though, that in no way raises its credibility, it does make them crucial if these internal reports stand in stark contradiction to another official case made by the same agency on the same matter.

At the same time, IRs in themselves are of no evidentiary value in any court of law, nor do they have any inherent truth value as they could be lacking in any material basis as the information obtained by the police could be through the use of third degree and the person may be compelled to state what the agency *wants* to hear rather than the truth. Even in the realm of the commonsensical, the IRs are just that-reports prepared by the police of a suspect's interrogation, with no value whatsoever but as investigative leads. Since Mr. Khetan does not reveal the source and content of these IRs, one has to largely and only accept his word about there being anything in the IR's about the IM, if at all.

However, it is inconsequetial if there is anything in the IR's about the IM or not. The credibility of the previous work by Mr. Khetan, stems not from any inherent truth value of the IR's, but from something entirely different-the fact that these reports, prepared by the police themselves, *were contradictory* to the official case. And hence, a crucial part of the defence case against the official prosecution.

The plea for the innocence of those prosecuted by the revelation of the IRs, has nothing to do with whether the IRs are true or not, but rests on contradictory evidence being available and the conscious and deliberate suppression of the same by the police. To put it simply while it is the job of the court to weigh the evidence and make a value judgment as to the truth or otherwise of the prosecution's case, the prosecution itself cannot act knowing that its case is false.

In these cases, the IRs revealed that not only did the prosecution itself not believe in its own case, it infact had reason to believe that it was false. The good faith of the prosecution was hence absent and the prosecution was proved to have acted in bad faith. The IRs, in themselves are in no way any proof of the guilt of Sadiq sheikh or any others who have been clubbed together with the overarching term of the Indian Mujahideen. It would be enlightening to look at what Justice A.M Thipsey of the Bombay High Court who dealt with this issue in the 7/11 case had to say regarding this very point.

Much before the revelation by Mr. Khetan, the defence council of the 13 accused in the 7/11 train blast case wanted to tender as part of the evidence the confession of Sadiq Sheikh who claimed to have done the blast. The prosecution objected to the confession being tendered as evidence in this case by arguing, among other things, that the confession if admitted here would be:

"inconsistent with the guilt of the accused in this case...[and that]it would prejudice the accused in that case(Crime Branch IM case-MCOCA Special case no.4 of 2009) and would not afford them the chance." (Pg 37.)

The trial Court accepted the prosecution's argument. When the defense took it to the High court, Justice A.M. Thipsey setting aside the order explicitly pointed out:

" It is not possible to accept the view of the learned judge. In the first place, the appellants had not claimed-and could not have claimed that the confessions of those accused 'were true'. They were not expecting to 'prove' those confessions against those accused. What they were saying is that someone else has confessed of having committed the offense with which they are charged...and it is the court that decides whether the fact of a confession having been made is true and also whether the facts stated in the confession are true. Confessions are treated as circumstantial evidence of the truth of the facts stated therein and it is the court that decides whether the facts stated in a confession are to be believed or not in a given case. It is a matter of evaluation of evidence to be done by the court after it is tendered."(Pg 26,29)

It is important to note that a confession is immeasurably more valuable when compared to an Interrogation report. It can be tendered as evidence in court. Despite this, as the High court points out and rightly so, that even then there is no presumption to their inherent truth value, and, it is the job of the court of law to evaluate if they do and can be believed and relief upon. For, the court remains the final arbitrator of guilt or innocence.

How is it possible, then, to proclaim the guilt of the IM based on Interrogation reports, even when the cases of Sadiq Sheikh and the rest, under the rubric of the IM, are still sub-judice? Can a claim be made even on the basis of certain facts which journalistic research might have brought to light, when those facts are yet to be tested in court?

Mr Khetan offers us neither proofs nor explanations. What is offered instead is a narrative of how 5 people-Sadiq Sheikh, Mujahid Saleem, Asif and Amir Reza Khan, and Riaz Bhatkal-fired by ideas of Jihad and retributive justice, bankrolled by forces across the border, went about bombing places one after the other.

The preposterousness of the claim, in the sheer absence of any proof offered, even when all these cases are sub-judice, do not warrant a rebuttal. If anything, it warrants the forceful disciplining of the clause of 'contempt of court'-for the sheer damage that the claim could possible wreck for all the cases that are presently under trial at a time when the 'collective conscience of the people' has assumed legal weight.

And yet, as the narrative has been expounded by Mr. Khetan, I shall take it seriously within the bounds of this chapter, as, unfortunately the entire fabric of the discourse of terror has been created by such unsubstantiated and baseless allegations. Allegations which have assumed the status of commonsense-and through repetition-gained legitimacy and have become the "truth". And it needs to be said that this narrative is thoroughly contested-factually.

For the last one year, as a Research Fellow at the Tata Institute of Social Sciences, I have been researching on terror cases across the 4 cities-Hyderabad, Mumbai, Bangalore and Kolkata. Over this period, I have gone through all relevant documents-legal and otherwise-, met lawyers (both prosecution and defense) as well as accused and their families, of almost all the cases of bomb blasts and attacks in these four cities. This research has encompassed the criminal and social history of two of the 5 people that Mr. Khetan authoritatively mentions as the original member who started the Indian Mujahideen-Mujahid Saleem, and Asif Reza Khan. And the picture that emerges is completely different from what Mr Khetan has attributed to them without proofs or explanations.

Mujahid Saleem: A study of the 4 bomb blast cases of Hyderabad (*forthcoming in EPW*), as well as my meeting with the lawyer associated with his encounter case, his friends, as well as his father Aleem Islahi (whose provocative writing on Jihad and Babri Masjid is the sudden and only explanation offered by Mr. Khetan of Mujahid's crime) makes a story worth telling.

But, it is Maulana Naseeruddin, a cleric who has been a friend of Aleem Islahi as well as his son, whose story of prosecution is directly linked to that of Mujahid. The families of both Maulana Naseeruddin and Aleem Islahi live next to each other in Saidabad-a densely populated Muslim pocket of Hyderabad. Maulana Naseeruddin was first arrested in 1992 when he organized public prayer for the 'martyrship' of the Babri Masjid. He was arrested along with 62 other young men under TADA. Since then Maulana

Naseeruddin has been accused in several cases of terror in Hyderabad, including the famous case of the murder of the Haren Pandya. Last year Maulana Naseeruddin, after spending almost 2 decades in prison, was acquitted of *all* charges in*all* the cases. A minor case is still pending against him. In 2004, when Naseerudin was first accused in the Haren Pandya murder case, there were protests and people had gathered when the Gujarat contingent came to arrest him. The Gujarat contingent was led by IPS officer Narendra Amin who is presently an accused in the Ishrat Jahan fake encounter case. Mujahid Saleem, then a 20 year old boy, was standing the closest to Naseeruddin, protesting with the others. He was shot at point blank range by Narendra Amin. At the time of his death, there was not a single case against him.

Md Rayeesuddin, a friend of Mujahid, was also there that day. He is the prime witness in the case of encounter against Narendra Amin. The case is presently lying dormant. Since the time time Md Rayeesuddin listed as a witness, he has been arrested and interrogated, in every single case of bomb blast in Hyderabad. He was Accused no 16 in the case no 198/2007, one of the 4 Mecca Masjid Blast cases. In that case, his name was included in the chargesheet after he refused to step down as a witness. Even after receiving compensation for the false framing, he has been picked up and tortured after the recent 2013 Dilsukhnagar blast. Ironically, previously listed in the chargesheet as a member of Huji, Rayeesuddin was picked up and interrogated even as the police claimed that it was the Indian Mujahideen. He still refuses to step down as a witness in the day-light encounter of his friend Mujahid Saleem.

Aleem Islahi: The mere holding of an opinion, irrespective of its nature, does not constitute crime, unless an overtly violent act has been done. Though it is difficult to understand the link with the opinions of Aleem Islahi with the guilt of his son Mujahid, it remains a fact that Aleem Islahi has not been accused in a single case of crime or terror in Hyderabad. His name was in the FIR in case no 198/2007, it was however not included in the chargesheet.

Asif Reza Khan: Asif Reza Khan, a resident of Kolkata, was 22 years old when he was first arrested in 1994 under TADA. A student at Aligarh Muslim University then, Asif had just finished his graduation from the well known Maulana Azad College in Calcutta. At AMU, Asif had Kashmiri friends with whom he lived in the hostel. The arrest was among the hundreds of arrests of Muslims across the country for alleged 'Jihadi' links and disruptive activities pertaining to Kashmir. Also arrested under TADA at the same time was ShahidAzmi-the lawyer who was later killed defending those who were falsely accused in terror cases.

Asif Reza and Shahid Azmi spent 5 years in Delhi's Tihar Jail. Released in 1999, after the Supreme Court acquitted them of all charges, both Asif and Shahid, like most others who were released, were re-arrested in several cases, especially in the many hi-profile cases of kidnapping of businessman in the country. After their release, all three of them-Shahid and Asif and Aftab-were accused in the kidnapping of Partha Roy Burman, the 'Khadim's' shoe baron from Kolkata. Shahid and Asif were taken in custody and interrogated. Asif was also accused in the kidnapping of a Gujarat diamond merchant, Bhaskar Parekh. *(Gathered from my conversation with Abdul Azeez, JamiluddinNasir, Aftab Ansari. Abdul Azeez is friend of the Asif Reza family and knew Asif well. The facts are corroborated in the deposition of Ali Reza Khan, the brother of Asif.)*

In 2001, immidietly after SIMI was banned, the Gujarat police took Asif into police custody, and took him to Rajkot where they shot him on December 7 -one and half months before the American Centre attack. The police said, officially, that Asif, a member of SIMI, in a bid to escape, fired upon them by snatching the AK-47 of one of the policemen. They shot him in retaliation. None of the policemen were hurt.

The entire case of the Calcutta attack is built on the assumption that Asif Reza Khan was a terrorist with links with 'Jihadi organisations'. An assumption which is not substantiated by any proof or corroboration.

According to the official case, the American Centre attack which was a ride by shooting of the guards stationed outside the United States Information Service which lasted 40s, was carried out by friends of Asif (one of the two shooters was Sadiq Sheikh according to the police) who wanted to avenge his death. Strangely, the attack took place in Kolkata, even though Asif was killed in Gujarat, as Asif was initially in custody of the Kolkata police according to a confession in the case. Out of the total of 9 accused, 7 were sentence to death by the trial court. The High court acquitted two of them and reduced the punishment of 3 others to 5 years of imprisonment. Two of the accused who presently stand between the complete collapse of the case, face the death penalty in a case which is laced with irregularities, and where the possibility of fabricated evidence cannot be ruled out, as I have concluded after studying the records of the case and speaking to people concerned.. The appeal by the two accused against their convictions is up for hearing in the Supreme Court the next month, where the entire narrative of Asif as well as the attacks by his friends, including Sadiq Sheikh, will be put to test. Strangely, in this case where the accused have veered between two judicial extremes-from death penalty to acquittal-Sadiq Sheikh, the prime accused who was shown as absconding till 2008, is yet to be tried even though the final appeal of the other two who only have minor conspiratorial roles is being heard.

The reality of the IM is sub-judice in many courts of the country with the allegations against them yet to be evaluated and appraised by examination to the level of evidence. For, along with allegations, are also irregularities, severe contestations and allegation of possible fabrication as well as violence-as the legal and extra legal stories of two out of the five named by Mr. Khetan reveal. And this, here, is the crucial point: this is not a contestation of facts. The above facts about the individuals who have been condemned unheard by Mr. Khetan, have not been narrated here to proclaim the innocence of Asif Reza Khan or Mujahid Saleem, but rather, to reveal the falsity of the innuendos which form the basis of Mr. Khetan's proclamation of their guilt.

This chapter is also not a proclamation of the innocence of the Indian Mujahideen. What is intended here is to raise a crucial question: On what basis can the Indian Mujahideen be declared as a reality responsible for many blasts across the country – without evidence-when the matter is sub-judice and also deeply riven with contestation and stories of state violence?

Purely on the basis of a personal, closeted reading of Interrogation reports whose validity is less reliable than the facts pointed out above or the testimonies of all those who are willing to testify in court against it?

TERRORIST GROUPS, AL-QAEDA AND U.S. POLICY IMPLICATIONS

Al-Qaeda's Fluid organization, methods of recruitment, funding, and means of communication distinguish it as an advancement in twenty-first-century terrorist groups. Al-Qaeda is a product of the times. Yet it also echoes historical predecessors, expanding on such factors as the international links and ideological drive of nineteenth-century anarchists, the open-ended aims of Aum Shinrikyo, the brilliance in public communications of the early PLO, and the taste for mass casualty attacks of twentieth-century Sikh separatists or Hezbollah.

Al-Qaeda is an amalgam of old and new, reflecting twenty-first century advances in means or matters of degree rather than true originality; still, most analysts miss the connections with its predecessors and are blinded by its solipsistic rhetoric. That is a mistake. The pressing challenge is to determine which lessons from the decline of earlier terrorist groups are relevant to al-Qaeda and which are not.

First, past experience with terrorism indicates that al-Qaeda will not end if Osama bin Laden is killed. There are many other reasons to pursue him, including bringing him to justice, removing his leadership and expertise, and increasing esprit de corps on the Western side (whose credibility is sapped because of bin Laden's enduring elusiveness). The argument that his demise will end al-Qaeda is tinged with emotion, not dispassionate analysis. Organizations that have been crippled by the killing of their leader have been hierarchically structured, reflecting to some degree a cult of personality, and have lacked a viable successor. Al-Qaeda meets neither of these criteria: it has a mutable structure with a strong, even increasing, emphasis on individual cells and local initiative. It is not the first organization to operate in this way; and the demise of similar terrorist groups required much more than the death of one person. Unlike the PKK and Shining Path, al-Qaeda is not driven by a cult of personality; despite his astonishing popularity, bin Laden has deliberately avoided allowing the movement to revolve around his own persona, preferring instead to keep his personal habits private, to talk of the insignificance of his own fate, and to project the image of a humble man eager to die for his beliefs. As for a viable replacement, bin Laden has often spoken openly of a succession plan, and that plan has to a large degree already taken effect. Furthermore, his capture or killing would produce its own countervailing negative consequences, including (most likely) the creation of a powerful martyr. On balance, the removal of bin Laden would have important potential benefits, but to believe that it would kill al-Qaeda is to be ahistorical and naive.

Second, although there was a time when the failure to transition to a new generation might have been a viable finale for al-Qaeda, that time is long past. Al-Qaeda has transitioned to a second, third, and arguably fourth generation. The reason relates especially to the second distinctive element of al-Qaeda: its method of recruitment or, more accurately, its attraction of radicalized followers (both individuals and groups), many of whom in turn are connected to existing local networks. Al-Qaeda's spread has been compared to a virus or a bacterium, dispersing its contagion to disparate sites. Although this is a seductive analogy, it is also misleading: the perpetuation of al-Qaeda is a sentient process involving well-considered marketing strategies and deliberate tactical decisions, not a mindless "disease" process; thinking of it as a "disease" shores up the unfortunate American tendency to avoid analyzing the mentality of the enemy.

Al-Qaeda is operating with a long-term strategy and is certainly not following the left-wing groups of the 1970s in their failure to articulate a coherent ideological vision or the peripatetic right-wing groups of the twentieth century. It has transitioned beyond its original structure and now represents a multigenerational threat with staying power comparable to the enthonationalist groups of the twentieth century. Likewise, arguments about whether al-Qaeda is best described primarily as an ideology or by its opposition to foreign occupation of Muslim lands are specious: al-Qaeda's adherents use both rationales to spread their links. The movement is opportunistic. The challenge for the United States and its allies is to move beyond rigid mind-sets and paradigms, do more in-depth analysis, and be more nimble and strategic in response to al-Qaeda's fluid agenda.

The third and fourth models of a terrorist organization's end—achievement of the group's cause and transition toward a political role, negotiations, or amnesty—also bear little relevance to al-Qaeda today. It is hard to conceive of al-Qaeda fully achieving its aims, in part because those aims have evolved over time, variably including achievement of a pan-Islamic caliphate, the overthrow of non-Islamic regimes, and the expulsion of all infidels from Muslim countries, not to mention support for the Palestinian cause and the killing of Americans and other so-called infidels. Historically, terrorist groups that have achieved their ends have done so by articulating clear, limited objectives. Al-Qaeda's goals, at least as articulated over recent years, could not be achieved without overturning an international political and economic system characterized by globalization and predominant U.S. power. As the historical record indicates, negotiations or a transition to a legitimate political process requires feasible terms and a sense of stalemate in the struggle. Also, members of terrorist groups seeking negotiations often have an incentive to find a way out of what they consider a losing cause. None of this describes bin Laden's al-Qaeda.

This points to another issue. As al-Qaeda has become a hybrid or "virtual organization," rather than a coherent hierarchical organization, swallowing its propaganda and treating it as a unified whole is a mistake. It is possible that bin Laden and his lieutenants have attempted to cobble together such disparate entities (or those entities have opportunistically attached themselves to al-Qaeda) that they have stretched beyond the point at which their interests can be represented in this movement. Some of the local groups that have recently claimed an association with al-Qaeda have in the past borne more resemblance to ethnonationalist/separatist groups such as the PLO, the IRA, and the LTTE. Examples include local affiliates in Indonesia, Morocco, Tunisia, and Turkey. This is not to argue that these groups' aims are rightful or that their tactics are legitimate. Rather, because of its obsession with the notion of a monolithic al-Qaeda, the United States is glossing over both the extensive local variation within terrorist groups and their different goals; these groups have important points of divergence with al-Qaeda's agenda, and the United States does no one any favors by failing to seriously analyse and exploit those local differences (except perhaps al-Qaeda). The U.S. objective must be to enlarge the movement's internal inconsistencies and differences. Al-Qaeda's aims have become so sweeping that one might wonder whether they genuinely carry within them the achievement of specific local grievances. There is more hope of ending such groups through traditional methods if they are dealt with using traditional tools, even including, on a case-by-case basis, concessions or negotiations with specific local elements that may have negotiable or justifiable terms (albeit pursued through an illegitimate tactic). The key is to emphasize the differences with al-Qaeda's agenda and to drive a wedge between the movement and its recent adherents.

The historical record of other terrorist groups indicates that it is a mistake to treat al-Qaeda as a monolith, to lionize it as if it is an unprecedented phenomenon with all elements equally committed to its aims, for that eliminates a range of proven counterterrorist tools and techniques for ending it. It is also a mistake to nurture al-Qaeda's rallying point, a hatred of Americans and a resentment of U.S. policies (especially in Iraq and between Israel and the Palestinians), thereby conveniently facilitating the glossing over of differences within. Fifth, reducing popular support, both active and passive, is an effective means of hastening the demise of some terrorist groups. This technique has received much attention among critics of George W. Bush and his administration's policies, many of whom argue that concentrating on the "roots" of terrorism is a necessary alternative to the current policy of emphasizing military force.

This is a superficial argument, however, as it can be countered that a "roots" approach is precisely at the heart of current U.S. policy: the promotion of democracy may be seen as an idealistic effort to provide an alternative to populations in the Muslim world, frustrated by corrupt governance, discrimination, unemployment, and stagnation. But the participants in this debate are missing the point. The problem is timing: democratization is a decades-long approach to a short-term and immediate problem whose solution must also be measured in months, not just years. The efforts being undertaken are unlikely to have a rapid enough effect to counter the anger, frustration, and sense of humiliation that characterize passive supporters. As for those who actively sustain the movement through terrorist acts, it is obviously a discouraging development that many recent operatives have lived in, or even been natives of, democratic countries—the March 2004 train attacks in Madrid and 2005 bombings in London being notable examples.

The history of terrorism provides little comfort to those who believe that democratization is a good method to reduce active and passive support for terrorist attacks. There is no evidence that democratization correlates with a reduction in terrorism; in fact, available historical data suggest the opposite. Democratization was arguably the cause of much of the terrorism of the twentieth century. Moreover, democracy in the absence of strong political institutions and civil society could very well bring about radical Islamist governments over which the West would have little influence. There are much worse things than terrorism, and it might continue to be treated as a regrettable but necessary accompaniment to change were it not for two potentially serious developments in the twenty-first century: (1) the use of increasingly destructive weapons that push terrorist attacks well beyond the "nuisance" level, and (2) the growing likelihood that terrorism will lead to future systemic war. In any case, the long-term, idealistic, and otherwise admirable policy of democratization, viewed as "Americanization" in many parts of the world, does not represent a sufficiently targeted response to undercutting popular support for al-Qaeda. There are two vulnerabilities, however, where cutting the links between al-Qaeda and its supporters hold promise: its means of funding and its means of communication. Efforts to cut off funding through traditional avenues have had some results.

But not nearly enough attention is being paid to twenty-first-century communications, especially al-Qaeda's presence on the internet. The time has come to recognize that the stateless, anarchical realm of cyberspace requires better tools for monitoring, countermeasures, and, potentially, even control. Previous leaps in cross-border communication such as the telegraph, radio, and telephone engendered counteracting developments in code breaking, monitoring, interception, and wiretapping. This may seem a heretical suggestion for liberal states, especially for a state founded on the right of free speech; however, the international community will inevitably be driven to take countermeasures in response to future attacks. It is time to devote more resources to addressing this problem now. Western analysts have been misguided in focusing on the potential use of the internet for so-called cyberterrorism (i.e., its use in carrying out attacks); the internet is far more dangerous as a tool to shore up and perpetuate the al-Qaeda movement's constituency. Preventing or interdicting al-Qaeda's ability to disseminate its message and draw adherents into its orbit is crucial. Countering its messages in serious ways, not through the outdated and stilted vehicles of government websites and official statements but through sophisticated alternative sites and images attractive to a new generation, is an urgent priority.

As for the opponent's marketing strategy, al-Qaeda and its associates have made serious mistakes of timing, choice of targets, and technique; yet the United States and its allies have done very little to capitalize on them. In particular, the United States tends to act as if al-Qaeda is essentially a static enemy that will react to its actions, but then fails to react effectively and strategically to the movement's missteps.

The Bali attacks, the May 2003 attacks in Saudi Arabia, the Madrid attacks, the July 2005 London attacks—all were immediately and deliberately trumpeted by al-Qaeda associates. Where was the coordinated counterterrorist multimedia response? There is nothing so effective at engendering public revulsion as images of murdered and maimed victims, many of whom resemble family members of would-be recruits, lying on the ground as the result of a terrorist act. Outrage is appropriate. Currently, however, those images are dominated by would-be family members in Iraq, the Palestinian territories, Abu Ghraib, and Guantanamo Bay.

The West is completely outflanked on the airwaves, and its countermeasures are virtually nonexistent on the internet. But as the RIRA, PFLP-GC, and ETA cases demonstrate, the al-Qaeda movement can undermine itself, if it is given help. A large part of this "war" is arguably being fought not on a battlefield but in cyberspace. The time-honoured technique of undermining active and passive support for a terrorist group through in-depth analysis, agile responses to missteps, carefully targeted messages, and cutting-edge technological solutions is a top priority.

This is a crucial moment of opportunity. Polls indicate that many of al-Qaeda's potential constituents have been deeply repulsed by recent attacks. According to the Pew Global Attitudes Project, publics in many predominantly Muslim states increasingly see Islamic extremism as a threat to their own countries, express less support for terrorism, have less confidence in bin Laden, and reflect a declining belief in the usefulness of suicide attacks. In these respects, there is a growing range of commonality in the attitudes of Muslim and non-Muslim publics; yet the United States focuses on itself and does little to nurture cooperation. American public diplomacy is the wrong concept. This is not about the United States and its ideals, values, culture, and image abroad: this is about tapping into a growing international norm against killing innocent civilians—whether, for example, on vacation or on their way to work or school—many of whom are deeply religious and many of whom also happen to be Muslims. If the United States and its allies fail to grasp this concept, to work with local cultures and local people to build on common goals and increase their alienation from this movement, then they will have missed a long-established and promising technique for ending a terrorist group such as al-Qaeda.

There is little to say about the sixth factor, the use of military repression, in ending al-Qaeda. Even though the U.S. military has made important progress in tracking down and killing senior operatives, the movement's ability to evolve has demonstrated the limits of such action, especially when poorly coordinated with other comparatively underfunded approaches and engaged in by a democracy. Although apparently effective, the Turkish government's repression of the PKK and the Peruvian government's suppression of Shining Path, for example, yield few desirable parallels for the current counterterrorist campaign.

Transitioning out of terrorism and toward either criminality or full insurgency is the final, worrisome historical precedent for al-Qaeda. In a sense, the network is already doing both. Efforts to cut off funding through the formal banking system have ironically heightened the incentive and necessity to en-gage in illicit activities, especially narcotics trafficking. With the increasing amount of poppy seed production in Afghanistan, al-Qaeda has a natural pipeline to riches. This process is well under way. As for al-Qaeda becoming a full insurgency, some analysts believe this has already occurred. Certainly to the extent that Abu Musab al-Zarqawi and his associates in Iraq truly represent an arm of the movement (i.e., al-Qaeda in Iraq), that transition is likewise well along.

The alliance negotiated between bin Laden and al-Zarqawi is another example of an effective strategic and public relations move for both parties, giving new life to the al-Qaeda movement at a time when its leaders are clearly on the run and providing legitimacy and fresh recruits for the insurgency in Iraq. As many commentators have observed, Iraq is an ideal focal point and training ground for this putative global insurgency. The glimmer of hope in this scenario, however, is that the foreigners associated with al-Qaeda are not tied to the territory of Iraq in the same way the local population is, and the tensions that will arise between those who want a future for the nascent Iraqi state and those who want a proving ground for a largely alien ideology and virtual organization are likely to increase—especially as the victims of the civil war now unfolding there continue increasingly to be Iraqi civilians. The counter to al-Zarqawi's al-Qaeda in Iraq, as it is for other areas of the world with local al-Qaeda affiliates, is to tap into the long-standing and deep association between peoples and their territory and to exploit the inevitable resentment toward foreign terrorist agendas, while scrupulously ensuring that the United States is not perceived to be part of those agendas. If the United States continues to treat al-Qaeda as if it were utterly unprecedented, as if the decades-long experience with fighting modern terrorism were totally irrelevant, then it will continue to make predictable and avoidable mistakes in responding to this threat. It will also miss important strategic opportunities. That experience points particularly toward dividing new local affiliates from al-Qaeda by understanding and exploiting their differences with the movement, rather than treating the movement as a monolith. It is also crucial to more effectively break the political and logistical connections between the movement and its supporters, reinvigorating time-honoured counterterrorism tactics targeted at al-Qaeda's unique characteristics, including the perpetuation of its message, its funding, and its communications. Al-Qaeda continues to exploit what is essentially a civil war within the Muslim world, attracting alienated Muslims around the globe to its rage-filled movement. Al-Qaeda will end when the West removes itself from the heart of this fight, shores up international norms against terrorism, undermines al-Qaeda's ties with its followers, and begins to exploit the movement's abundant missteps.

THE IM'S DEVELOPING IDEOLOGY: THREE DISTINCT PHASES

On 17 July 2013, the National Investigation Agency (NIA), the organization that New Delhi set up after the 2008 Mumbai terrorist attacks as the primary agency to investigate all terrorist incidents in India, stated in its charge sheet that the IM "was formed in 2003 after ultra-radicalised Muslim youth segregated from the Students Islamic Movement of India." Similar to the IMMM and the MIH, the IM has its roots in the avowed need to radicalize the SIMI's plan of action even further. In 2001 and 2002, a rebellion of sorts was brewing within the SIMI. A faction broke away from the less-radical parent organization and sought new cadres who were already sufficiently radicalized; their extremism was further boosted by contact with external militants such as the LeT. This new faction became the IM. The IM, in a way, was also a result of the LeT's "Karachi Project," which had sought to raise a new network of jihadists. In its 17 July 2013 charge sheet, the NIA added that the IM cadres "do not believe in India's Constitution and IM's members nurse communal hatred against the Hindu community."

Since the IM had been formed on an agenda of waging a violent war against Hindu India, no spell of moderate militancy separated the IM's birth from its first act of violence. Within a relatively short time period, however, the IM underwent three distinct phases of ideological expansion: traversing from a narrow India-centric ideology to revenge-seeking and eventually embracing the concerns of Muslims in other countries. This is not to suggest that the IM abandoned or progressed beyond any of the causes that it initially championed. Rather, it acquired new additional causes to fight for. In effect, the IM's successes in the Indian theater and its constant ideological oscillation demonstrated the IM's widening profile and proclivity for becoming an integral part of the global Jihad. Such a broadening of ideology was important, for it fit in well with the amplification of jihadist terrorism in South Asia, especially boosted by the prospects of instability in post-2014 Afghanistan.

Guardian of Wronged Muslims in India

According to an estimate by an intelligence agency,

By 2005, the IM had firmly established a complete terror outfit, with different sections in charge of providing manpower and sourcing explosives and bomb components. A specialist computer-services cell was already in place. Different leaders were already travelling countrywide, liaising between cells.

The IM's war on Hindu India began in 2005 with a string of urban attacks, which included serial explosions in the national capital, Delhi—two bombs exploded at busy marketplaces and a third exploded inside a Delhi Transport Corporation bus, killing 62 people. There was some question about who had carried out the attacks. The LeT was initially suspected. A Delhi Police special cell team also claimed to have killed the mastermind of the blasts in an operation in the Indian state of Jammu and Kashmir in 2007.

In 2006, the IM carried out serial bombings in the Hindu pilgrimage town of Varanasi, in the state of Uttar Pradesh. Three explosions, one in a crowded temple and two in a railway station, killed 21 people and injured 62 others. In 2013, an arrested IM cadre who had participated in the 2006 bombings told his interrogators that the timers and improvised explosive devices (IEDs) used in the Varanasi blasts were similar to the ones used in the 2005 Delhi blasts. Since the formation of the IM had remained unannounced, these attacks were thought to have been perpetrated by Pakistan-based outfits, like the LeT, and the Bangladesh-based Harkat-ul Jihad-al-Islami. The fact that the LeT was still perpetrating large-scale attacks, like the July 2006 explosions that targeted the train systems in Mumbai and killed 200 people, made the task of looking for another perpetrator seem unnecessary. Indian security personnel felt comfortable in the assumption that because the LeT was still active within India, the LeT must be behind the Varanasi attacks.

The IM's first-ever ideological affirmation came in the form of its first manifesto, which the group released in 2007 after it had bombed court complexes in Lucknow, Varanasi, and Faizabad. The manifesto claimed that the blasts were intended to "punish local lawyers" who had physically attacked some suspects who were being held for an abortive kidnap plot against politician Rahul Gandhi by the terrorist group Jaish-e-Muhammad (JeM). The manifesto, however, spoke broadly of "wounds given by the idol worshippers to the Indian Muslims" and the demolition of the Babri Masjid, a disputed mosque in the state of Uttar Pradesh that Hindu radicals had demolished in 1992 following violent countrywide communal riots. Emphasizing the miserable condition of the Muslims in the country, the manifesto concluded, "If you want to be a successful person in India, then you should be an idol worshipper and kill Muslims."

The IM released two other manifestos in 2008 and 2010, following more bombings in Delhi and Varanasi, respectively. Both documents pointed at the role of "the Supreme Court, the high courts, the lower courts and all the commissions" for failing the Muslims in India. The 2008 manifesto, running nearly 14 pages and titled The Rise of Jihad, indicated that the bombings were carried out to avenge the 2002 anti-Muslim violence in Gujarat. "In the light of the injustice and wrongs on the Muslims of Gujarat, we advance our Jihad and call all our brethren under it to unite and answer these irresolute kafireen [infidels] of India," it said. The 2010 manifesto, titled Let's Feel the Pain Together, said that the attack in 2010 served as a reminder to Hindus that the IM had "resolved that none of your mandirs [temples] will remain safe until and unless all our occupied Masjids [mosques] throughout India are returned back to the Muslims."

When the IM targeted the Indian judiciary in explosions outside the Delhi high court in 2011, its attacks had already spanned the entire country and were being carried out in almost all of the major urban centers, including New Delhi and the country's FINANCIAL capital, Mumbai. Attacks in Ahmedabad and Pune in the west, Hyderabad and Bangalore in the south, Patna and Bodh Gaya in the east, and Delhi in the north made the IM look like a pan-Indian outfit capable of taking its activities to almost any corner of the country. Among these attacks was a 2010 incident in which two bikers fired on tourists gathered at the gate of the Jama Masjid in the Old Delhi area. The drive-by shooting, the only attack of this nature carried out by the IM so far, was to be followed by an explosion, but the explosive, which was fitted into a car parked in the area, did not go off due to faulty circuitry. This attack was carried out on 19 September 2010, days before the opening of the Commonwealth Games in the national capital. Two Taiwanese nationals sustained bullet wounds.

By the time of the Jama Masjid attack in 2010, the IM had stopped mailing its usual manifestos claiming responsibility for its attacks, so investigative agencies had to rely on interrogations of arrested IM cadres to unravel the intentions behind the explosions. The IM had also diversified its target selection, demonstrating that it was indeed willing to go after almost any target, with the sole intention of maximizing fatalities. Revenge against Hindus and the institutions facilitating the dominance of Hinduism over the Muslims remained the proclaimed raison d'être of the IM—at least for awhile.

Avenging the Deaths of Its Cadres

Over a period of time, the IM began perpetrating terror attacks even to avenge the deaths of its cadres, representing a drastic climbdown from its larger goal of fighting on behalf of the Muslim community. According to interrogation reports, the explosions in Pune, Maharashtra, on 1 August 2012 were intended to avenge the killing of imprisoned IM cadre Qateel Siddique by his cell mates in a Pune prison a couple of months earlier. The attack included five coordinated low-intensity explosions on a busy road in the heart of Pune, injuring one person. Another live IED was later recovered from the area.

Within a year of the Pune attack, the IM had expanded its worldview, aiming to take up the causes of persecuted Muslims outside of India. Blasts that targeted the Buddhist shrine in Bodh Gaya, Bihar, in July 2013 were said to have been in response to violence against the Rohingyas, a Muslim population in Myanmar, by members of the ethnic Buddhist majority. Arrested IM cadre Umair Siddiqui told his interrogators that he had been approached by another IM cadre, Haider Ali, about the Rohingyas' situation, and both had finalized the plan to carry out the attack at the Buddhist shrine. Earlier, arrested LeT cadre Abdul Karim Tunda revealed that the LeT had also been part of the Bodh Gaya attack; during his interrogation, Tunda detailed the LeT's plan, in collaboration with the IM, to recruit Rohingyas and carry out the attack.

On 27 October 2013, explosions in Patna, Bihar, were reportedly carried out to protest communal riots in Muzaffarnagar, in the neighbouring state of Uttar Pradesh. The recovery of a large amount of explosives at Ranchi, Jharkhand, on 4 November 2013 demonstrated the IM's plan to maintain the momentum in its violent campaign. Similarly, the recovery of documents from an IM safe house in Ranchi, including handwritten notes from IM members detailing future action plans, pointed to the possibility that the IM would carry out future attacks on Buddhist shrines, foreign tourists, and public installations in the state of Chhattisgarh.

The IM's wide array of unconnected objectives underscores the fact that, instead of remaining a purely ideology-based organization with both local and global aspirations, the IM could be willing to carry out attacks for almost any cause that suits its convenience. Believed to be controlled by external forces (including the JeM, the LeT, and the Pakistani external intelligence agency known as Inter-Services Intelligence [ISI]), and to nurture the aspiration of making common cause with al Qaeda, IM leaders could be looking well beyond the traditional outfit that was triggering explosions only on behalf of wronged Indian Muslims. Although the IM is largely defined as an indigenous or homegrown terror organization within India, its leadership does not appear to be averse to eventually transforming the outfit into a pan-Islamist terrorist operation.

THE GLOBAL WAR ON TERROR

Using the opportunities therefore afforded by the global war on terror, the Pakistani security services systematically eliminated many sources of sectarian violence within two years of the campaign's initiation, even though they have been unable to conclusively eradicate the cancer of sectarian bloodshed within Pakistan itself. In part, this is due to the selectivity of Musharraf's antisectarian campaign. But the continuing fragmentation of these violent groups; their links to the wider networks of international terrorism now resident in Pakistan, various foreign sponsors abroad, and the flourishing madaris within the country; and the continuing utility of their gun- toting membership to different political parties and occasionally to governmental organs themselves imply that sectarian threats will be impossible to extinguish so long as "state policies of Islamisation and [the] marginalization of secular democratic forces" continue to persist in Pakistan.

The second set of groups, the terrorist outfits operating with Pakistan Army and ISID support against India in Kashmir, was treated in a remarkably different way compared with the anti-national sectarian militants inside Pakistan. These groups, such as the Lashkar- e- Toiba, the Jaish- e- Muhammad, and the Harkat-ul- Mujahideen, for example, were the long lances in the Pakistani campaign to wrest the disputed state of Jammu and Kashmir from

India. Since the late 1980s, the Pakistani military has financed, trained, armed, and launched these cadres on their murderous missions into Kashmir and elsewhere inside the Indian union. Because the struggle for control over the disputed Himalayan state was fully under way by the time the global war on terror was inaugurated, these terrorist groups were more or less exempted from Musharraf's domestic campaign against violence and extremism.

This exclusion was justified both on the strategic rationale that Pakistan's participation in the war on terror was intended, among other things, to protect its freedom of action in Kashmir and on the repeated, though fraudulent, assertion that these groups, far from being terrorists, only personified the legitimate Kashmiri struggle for self- determination against India. In fact, of all the Pakistani- sponsored Deobandi terrorist groups operating against India in Kashmir and elsewhere, only one entity— the Hizbul Mujahideen— began life as an indigenous Kashmiri insurgent group; the others, including the most violent organizations such as the Lashkar- e- Toiba, the Jaish- e- Muhammad, and the Harkat- ul- Mujahideen, are all led, manned, and financed by native Pakistanis. This reality notwithstanding— and perhaps because of it— Islamabad continued to sustain the operations of these groups against India but, in an effort to maintain the consistency of its commitments to the global war on terror, now began to emphasize that its support took only the form of moral, and not material, encouragement.

This charade was rudely interrupted by the December 13, 2001, terrorist attack on India's parliament when, in response to New Delhi's subsequent military mobilization, Pakistan was compelled by U.S. diplomacy to initiate a series of measures to restrict the activities of its terrorist clients. The implementation of these actions, however, was at best halfhearted and inconsistent.

Far from seeking to extirpate these terrorist groups permanently, Musharraf sought mainly to defang India's threats of military action and to alleviate Washington's fears of an inconvenient Indo- Pakistani war. His overarching objective consisted of protecting these terrorist assets to the extent possible because they represented national investments— a "strategic reserve"—in Islamabad's subconventional war against New Delhi.

Consequently, to this day, Musharraf has not sought to eliminate the Deobandi terrorist groups operating against India in Kashmir and elsewhere; he has instead sought only to modulate their activities, depending on the extent of satisfaction he derives from the prevailing state of diplomatic relations with New Delhi and the progress secured in the ongoing Indo- Pakistani peace process.

Although the Pakistani- supported infiltration of terrorist groups into Kashmir— but not into the rest of India— appears to have abated in recent years, most observers conclude that this phenomenon is linked either to Musharraf's desire not to provide India with any excuses to abandon the generally fragile peace process or to domestic crises within Pakistan. In any event, it is agreed that Musharraf simply has not made the decisive decision to abandon or eliminate the terrorist groups operating against India in the manner witnessed, for example, in the case of the more virulent anti- national sectarian entities operating within Pakistan.

The third group relevant to the Pakistani decision to join the U.S.-led coalition against terrorism consisted of the Taliban, that is, the Pashtun remnants of the regime ejected from power in Kabul as a result of the initial success of Operation Enduring Freedom. After their defeat at the hands of the Northern Alliance, the Taliban cadres hastily returned to the regions whence they originated.

Many in the rank and file withdrew to their villages in the southern Afghan provinces of Helmand, Kandahar, Oruzgan, and Zabol as well as along the border areas on the western side of the Durand Line separating Afghanistan from Pakistan, that is, in the eastern Afghan provinces of Paktika, Paktia, Khowst, Nangarhar, and Konar. Given their significance as high- value targets, the core Taliban leadership— along with those Pakistani Pashtuns who had joined their movement— crossed over the Afghanistan-Pakistan border into the relative safety of the FATA.

Because most of the Taliban's fighters originally mobilized by the Pakistani ISID were drawn from the Ghilzai confederation of

Pashtuns, which dominates eastern and southeastern Afghanistan, and from the other Pashtun tribes inhabiting the FATA, their return to these ancestral lands was not surprising. In fact, all the evidence relating to the incidence of terrorist attacks since 2001 suggests strongly that the war- fighting cadres of the Taliban continue to remain bivouacked in these areas.

The exact location of the supreme leadership of the Taliban movement, however, cannot be established with any self- evident clarity. Irrespective of where the rahbari shura (leadership council) centred on Mullah Omar and his closest associates found shelter in the immediate aftermath of their defeat, Afghan military and civilian intelligence officials as well as NATO commanders today believe that this coterie eventually found refuge in Quetta, the largest city and capital of Pakistan's Baluchistan Province, from where they continue to operate to this day.

As Col. Chris Vernon, NATO's chief of staff for southern Afghanistan, declared forthrightly, "The thinking piece of the Taliban [operates] out of Quetta in Pakistan. It's the major headquarters— they use it to run a series of networks in Afghanistan."

These networks, in turn, are judged to be directed by four subsidiary shuras based in Quetta, Miran Shah, Peshawar, and Karachi: the first three actually control or coordinate most of the ongoing terrorist operations occurring, respectively, along the southern, central, and northern "fronts" in Afghanistan, whereas the fourth is believed to connect the Taliban with the logistics, financial, and technical assistance conduits emanating from the wider Islamic world. The pattern of terrorist attacks occurring in Afghanistan from 2002 to 2007, again corroborates this judgment.

Because the Pakistani state was most intimately involved in the creation of the Taliban before their fall, Musharraf's antiterrorism campaign after September 11, 2001, deliberately avoided any concerted targeting of this group and, in particular, its senior leadership. No other explanation is consistent with the fact that, although Pakistani military, intelligence, and paramilitary forces apprehended scores of al- Qaeda operatives, including numerous key individuals in the al- Qaeda hierarchy, the senior

Taliban leaders killed or captured in southern Afghanistan or in the FATA have numbered literally a handful in comparison.

This asymmetry in seizures is all the more odd because, prior to Operation Enduring Freedom, Pakistani military and ISID liaison elements were deeply intertwined with all levels of the Taliban mand structure and its war fighters in the field. In contrast, the Pakistani intelligence relationship with al- Qaeda in Afghanistan was more tenuous, yet Pakistan's military forces were able to apprehend far more al- Qaeda cadres than Taliban operatives.

These successes in regard to al- Qaeda have invariably been attributed by Pakistanis, including General Musharraf, to the fact that it was always easier to identify the ethnically alien al- Qaeda elements along the frontier in comparison with the Taliban who, being ethnically Pashtun, were able to disguise their identities by assimilating into the larger tribal population.

While this explanation is only partly true— non- native fighters have lived in and become amalgamated into the social structures of the Afghan- Pakistani frontier since at least the anti-Soviet jihad of the 1980s— it is also disingenuous because the Pakistani ISID was not only deeply involved in the recruitment, training, arming, and operations of Taliban fighters at multiple bureaucratic levels, but it also maintained an intense liaison relationship with the Ghilzai tribes whose population has been disproportionately represented in the Taliban. Since protecting these relationships was deemed to be especially critical for Pakistan's national security interests in the aftermath of the Northern Alliance victory in Kabul, the large number of Taliban foot soldiers who made their way into the FATA were largely ignored by Pakistani counterterrorism operations so long as they did not engage in any untoward activities that either called attention to their presence or magnified the troubles confronting the Pakistani state.

All told, then, the Taliban network, just like the Pakistani-aided terrorist groups operating in Kashmir and elsewhere in India, was deliberately permitted to escape the wrath of General Musharraf's counterterrorism operations in the initial phase of the war on terror.

Such an approach, however, could not be extended to the fourth group, al- Qaeda, which had also taken up sanctuary in the FATA, particularly in South Waziristan initially. Although al- Qaeda continued to have sympathizers within the extreme fringes of Pakistani society even after the terrible events of September 11 were conclusively attributed to its operations, the Pakistani military establishment did not enjoy the luxury of slackening its campaign against this target because of the consequences for U.S.-Pakistani relations at a time when bilateral ties were just recovering after a decade of U.S. disfavor and when Washington had just embarked on a ferocious campaign against al- Qaeda worldwide.

Most senior Pakistani military officers at the corps command level were also genuinely horrified by the destruction that al-Qaeda wreaked in New York and Washington and, fearing for their country's own future in the face of the monster now present in their midst, supported Musharraf's decision to engage and destroy this terrorist organization of global reach.

Pakistan's military, accordingly, began to prosecute the war against al- Qaeda with great vigor, if not always with finesse, through multiple instruments. These included providing the United States and its military with facilities and access for the prosecution of Operation Enduring Freedom in Afghanistan, and conducting various law enforcement and internal security operations (sometimes in cooperation with their U.S. counterparts) aimed at interdicting terrorist financing and apprehending and rendering terrorist targets for prosecution abroad.

Most important, however, the Pakistani military initiated Operation Al Mizan, a large- scale effort that involved moving major military formations from the Army's XI Corps and elite Special Services Group (SSG) battalions into the FATA, an area where regular army units had not ordinarily been deployed for decades.

These infantry forces joined the Frontier Corps regiments—the paramilitary formations usually located in the region— as a show of force in order to both reassert the strong state presence that historically was lacking and apprehend the al- Qaeda elements that had taken shelter within the area.

This military campaign, which took the form of a gigantic cordon- and- search operation, had several consequences. First, it resulted in the capture of numerous al- Qaeda and other extremist operatives— some 700 at last count— who have since been turned over to the United States.

Because these individuals are mostly foreigners— non–South Asian arrivals living in what are essentially Pashtun lands— detecting their presence, while not easy because of the local support they receive from the natives for ideological reasons and sometimes simply out of greed or fear, was certainly easier.

Second, it forced some though by no means all senior al-Qaeda operatives— for example, Khalid Sheikh Muhammad and Ramzi Binalshibh— to leave the relatively secure FATA sanctuary and disperse further inward into Pakistan, where their insertion into less ideologically congenial surroundings and their need to rely on more complex means of communication increased their susceptibility to detection and arrest.

Third, the dramatic irruption of the Pakistani state into the FATA, through a significant military presence of the kind not seen in more than a century, resulted in making conditions sufficiently inhospitable for al- Qaeda such that its senior leadership and cadres were compelled to relocate under fire from South to North Waziristan and beyond, where they operate to this day.

This forced displacement, which unfortunately remains at continuous risk of reversal, nonetheless had the beneficial effect of disrupting many planned terrorist operations, but the dispersal of the organization's leadership in the northern FATA, especially in the Bajaur Agency where the terrain is inhospitable, the population is violently pro- Taliban, and the presence of the Pakistan Army is thin, has inadvertently made the task of destroying the al- Qaeda core all the more difficult.

In any event, these outcomes suggest that although Pakistan began as a reluctant entrant into the global war on terrorism, it has since become an active participant in the struggle. More than 85,000 Pakistani troops remain garrisoned along the Afghanistan-Pakistan border— a deployment that predates the initiation of the global war on terror.

A significant fraction of these forces, however, is engaged today in counterterrorism operations in the border areas, and more than 600 soldiers have already sacrificed their lives in this effort.

Further, Islamabad itself has now become a victim of terrorism as a variety of groups, ranging from those previously nurtured and now discarded by the Pakistani state, such as the al-Alami faction of the Harkat- ul- Mujahideen, to more distant beneficiaries of past Pakistani policies, such as al- Qaeda, seek to wreak an orgy of revenge against institutions and individuals whom they had previously counted among their sponsors and friends.

That Pakistan has made significant contributions to defeating various terrorist groups is therefore undeniable, yet its larger campaign against terrorism has also been conspicuously selective and perhaps self- serving. While it has secured major gains in eradicating some domestic anti- national sectarian terrorist groups and has contributed disproportionately to the ongoing campaign against al- Qaeda, it has been much more reluctant to conclusively eliminate those terrorist entities operating against India in Kashmir and elsewhere and against Afghanistan both in the FATA and in transit back and forth to the southern and eastern Afghan provinces. Further, the protection of the terrorist infrastructure that supports these groups has produced undesirable blowback because the actors traditionally involved in perpetrating terrorism in Kashmir increasingly either coordinate with or directly assist the Taliban and al- Qaeda in operations against not only Afghanistan but also the United States and even Pakistan itself.

Clearly, strategic and geopolitical calculations play an important part in accounting for this segmented Pakistani response. Islamabad, for example, has long viewed the terrorist groups operating in Kashmir and now in other Indian states as useful instruments for executing its policy of "strategic diversion" against New Delhi. For this reason, Pakistan has been reluctant to target and eliminate these groups conclusively, preferring instead to alternately tighten and loosen control over their operations depending on how much satisfaction it receives from India at any given moment.

The decision to avoid targeting the Taliban was born of similar calculations. Initially, it was owed simply to the inclinations of senior Pakistani military commanders who were just not prepared to add insult to injury by physically eliminating the very forces they had long invested in, especially because they had now suffered the ignominy of having to consent to their client's defeat.

Over time, however, the reasons for protecting the Taliban only grew stronger: India's growing prominence in Afghan reconstruction, its increased influence and presence in Afghanistan more generally, the weakening of the Hamid Karzai government in Kabul, the progressive souring of Pakistani- Afghan relations (including those between Karzai and Musharraf personally), and the disquiet about a possible U.S. exit from Afghanistan (a prospect inferred from the mid-2005 announcement that the United States would divest full command of Afghan combat operations to NATO) once again increased Pakistan's paranoia about the prospect of a hostile western frontier.

It was exactly the desire to avert this outcome that led to the initial Pakistani decision to invest in sustaining the Taliban. And with fear of the wheel turning full circle gaining strength in Islamabad since at least 2005, the temptation to hedge against potentially unfavorable outcomes in Kabul— by protecting the Taliban as some sort of a "force- in- being"—only appeared more and more attractive and reasonable to Pakistan.

Although Pakistan's discriminative approach to fighting terrorism was shaped and implemented by General Musharraf in his dual capacity as president and previously chief of army staff, it would be erroneous to conclude that this prevailing strategy is owed simply to the whim of one man.

This is particularly relevant today when Musharraf's hold on power has become progressively weaker and the future of his political status and effectiveness increasingly clouded. Rather, Musharraf's decisions in regard to counterterrorism strategy since 2001, although publicly perceived as personal dicta, invariably reflected the consensus among the corps commanders of the Pakistan Army and, hence, represent the preferences of Pakistan's military- dominated state.

In other words, even if Musharraf were to suddenly exit the Pakistani political scene at some point, Islamabad's currently disconsonant counterterrorism strategy would still survive so long as the men on horseback continue to be the principal guardians of national security policy making in Islamabad.

Because it is unreasonable to expect that the uniformed military will give up its privileges in this regard anytime soon— even if a civilian regime were to return to the helm in the future— the internally segmented counterterrorism policy currently pursued by Pakistan will likely persist for some time to come.

Even if it could be imagined that a civilian dispensation could wrest some control of Pakistan's national security policy from the military, it is not at all certain that the current strategic direction would change dramatically: a civilian regime would probably have greater incentives to combat all sectarian terrorist groups more evenhandedly, but that too is uncertain. After all, both the Pakistan People's Party led by the late Benazir Bhutto and the Pakistan Muslim League led by Nawaz Sharif have had problematic Islamist political allies in the past and, depending on the political exigencies of the moment, could harbor incentives to give even sectarian or otherwise radical entities a breather from prosecution, although that would likely be justified as only a temporary expedient.

Both civilian parties historically also permitted the Pakistani military and intelligence services to aid, abet, and arm the terrorist groups operating in Kashmir and elsewhere in India, sometimes because they were simply powerless to prevent it but at other times with their full knowledge and consent.

It also ought not to be forgotten that even a radically atavistic Islamist group such as the Taliban was raised, promoted, and unleashed by the civilian government of the late Benazir Bhutto (during her second term in office from 1993 to 1996) with the full collaboration of the Pakistani military and intelligence services— and that the Taliban continued to receive complete moral and material support under her civilian successor, the then prime minister, Nawaz Sharif.

3

Countering the Indian Mujahideen: India's Counter Terrorism Success

The arrest of Tahseen Akhtar alias Monu current leader of the Indian Mujahideen in Ajmer Rajasthan on 25 March 2013 marks significant success achieved by India's counter terrorism agencies adopting decapacitation as the principal strategy. This comes days after IM's Pakistani bomb-maker Zia-ur-Rehman alias Waqas was also arrested in Rajasthan.

Central to the strategy was creation of the National Investigation Agency (NIA). Contrary to popular belief the NIA can act on proactive information, provide inputs to the state anti terrorism squads and make arrests.

The focus of the NIA was the Indian Mujahideen after the terrorist outfit had carried out a series of attacks in the recent past starting with the Hyderabad Serial blasts in February 2013. These were followed by the Bodh Gaya and the Patna blasts the same year.

The breakthrough however came with the arrest of Yasin Bhatkal who was operating incognito from Nepal. In a cloak and dagger operation, Bhatkal was apprehended along with the group's chief bomb-maker Asadullah Akhtar. Bhatkal confessed to have carried out a large number of bomb attacks in the country including planning and in some cases actual execution. Bhatkal was reportedly apprehended by the Intelligence Bureau (IB) from deep inside Nepal though the home ministry said Bhatkal and Akhtar were arrested from Raxaul in Bihar.

Bhatkal was being tracked after his face came up in the CCTV footage of Hyderabad's Dilsukh Nagar where he was seen planting a bomb that killed 17 people in February 2013. Bhatkal whose real name is Mohammed Ahmed Sidibapa is accused of being involved in at least six other major blasts since 2008. Bhatkal's arrest follows that of LeT terrorist Abdul Karim Tunda, also with Nepal's help.

The interrogation of Yasin Bhatkal led to wealth of information on the activity and profile of the group across the country given that he was leading the network for a number of years. The NIA acting on this information had build up profile of the entire network identified key leaders and declared huge awards to the tune of Rs 10 Lakh (1 Million) for information leading to capture of key leaders as Tahseen Akhtar or Monu.

Tahseen Akhtar alias Monu reportedly replaced Yasin Bhatkal though some reports say and Dr Shahnawaz has taken over. Dr Shahnawaz is a leader of IM's Azamgarh module and escaped from India after the September 2008 Batla House encounter in Delhi as per a report in the India Today. He is known to be an expert in Improvised Explosive Device (IED) and was a link between SIMI and IM. He was also responsible for indoctrinating new members into IM. Tahseen Akhtar alias Monu belongs to Samastipur in Bihar has motivated and set up several modules in Bihar.

In February 2014, suspected key IM operative in Abu Dhabi believed to be Abdul Wahid Siddibapa was another major blow to the IM and particularly the Bhatkal cell which is based on youth from the coastal Karnataka town of Bhatkal. Siddibapa is also related to the IM founders Riyaz and Yasin Bhatkal. Wahid is obviously the linkman for the group in Abu Dhabi possibly carrying out liaison activities for the group in the Gulf thus resulting in contacting Indians who frequent the region as well as providing money flow.

With the Bhatkal or Karnataka Cell and Ranchi Cells of the IM effectively neutralized Azamgarh Cell in UP and remains underground. The regional spread with contacts in Karachi in

Pakistan will pose challenge for targeting the group completely. Indian Mujahideen is also trying to expand the terror network like Al-Qaida, keeping a close liaison with Pakistan based Tehreek-E –Taliban. Thus sustained pursuit of the outfit would be necessary.

Decapacitation strategy has produced similar results for Indian agencies in neutralizing the Naxals with leadership of the politburo either killed in encounters, apprehended by the police or surrendered. In January a key Naxal leader and spokesperson of the Maoist party in Chhattisgarh's Dandakaranya surrendered along with his wife. Gudsa Usendi alias G V K Prasad, a high ranking member and spokesperson of the Dandakaranya Special Zonal Committee (DKSZC) of the banned Communist Party of India (Maoist) who joined the mainstream carried a cash reward of Rs 20 lakh on his head.

Indian counter terrorism agencies seem to be specializing in decapacitation strategy though the Naxal and Indian Mujahideen threat is far from completely eliminated and will need sustained follow up.

THE INDIAN MUJAHIDEEN: A RESURGENCE OF TERROR

The blood that flowed through Varanasi on the evening of December 7, 2010, marked yet another appalling episode in the history of India's prolonged combat with the various subversive elements spread throughout the length and breadth of the country. Soon after the devastating attack that rocked the portals of the temple town, an e-mail was sent to various prominent media houses by the Indian Mujahideen claiming responsibility for the attack. The e-mail claimed that the blast was in retaliation to the verdict in the Babri Masjid-Ram Janambhoomi title suit case. Security agencies traced the Internet Protocol address of the five-page e-mail signed by 'Al-Arbi' to the suburbs of Mumbai.i Police teams were immediately despatched to the area for further investigation, the results of which are awaited.

At this juncture, it would be prudent to look into the inception as well the activities of the Indian Mujahideen (IM) in order to understand their composition, terror tactics, modus operandi, as well as the issues that inflame their operations. Thus, this chapter focuses on the inception of the IM, their links with the Students Islamic Movement of India (SIMI), the ideology that they profess, and the various attacks that have been attributed to the same. Since the subject requires an in-depth research into the intricacies of the terror group as well as its links with other groups, this chapter deals with certain aspects of the same. It is the initial part of a series of papers based on a study of the Indian Mujahideen.

INDIA'S HOME-GROWN JIHADI THREAT: A PROFILE OF THE INDIAN MUJAHIDEEN

Unknown before 2008, the Indian Mujahedeen (IM) has emerged as a well-organized jihadi terrorist group in India, claiming responsibility for a number of terror attacks perpetrated in various urban centers of India during 2007-2008. Even though the exact moment of IM's formation is not known, the recent arrest of a number of IM operatives has revealed its possible existence and involvement in terror strikes in India as far back as late October 2005. The name "Indian Mujahideen" was reportedly conceived at a terrorist conclave attended by top leaders of the Lashkar-e-Taiba (LeT) and Harkat-ul-Jehadi Islami (HuJI) in Pakistani-administered Kashmir in early May 2008 (Rediff.com, July 29, 2008).

The well-concealed rise of the Indian Mujahedeen as a home grown jihadi organization is not a good omen for India's security. IM came into the open for the first time in November 2007, when simultaneous bomb blasts targeted lawyers in court premises in three Uttar Pradesh cities—Varanasi, Faizabad (Ayodhya), and Lucknow (NDTV, November 23, 2007). IM described the attacks as "Islamic raids" and justified them as revenge against lawyers who had allegedly assaulted a couple of Jaish-e-Muhammad terrorist suspects. IM also alleged that the lawyers had refused to take cases involving other alleged terrorists, including suspected HuJI leader and Phulpur-based Islamic cleric Muhammad Waliullah, the alleged mastermind of the March 2006 Sankatmochan temple blasts in Varanasi.

In IM terror strikes, email messages have typically been sent out to the media prior to the attacks, describing IM viewpoints on issues such as the Babri mosque demolition, the Mumbai riots, the communal violence in Gujarat that followed the 2002 torching of a train carrying Hindus, and various atrocities against the Muslim community in Gujarat and beyond. IM cites these incidents as reasons for their Islamic Jihad. IM's email manifestos shed some light on its objectives. The group calls for spreading Islam in India and waging Jihad against the "infidels" (non-Muslims, i.e. Hindus) and establishing "God's government" according to Quranic tenets.

After prolonged investigations, Indian intelligence agencies have corroborated that members of IM are mainly drawn from proscribed outfits such as the Students Islamic Movement of India (SIMI), the Pakistan-based LeT and the Bangladesh-based HuJI. IM's email statements indicate their ties with SIMI when they put forward demands for the release of SIMI cadres under detention or serving jail terms. However, the newly emerged IM continues to deny any connection with Pakistan, Bangladesh, or any of their agencies (e.g. Pakistan's Inter-Services Intelligence [ISI] and Bangladesh's Directorate General of Forces Intelligence [DGFI]). It also denies any links with terrorist groups such as LeT and HuJI.

The Indian Mujahideen has been trying to garner support from India's teeming Muslim population, often by raising indigenous issues in its manifestos. Since the Uttar Pradesh Court attacks, IM, as a home-grown jihadi outfit, has claimed responsibility for at least four major terror strikes in 2008 that targeted civilians. Each attack came with prior emails to media citing a list of anti-Muslim atrocities in the country. The group justifies the violence by tagging the terror campaign as the "rise of Jihad" and the "revenge of Gujarat."

THE INDIAN MUJAHIDEEN'S URBAN MAYHEM

Massive IM terrorist attacks occurred throughout India in 2008, all apparently designed to inflict maximum civilian casualties:

- May 13, 2008: Jaipur, the capital city of Rajasthan State, suffered nine bomb blasts that killed over 60 and injured scores of people. The explosions occurred in busy MARKET places, including Tripolia market, Manek Chowk and Johri Bazaar.

- July 25, 2008: IM struck again in India's IT capital, Bengaluru (Bangalore, Karnataka State), with eight simultaneous low-intensity blasts, in which at least two people were killed and seven injured. The explosions occurred near the Madivala check point in Hosur Road, the Adugodi area, a place near the Mallya Hospital, and another site near the Rashtriya Military School.
- July 26, 2008: A series of over 16 synchronized bomb blasts hit Ahmadabad (Gujarat State), in which as many as 38 people were killed and more than 100 others injured. Most of the blasts occurred in crowded places like Hatkeshwar, Bapunagar, Narol, Ishanpur, Saraspur, Sarangpur, and L.G. General Hospital in Maninagar.
- September 13, 2008: The national capital, New Delhi, was hit by a series of five bomb blasts that killed nearly 30 people and injured over 100 others. The explosions took place in the crowded Karol Bagh area, the busy Barakhamba Road, the MARKET place at Greater Kailash, and the Central Park in Cannaught Place area.

After widespread mayhem in these vital urban centers, the organization was subject to a stepped-up counterterrorist crackdown on its operatives and hideouts across the country. At least six senior IM leaders are reported to have fled to Pakistan or Bangladesh after the Delhi serial blasts. They were identified by Mumbai's Crime Branch as Riyaz Bhatkal, Amir Reza, Iqbal Bhatkal, Muhammad Khalid, Shahzad Ahmed, and Ariz Khan.

After months of investigations it is widely believed by intelligence agencies in India that the IM was created by Pakistan's ISI to operate beyond Kashmir. However, no conclusive evidence has been gathered to implicate the ISI in such an alliance. The alleged Pakistani connection has not been supported by the large number of arrests of Indian operatives after the recent terrorist attacks.

Terror Tentacles

Though many details of IM's organization remain unclear, some facets of the mystery were unraveled during the interrogations of arrested cadres, documented in the 1,809-page charge sheet filed by the Mumbai Crime Branch. 21 IM members have been charged for conspiracy, damaging a place of worship with intent to insult a particular religion, collecting arms for waging war, and waging war against the country. Most of the accused are from Azamgarh in Uttar Pradesh and are well-qualified professionals (The Hindu, February 18). Among the 21 suspects is Muhammed Saif, who was involved in the September 13, 2008, New Delhi serial blasts and was later captured during the controversial October 19, 2008, Batla House raids, in which two suspects were killed.

Since his arrest, Muhammad Saif has provided details of the IM organization and its countrywide activities. According to his confession, the Indian Mujahedeen has four wings, each wing having a distinct responsibility for spreading terror in India with the LeT's active assistance (Bangalore Mirror, February 18; Rediff.com, February 10):

(1) Shahabuddin Ghouri Brigade: Headed by Amir Raza; responsible for planning and executing attacks in southern India, headquartered in Kerala
(2) Muhammad Ghaznavi Brigade: Responsible for planning and executing terror strikes in northern India
(3) Shaheed-al-Zarqawi Brigade: Responsible for targeting political and other important personalities of the country as well as organizing suicide attacks
(4) Media Wing: Headquartered in Pune, Maharashtra, the wing was responsible for email and print media communications/press release of manifestos before or after the blasts

The arrest of IM cadres from different locations demonstrates the geographical spread of a terror network that now spans the length and breadth of India—possibly even extending into neighbouring states.

Indian Mujahideen Who's Who

After months of speculation on the leadership hierarchy of IM, investigating agencies finally sketched a relatively clear picture of who's who in IM. Earlier, it had been speculated that the group's leader was Abdul Subhan Qureshi (a.k.a. Taqueer), a former SIMI cadre and software engineer by profession. However, instead the credit of founding the first home-grown Indian jihadi outfit goes to Sadiq Israr Sheikh of Azamgarh. A former SIMI member and an electronics engineer by profession, Sheikh has been identified as the co-founder and leader of the IM. Sheikh is alleged to have contacts with LeT in Pakistan through his brother-in-law, Mujahid Salim (The Hindu, February 22). The anti-terrorism squad of the Maharashtra police has been interrogating Sheikh regarding his role in the group's July 2006 serial train blasts in Mumbai. Sheikh has described how the group planted seven cookers filled with explosives on the train before getting off in advance of the blasts (Times of India, February 27). Sheikh's confession also indicates IM's hand in the March 2006 attack on the Sankat Mochan temple in Varanasi.

Riyaz Bhatkal (a.k.a. Ismail Shahbandri), who has eluded police so far, is the commander of the southern region. Iqbal Bhatkal, Riyaz's brother, has a senior position in the IM hierarchy, according to police sources. Riyaz Bhatkal was previously involved in organized crime in Mumbai as part of the infamous Fazlu Rehman gang (Chennai Online, September 27, 2008). Interrogation of arrested IM members revealed that Bhatkal was a key LeT operative in south India who had planned the Hyderabad, Bengaluru, Ahmadabad, and New Delhi serial blasts (Rediff.com, January 5). Abdul Subhan Qureshi, still on the run and formerly believed to be IM's leader, has now been confirmed as the IM second-in-command. Despite previously being named as one of the country's most wanted terrorist masterminds, Abdul Subhan's name did not appear in the recently filed chargesheet (Indian Express, February 19).

The most surprising revelation has been the many IT professionals found to be involved in IM's activities, including wealthy professionals Asghar Peerbhoy, Salman Kadar Shaikhand, and Asif Bashiruddin Shaikh, who have played pivotal roles in generating FUNDS for the outfit and planning attacks. Peerbhoy, believed to have headed IM's media wing, reportedly worked for Yahoo.com before being arrested by the Mumbai Anti-Terror Squad in October 2008 (Indian Express, February 5, 2009).

DEALING WITH THE AFTERMATH OF ATTACKS

The Mumbai November 26 attacks were marked by several new features though less in casualties than earlier incidents. For the first time heavily armed terrorists*invaded* India through a sea route and engaged in active combat for almost 68 hours. All earlier attacks on Mumbai were explosions through timed devices. It was also the first time that many foreigners were killed, mostly in 5 star hotels. Although casualties were less, the psych ological damage and panic it created on civil population resulted in severe public anger resulting in the resignation of several senior politicians including the State Chief Minister and Union Home Minister.

The attacks unveiled a number of innovations in terrorist methodology. The most important was the handlers ability to direct action from a foreign country. Next was their ability in utilizing target country s free electronic media as guide for further killing. Competitive visual media covering the attack beamed minute to minute details which were relayed back to killer teams by handlers through cell phones. Simultaneous attacks on all the five targets totally confused an unprepared Mumbai Police and public much like the September 11 attacks did to the Americans. The elaborate subterfuge which the handlers organized in their communications with terrorists was yet another innovation.

Unlike many other earlier attacks in India, during this incident real time operational co-operation between foreign and Indian agencies in tracking down communications between terrorists and handlers took place. This helped immediate tactical planning for counter measures. Foreign cooperation also helped to secure scientific evidence in tracking down the source of procurement of equipment used for the attack. Thus this incident provided a highly illustrative case for examining international cooperation in counter-terrorism.

The Mumbai attacks

In January 2008 India nationals Fahim Ansari and Sabuddin Shaikh handed over rough target maps to the "Lashkar-e-Taiba" (LeT) leadership. This was fed into five Garmin Rino GPS sets procured by the LeT. Fake Indian (Hindu) identity cards were prepared for ten terrorists (in five "buddy pairs") who were taught the Hindi spoken in Mumbai. To hide their communication, the LeT booked an account in October 2008 with Callphonex, a New Jersey (USA) VOIP service provider and obtained different cell numbers in an Indian fictitious name as a VOIP re-seller. Separate numbers were obtained for two way communications (handler to terrorists and terrorists to handler). Payments were made from different locations including Pakistan and Italy. Fictitious e-mail ID created by them was traced subsequently to ten IP addresses in Lahore, Chicago, Kuwait, Koroliov (Russia) and Rawalpindi. This was used for communication with Callphonex and also with an Indian TV channel claiming themselves as "Deccan Mujahideen". One IP address-that of Sajid Iftikar-was traced to "Special Communication Organization", Rawalpindi, which was suspected to be a government organization. An inflatable rubber dinghy was procured with a Yamaha outboard engine by "Busin ess and Engineering Trends", Lahore. Five cell phone handsets used by terrorists and abandoned in Mumbai were found procured from Nokia, in Dongguan, China by different addresses in Pakistan. Live hand grenades recovered from dead terrorists had "Arges" mark traced to the "Wah Nobel Company" located near Islamabad.

The fully trained terrorists left Pakistan i waters on November 23 in a Pakistani vessel "al-Husaini". Each was armed with a AK-47 rifle with 240 bullets, 10 grenades, one 7.62 pistol with 14 rounds, a Nokia cell phone, a RDX laden IED (Improvised explosive device) and dry fruits. The group had a satellite phone. On entering Indian waters off Saurashtra coast they hijacked an Indian vessel *M.V.Kuber* with five crew members. Four of them were led away in al-Husaini and reportedly killed. One was taken to Mumbai coast as a guide, until the last four nautical miles, and then killed. They then inflated the rubber boat with a foot pump, transferred all equipment and abandoned the *Kuber* with the dead sailor, and reached the Mumbai shoreline around 8:30pm on November 26. On landing in the thickly populated Machimar Nagar (Fishermen s Colony) opposite Badhwar Railway Officers quarters, they split themselves into five groups and went towards target areas. Some hired taxis while one team walked up to the Chabad House through narrow bye-lanes. All were guided by GPS instruments. Targets were: Leopold Café, Taj Palace Hotel, Chabad House, Railway Terminal and Oberoi/Trident Hotel. The Chabad House terrorists were the last to fall at about 4:00 pm on November 29 while the two terrorists in the Oberoi-Trident lasted until that morning. The two terrorists who attacked the railway terminal tried to escape through a narrow lane into Cama Hospital where they killed seven and hijacked a senior police officer s vehicle after killing nine, including three senior police officers, around midnight of November 26 and 27. However soon thereafter they were finally intercepted by a police road block on "Marine Drive". One terrorist was killed while the other was taken alive. He was Ajmal Kasab, the lone Pakistani terrorist who was caught alive, faced trial and was sentenced to death on May 6, 2010.

As far as can be ascertained this was the first time terrorist handlers actively guided attacks from Pakistan through cell phones with numbers appearing from European countries. Also almost certainly for the first time, the terrorist handlers were helped by a visual media broadcasting minute to minute details on attacks at different spots, casualties, persons who were trapped, public panic and all other operational details.

Policemen who saw visuals of their top leaders dying in ambush including an Inspector General in charge of the State anti-terrorist squad conveyed to the Enquiry Team that it seriously demoralized the entire force which was engaged in combat operations for 68 hours. Further and significant public panic also resulted from several bombs going off in different parts of the city. The terrorists had planted bombs in unsuspecting taxis which took them to target spots which later blew up in different parts of the city. Bombs planted in the Taj hotel, the Oberoi-Trident and Chabad House, exploded causing great damage. Rumours that started to spread claimed 60 terrorists had invaded the city.

Strategic failures of government machinery

Even though central agencies received a series of intelligence alerts from 2006 that the LeT was training teams for sea borne commando attacks on multiple targets including luxury hotels in Mumbai they did not lead to capacity building by the local police in Maharashtra state. No efforts were made to strengthen sea patrolling. In the Indian system, the State Police were responsible for guarding 12 nautical miles from shore line, the Defence Ministry s Coast Guards from 12 to 200 nautical miles and the rest is the responsibility of the Navy. Owing to several reasons the st ate of Maharashtra, which has 720 kilometres of coast line, could not set up satisfactory coastal security. The Central Government also failed to order the Coast Guards to keep vigilance despite generating terror alerts since 2006. Special ant i-terrorist squads created in Maharashtra to confront terrorists in the wake of earlier bomb attacks also proved inadequate. The terrorists used "area clearing weapons" like grenades against which the local police had no suitable equipment to counter.

Prior to the attacks the central and state governments neglected "open source intelligence" on such attacks. They failed to verify press reports that a suspected LeT vessel with terrorists was intercepted in March 2007 off the Mumbai coast by the Coast Guards. Similarly the Mumbai police failed to analyze capacity building by the terrorist groups concerned and their implications for Mumbai's own security following the Kabul Serena Hotel attack (January 2008) or Islamabad Marriot attack (September 2008).

The government s response was also let down by the time it took (almost 11 hours) for the National Security Guards (NSG), the specially trained commando force to counter terrorist attacks, to arrive at the scene since they had to be flown from a location near New Delhi. By the time they arrived most of the killings and arson had already taken place. The Army and Navy contingents who were deployed in the interim to help the local police proved ineffective in resisting the heavily armed and well trained terrorists. Even the NSG only managed to clear the last of the terrorists in the afternoon of November 29. The local police, although poorly equipped and took heavy casualties in the process, contributed most to containing the damage by avoiding the violence from spilling beyond the target spots. Its officers even ventured inside the narrow labyrinths of luxury hotels to keep terrorists at bay although they could not match the terrorists' skill.

A constitutional provision of division of power between the Union and the states is partly responsible for the poor preparedness of State Police forces. The primary responsibility for internal security affecting the 1.3 billion Indian people is with the civil police numbering about 1 million working under 28 state governments and seven Union territories. The Seventh Schedule of Indian Constitution provides for distribution of powers wherein "police" and "public order" is the state's responsibility. States have been reluctant to dilute this. The deployment of police is a prerogative of state governments and the Union government, as such, has no authority to order the deployment of police. Unlike other countries India has no law on "federal crime. Consequently terrorism even emanating from outside international borders is considered as crimes to be investigated only by state police. Training and deployment of state police are left to individual states. The quality of police training and preparedness thus differ from state to state. The Mumbai incident confirms long standing experience that this is a key weakness in India s anti-terrorist capacity.

Inexperience of local authorities also contributed to their failure in handling an attack on the scale of the Mumbai assaults. Ambulance services failed while fire engines ran out of water. Police vehicles had to be used to ferry the injured to hospitals and also as escorts for fire engines trying to replenish their water. Instead of having one centralized Operations Room, different sets of supervisory officials met in different "Control Rooms". The experience underlined the need to have an overall "Operational Incident Manager" to take charge of the situation.

Present features of Jehadi terrorism in South Asia and inter-state links

Educated Indian Jehadi recruits continue to h ave links with others including like minded extremists abroad as revealed by the terrorists arrested in September 2010 for the February 13, 2010 Pune (Maharashtra) "German Bakery" IED attack which killed 17 and injured 56. Footprints of the Indian Mujahideen (IM) and the LeT were clearly visible proving James Kitfield's premonition in 2006. The attack architecture was prepared in a remote town,

Udgir, 590 kilometers from Mumbai in a small Cyber Café owned by Mirza Himayat Baig. The 3 kilogram RDX bomb assembled here was carried all the way from Udgir to Pune (380Km) on a public bus! They also wanted to attack a major Indian Army camp in Deolali (Nashik District adjoining Pune District) to avenge the Malegaon Bomb attack on September 28, 2008 by a Hindu extremist group. The main terrorists were trained by the LeT in Pakistan and had used Bangladesh and Nepal for clandestine cross border journeys. Mirza Himayat Baig revealed that he received training in Colombo, a hitherto unknown training centre, in "Daura-e-aam" (Basic combat course) and "Daura-e-Khaas" (3 months advanced combat course). Colombo was preferred since Pakistan-Nepal or Pakistan-Bangladesh routes have been kept under close surveillance since November 26. He also said that terrorists preferred operating in small modules to prevent detection. Another terrorist Sheikh Hussain Fareed alias "Bilal" who lived as a Hindu in Nashik District said that he was indoctrinated in Qatar in 2007 while working as a mechanic. Bilal was then sent to Dubai and Iran to meet with LeT leadership. He said that Gulf countries continued to be key recruiting areas for Indian youths.

Some fringe organizations representing "marginalized sections" of Indian society with avowed political agenda were found instigating extremist activities clandestinely. Abdul Nasser Madani of Kerala State, leader of the Islamic Sevak Sangh (Islamic Service Society-ISS) and later of Peoples Democratic Party (PDP) when ISS was banned in 1992, was accused in the 1998 Coimbatore serial bomb blasts killing 60. After his acquittal in 2007 he was wooed by Kerala State political parties to garner Muslim votes. However he was again arrested in 2010 for inciting LeT terrorists responsible for several bomb blasts including the 2008 Bangalore serial bombing cases. Similarly some activists of the Popular Front of India (PFI) were accused of chopping off the right hand of Mr. Joseph, a Kerala College professor on July 4 2010, for alleged blasphemy in preparing a College question paper.

"Mega Cities": A big problem in developing Countries

South Asian cities are "Endless Cities" with nightmarish logistical problems for law and order even in normal times. India s Central Urban Development Ministry's "Expert Committee" has said that the projected slum population in or around major Indian cities would go up from the present 75.26 million to 93.06 million in 2011. Lopsided urban development in most major cities has created honey comb residential structures on narrow streets causing traffic snarls, water scarcity and a host of other problems. Mumbai, which had a population of 7 million in 1975, has 14 million now. Including its satellite cities it is 19 million. The entire population is confined to a land area of 604 square kilometers, with 54% living in slums occupying only 6% of the land area. Seven million travel daily by suburban trains while the volume of daily traffic by bus is four million. Flash riots take place if daily transit trains are delayed. Even in ordinary times emergency vehicles have grave difficulties in reaching trouble spots promptly.

INTER-STATE COUNTER-TERRORIST COOPERATION IN SOUTH ASIA

Terrorism was noticed as a new phenomenon in India only since the mid-1980s after Prime Minister Indira Gandhi s assassination by her police guards on October 31, 1984. India then created new Central anti-terrorist forces to help the state police in meeting terrorism which had raged in Punjab after Indian forces stormed the Sikh religious shrine in June 1984 to flush out militants. From 1989 onwards Kashmir related terrorism gave a new dimension to the problem while the Babri Masjid demolition by Hindu zealots on December 6, 1992 extended it to the rest of India. Communal strife gave way to Jehadi terrorism. However Indian Police did not evolve a holistic strategy to tackle terrorism since information on terrorist activities was scattered in different wings of the Security machinery. The March 12, 1993 serial blasts in Mumbai, which killed 257 in 13 "serial" explosions, were considered as the first manifestation of externally sponsored terrorism in the "rest of India". It was not so. Indian security forces forgot that an earlier externally sponsored attempt to spread strife to South India with similar *modus operandi* by bombing various targets including the Madras Stock Exchange. This series of attacks failed due to the chance arrest of the Toronto based Lal Singh on

July 16, 1992. The Central Bureau of Investigation which took over investigation from the local police in August 1992, failed to inform others of this methodology of serial bomb blasts-much like the failures of US authorities prior to September 11 where interrogation reports were not shared. Consequently the then Bombay Police Commissioner told the media that he suspected LTTE s hand immediately after the March 1993 blasts in which the Bombay Stock Exchange was also bombed.

The lack of a holistic understanding of the inter links between terrorists adversely affects not only the internal counter-terrorist operations within a country but also the countering of global terrorism. I first underlined the importance of understanding how terrorists operated trans-nationally during a lecture at the Seminar on Terrorism organized by the National Advisory Council on South Asian Affairs, Washington DC on June 19, 2003. It was the chance arrest of Noor Sikander by Mumbai Police in May 2003, who was responsible for the March 2003 serial Mulund blasts, that revealed Aftab Ansari – deported from Dubai to India in February 2002 – was involved in the January 2002 shooting of the Kolkata American Centre in Calcutta, and as the mastermind of the kidnapping for ransom of Partha Burman (Kadim shoes, Kolkata) in July 2001. The ransom (reportedly US$ 600,000 or $830,000) was sent through "Hawala" channels in Hyderabad or Dubai to Saeed Omar Sheikh of Jaish-e-Mohammad (the killer of Daniel Pearl) who forwarded it to Mahammed Atta before September 11. In other words the Kolkata ransom wholly or partially funded September 11 attacks. We came to know about this only in 2003. No state police with inherent handicaps would have learnt about this in advance since criminal activities spanned several states/ countries.

Counter-terrorist cooperation between different countries usually depends on bilateral political relations. If bilateral relations warm up there is some movement in cooperation as we see with India and Bangladesh. The present Bangladesh Government has handed over several fugitives of Unit ed Liberation Front of Assam (ULFA), a regional terrorist group hiding in Bangladesh. However by and large there has been no satisfactory cooperation among

South Asian countries due to historical factors. Despite reaching the "SAARC [South Asian Association for Regional Co-Operation] Regional Convention on Suppression on Terrorism" since 1987 no concrete steps have been taken by the signatories to establish intelligence sharing or arrest of fugitive terrorists. Sometimes even when political relations are normal such exchanges do not result in prompt action. Early in October 1994 Indian intelligence came to know LTTE preparations to assassinate Gamini Dissanayaka, one of Sri Lanka's brightest politicians. Sri Lankan authorities were immediately alerted through diplomatic channel. However this was lost in the bureaucratic chain and Gamini Dissanayaka was killed in a suicide bomb attack near Colombo on October 24, 1994 much like former Indian Prime Minister Rajiv Gandhi who was killed on May 21, 1991.

Studies of the Indo-Pakistani relations indicate that temporary groundswell of good dialogue is not translated into policy correction. The "Hawana Declaration" (September 16, 2006) between President Pervez Musharraf and Prime Minister Dr. Manmohan Singh on intelligence exchange was a non-starter. The bonhomie witnessed during SAARC Interior Ministers Conference (Islamabad, June 2010) and the warm sound bites between Indian and Pakistan Interior ministers during bilateral parleys, which also saw the first ever meeting between both countries Chiefs of Intelligence Bureaus, did not in fact result in any forward movement to implement "SAARC Convention on Mutual Assistance in Criminal Matters". Indeed, the verbal pyrotechnics witnessed later between both countries on Kashmir stone throwing and police action have almost wiped out the possibility of any movement by Pakistan pursuing the case against November 26 conspirators which were purely as a result of external pressure.

What is the way out?

It will be futile to imagine that relationship between some South Asian countries would improve in the near future to enable active counter terrorist cooperation to European standards. However, experience reveals that activities of scattered extremist modules in different countries pose threats not only to home countries but also to the rest of the world. Experience during the last thirty years has revealed that terrorism is not a conventional foreign intelligence problem. Yet most nations still entrust their foreign intelligence agencies with collection of intelligence on terrorism and liaison merely because terrorists usually live outside their national boundaries. Most intelligence agencies are organized on the basis of lessons learnt from World War II to support their foreign offices. They share the same professional culture and outlook, and often undertake intrusive and at times coercive operations under cover of diplomacy. Because of this they suffer from mutual distrust. In contrast, terrorism based on transnational religious extremism is a new phenomenon that uses organized crime's tradecraft. It is more of a policing problem than a foreign intelligence service problem. In this context it is useful to remember the main recommendation of the "John Major Enquiry Report" on the 1985 Air India Kanishka aircraft bombing. He advised the CSIS to upgrade their intelligence collection to the level of MI5 or ASIO in producing intelligence that can be used as evidence.

It is a generally accepted fact that police organizations enjoy better credibility even between less friendly nations since their activities are governed by national criminal laws supervised by courts. That is not the case with intelligence agencies, which are often suspected to be working against other countries or whose work are not subject to be tested in a court of law. It is for this reason why national crime investigating agencies like FBI or Australian National Police have foreign relations posts. Even New York Police and Los Angeles Police Departments have foreign liaison posts in view of the complex problems of terrorism originating from abroad. To make South Asia more effective in countering transnational terrorism, "Police Attaches" should be appointed to liaise with local police authorities where they are needed.

DEVELOPING STRATEGIC LEADERS FOR THE 21ST CENTURY

It is remarkable how the scope and focus of American national security policy have changed since September 11, 2001 (9/11). The United States has fought two major wars in Afghanistan and Iraq and is engaged in the daunting challenges of post-conflict stability operations in both countries. The "war on terrorism" continues both here in America as well as throughout the globe. Policymakers remain engaged with the challenges of globalization, international trade, the spread of AIDS, etc., that predate the 2001 terrorist attacks. Now, however, they must view these problems through a new lens and confront emerging challenges with Iran and North Korea. Finally, these conditions are not transitory—the nation must expect that the threat of multiple crises having an immediate effect on American security will continue indefinitely. The old adage that Washington is "a one crisis town" can no longer apply.

These events have changed how we think about "national security." They have dramatically expanded not only the number and scope of issues, but also the overall complexity of the process. Americans who felt safe at home and viewed security threats as distant from our shores no longer feel this way. The government that is supposed to protect us has also felt the winds of change. The requirement for interagency decisionmaking has accelerated, demands for greater policy flexibility have increased, and a process that was largely confined to a few agencies of the Federal government now involves a multitude of new players and allied states. Clearly, the sad and apparently unexpected aftermath of the Iraq War underscores the critical need for significant changes in the planning of military operations, preparation for post-conflict requirements, *and* oversight of their execution.

As the nation embarked on this new era at the turn of the century, the *2002 National Security Strategy* noted that we must "transform America's national security institutions to meet the challenges and opportunities of the 21st century." The Bush administration responded initially with the creation of the Department of Homeland Security, the largest change in the structure of the Federal government since the National Security Act of 1947. But we must also transform existing institutions, the policy process, and how we "think" about the defense of the nation. Furthermore, as General Richard Myers, former Chairman of the Joint Chiefs of Staff, observed, this transformation cannot wait—"It must take place as we wage the war on terrorism."

Crucial to this effort is developing a system that places the right people in the right places in government at the right moment. The nation critically needs civilian policymakers who can manage change and deal with the here and now. This monograph will examine the development of career civilian leaders for strategic decisionmaking in the national security policy process. Such development must include the recruitment of high-quality personnel, experiential learning through a series of positions of increasing responsibility, training for specific tasks or missions, and continuous education that considers both policy and process. Consequently, it requires people who are not only substantively qualified and knowledgeable of policy issues, but also possessed of the leadership abilities to direct large complex organizations.

This monograph will first consider existing efforts in the Office of the Secretary of Defense (OSD), State Department, and Central Intelligence Agency (CIA) and then make appropriate recommendations for each. It will further consider what changes must be made to existing personnel management systems and development programs to encourage the creation of an effective cadre of civilian "national security" professionals for the policy process. Such recommendations may be applicable to other executive agencies as well. These three departments were selected since they are in many ways those with a clear traditional role in the development of foreign and defense policy. Clearly, there are additional considerations with respect to current and growing requirements for those with technical expertise, human resource management, finance/comptroller skills, etc. The development of personnel with such talents for these three agencies will not be the subject of this monograph.

Some critics might observe from the outset that the nation is at war and can ill-afford reorganizations or changes at this critical moment. The sad tragedy that has been the Iraq War would suggest otherwise. It became clear almost immediately following the invasion in 2003 that fundamental errors had been made in intelligence and policy analysis. From the very beginning the United States not only required additional troops for the occupation of Iraq but also enhanced civilian leadership and capacity to reconstruct Iraqi society. Without both these components, efforts to forestall the ensuing chaos as well as the resultant insurgency were doomed to failure.

Poor civilian leadership and mismanagement have been clearly documented in numerous studies, books, reports, and articles. Official reports provided by Stuart W. Bowen, Jr., Special Inspector General for Iraq Reconstruction (SIGIR), are particularly critical of American efforts in Iraq. In early 2007, SIGIR reported that despite nearly $108 billion budgeted for the reconstruction of Iraq since 2003, the country's electricity output and oil production were still below prewar levels. Stocks of gasoline and kerosene had actually plummeted to their lowest levels in at least 2 years. Consequently, Mr. Bowen testified before the Senate Judiciary Committee in March 2007 that his office planned to "aggressively pursue" the suspension and prosecution of contractors who are determined to have engaged in fraudulent contracting activities in Iraq. He further observed that the failure of the American-financed reconstruction program in Iraq threatened to be repeated elsewhere unless structural changes were made in the U.S. Government. Mr. Bowen compared his recommendations to the Congress as not dissimilar to proposals made in the 1980s that resulted in legislation strengthening the Joint Chiefs of Staff.

Prior to this, the Iraq Study Group (ISG) noted in its comprehensive report in late 2006 that "civilian agencies also have little experience with complex overseas interventions to restore and maintain order—stability operations—outside of the normal embassy setting." The ISG described the mission in Iraq as "unfamiliar and dangerous." As a result, the report observed that the United States had great difficulty filling civilian assignments in Iraq with sufficient qualified personnel. The ISG recommended that the constituent agencies (State, Defense, the U.S. Agency for International Development [USAID], Treasury, Justice, Intelligence community, etc.) train for and conduct joint operations across agency boundaries. It further suggested that the State Department expand its efforts to train personnel to carry out civilian tasks associated with such complex stability operations, concluding that a Foreign Service Reserve Corps with personnel and expertise to provide surge capacity for such operations be established. This effort should provide a model for other civilian agencies to include Treasury, Justice, and Agriculture. Such ideas, however, were hardly new. They had been recommended a year or more prior to the release of the ISG report by leading government experts and officials.

As American patience wears thin over the failure to achieve progress in Iraq the argument might be presented that this venture has been a tragic aberration. Once the United States withdraws from Iraq, it can simply avoid future efforts to rebuild societies torn apart by conflict. Unfortunately, this global conflict will not allow us that luxury. We are confronted by an enemy who would replace secular governments with theocratic regimes hostile to our national interests and values. Their strategy amounts to "a global series of insurgencies, competing for the right to govern" in many predominantly Muslim nations around the globe. State collapse will continue to challenge the national interests of the United States and its allies for decades to come. If we are to prevail, we must mobilize and synchronize all elements of our national power—diplomatic, military, economic, social, and informational—to confront these new and extremely dangerous adversaries. The key actions required in a counterinsurgency involve "work we associate with civilian skill sets and even agencies—but the uniformed military is often placed in the position of having to undertake such activities." Consequently, a rebalancing of roles between military and civilian leaders is required. Regardless of what the final outcome is in Iraq, that outcome may not be our past so much as our future. This new security environment requires better qualified civilian leaders to think in different patterns in order to accomplish these daunting tasks.

Terms

Understanding certain assumptions is crucial to this analysis. First, some observers may take exception to the distinction between the words "training" and "education." They may argue that they are synonymous, as we frequently use them interchangeably. They are *not* the same, there being a significant denotative difference. While training is more concerned with teaching *what* to think and what the *answers* ought to be, education is all about teaching *how* to think and what the *questions* ought to be: "Training is focused on the development and performance of specific tasks or skills, and education is oriented toward more generalized and abstract knowledge that may or may not be tied to specific tasks or action." Training is most frequently used when the goal is to prepare an individual or an organization to execute specified tasks. It often includes repetition of tasks, not unlike an athletic team learning to execute plays. Finally, it is normally the preferred method of learning when the goal is to perform operations in which success, failure, and completion can be clearly measured. Education has more to do with how to think about problems and how to deal with those things that may not lend themselves to categorical solutions. It becomes a matter of intellect, thought, indirect leadership, advice, and consensus building.

Second, we must also differentiate between "leadership" and "management." *Management is about coping with complexity*. It is a response to a significant development of the 20th century, namely, the emer-gence of large, complex organizations. Good management brings order to what would otherwise be chaos. *Leadership, by contrast, is about coping with change.* An expert in human development once wisely observed, "If you don't like change, you will like irrelevancy even less." American business recognized this phenomenon as competition in the market and volatility in business cycles became more intensive and jarring. Doing the same thing only slightly better was no longer good enough. *Management* remains important for the day-to-day success of any organization, focusing as it does on such issues as planning/budgeting, organizing/staffing, and controlling/problem solving. By contrast, *leadership* begins with setting directions, aligning people, and motivating them to achieve success. The successful development of government policy for the war on terrorism is wholly dependent upon developing leaders of substance at all levels of executive agencies. They must be able balance the pressing requirements of management with the critical need to provide leadership for their organizations and the collective effort.

These expanding requirements for improved leadership and management preceded 9/11, and remain an integral part of dealing with the rapid pace of change. In his widely acclaimed book, *The Lexus and the Olive Tree,* Thomas Friedman described the importance of change in the international system along with the corresponding demands placed on both organizations and individuals. He argued that "Globalization" had replaced the Cold War as the new defining international system. But "the globalization system, unlike the Cold War system, is not frozen, but a dynamic ongoing process." Friedman observed that "if the Cold War were a sport, it would be sumo wrestling." Quoting Professor Michael Mandelbaum, he continued: "It would be two big fat guys in a ring, with all sorts of posturing and rituals and stomping of feet, but actually very little contact, until the end of the match, when there is a brief moment of shoving and the loser gets pushed out of the ring, but nobody gets killed." Globalization, by contrast, "would be the 100meter dash, over and over and over. And no matter how many times you win, you have to race again the next day. And if you lose by just one-hundredth of a second, it can be as if you lost by an hour."

In this new environment, any program that places "the right people, in the right place, at the right time" must acknowledge that it seeks to develop policy substance as well as management and leadership in its workforce to confront the changes engendered by globalization and the new security environment. If the policy process is to be improved, it must have well-qualified policymakers who understand the issues. Many must also develop into leaders as they move through their careers. These future leaders must be able to set goals, inspire performance, and monitor progress for the success of their organizations and the overall process.

INDIAN MUJAHIDEEN AND ITS DUBIOUS ORIGIN

For all the claims, the probing and prosecuting agencies have not come out with one individual who has a proven association with this so-called nationwide organization supposedly working at the behest of Lashkar e Toiba, Hizbul Mujahideen, Taliban and you name who, so how do we know IM really exists or is merely the figment of imagination of the IB/Saffron brigade happily lapped up by an already biased media?

But let us just glean through the official explanation. Wikipedia says, "Investigators believe that Indian Mujahideen is one of many groups composed of lower-tier SIMI members. According to the Indian Intelligence Bureau, SIMI took new titles because the top leadership of SIMI have been detained and would be available for interrogation. The change in name is believed to signal a change in tactics as SIMI affiliated militants attempt to garner more support from India's Muslim community rather than be seen as a group consisting of foreigners. Two days after the 13 May 2008 Jaipur bombings, the extremist group sent an e-mail to Indian media in which they claimed responsibility for the attacks and said they would "demolish the faiths (all religions apart from Islam) of the infidels of India". The biggest and boldest attack to date by the group was the 2008 Ahmedabad serial blasts, where it gained national notoriety with a casualty count towards 50."

Now who banned SIMI and when was it banned and on what grounds? First came the terror attack on the Indian Parliament on December 13, 2001, which is a grey area because of the apprehension of the whole exercise sponsored by the then NDA-led government and specifically the Union Home ministry under the then Home Minister LK Advani. Soon thereafter Narendra Modi led Gujarat government patronized the pogrom of Muslims ostensibly to avenge the burning down of kar sevaks in coach number S-6, in the Sabarmati Express on February 27, 2002, just two months after the Parliament attack. Those who don't suffer from a memory loss remember the whole charged atmosphere created by Advani-Modi and Jaitley combine against the Muslim youth in preparation of bringing in POTA and to justify POTA SIMI was banned just a little before POTA was conceived. While announcing the ban Advani held a press conference in North Block and distributed to the media some SIMI posters in Urdu, none of which carried any seditious material. All these were expressions of anger and frustration over the Gujarat pogrom and the inability of anyone to counter Modi.

So what is wrong in saying that IM is an outcome of Gujarat pogrom? When did IM come into prominence and how? The official version says, "Two days after the 13 May 2008 Jaipur bombings, IM sent an e-mail to the Indian media in which they claimed responsibility for the attacks and said they would "demolish the faiths of the infidels of India". The biggest and boldest attack to date by the group was the 2008 Ahmedabad serial blasts, where it gained national notoriety when 56 people were killed in those serial blasts." This is the official version.

Who according to the official version are prominent leaders of IM:

1. Abdus Subhan Qureshi, alias Ali Tauqeeer a Gujarati software engineer from Mumbai
2. Safdar Nagori from Indore
3. Qayamuddin Kapadia, a TRADER from Vadodra
4. Usman Agarbattiwala, a PG diploma holder from Vadodra
5. Alazeb Afridi, a jobless youth from Ahmedabad
6. Abdul Razzzak Mansuri, an embroidery unit owner from Gujarat
7. Mujib Shaikh, a stone polishing artisan from Gujarat
8. Zahid Sheikh, a mobile repair owner from Ahmedabad
9. Amil Parvaiz, a native of Ujjain. These were the original IM men according to the IB along with just one Mufti Abu Bashir from Azamgarh. Later after the Batla House incident of Delhi, according to the investigative agencies it had also spread its tentacles in UP as well, and in particular in Azamgarh district.

But then stating the obvious becomes a crime and the BJP cries hoarse attacking poor Shakeel Ahmad while the Congress always lacking spunk, hurriedly withdraws what with the Heir Apparent in the ruling party advising everyone not to irritate BJP/Modi too much and so poor Shakeel has to shut up.

4

Indian Mujahideen: Terrorist Group and Great Threat to India

WHAT IS MUJAHIDEEN?

The actual meaning of Mujahideen is a struggler. However in practice, it has been identified with such men who are fighting Jihad (in their own way) for self glorified Islamic cause. Now, it is always related to religious and Islamic connection. The word is also used as some sort of title to Islamic names.

Many names of Muslims proudly carry the word Mujahid because the acts of those who fight for the religion are glorified in Islamic scriptures. As it is, Holy Qoran prescribes that those who die in the cause of Islam and become martyrs attain paradise directly to enjoy all comforts such as company of many virgins. Thus, the word Mujahideen has come to stand for a religious fighter although in real sense the word is not connected to religion.

In the late 20th century and early 21st century, the term "Mujahideen" became the name of various armed fighters who subscribe to militant Islamic ideologies and identify themselves as Mujahideen, although there is not always an explicit "holy" or "warrior" meaning of the word. Indian Mujahideen are a recent terror outfit active in India, that has claimed the responsibility for several attacks on unarmed unsuspecting civilians in India . Indian Mujahideen are no special men. They are motivated fundamentalists, blood thirsty and misguided men who aim at Islamizing India at all costs. They are motivated by the false propaganda that India belonged to Muslims as they ruled for many years. They of course forget that Islam is only 1500 years old while Hinduism is very old and was ruled by Hindu kings. Thus it no way belongs to Muslims. It is not necessary that these men are not educated in modern way and Madrasa (religious school) bred always like Taliban now hiding desperately in Pakistan saving their skins. Even highly educated youth and even professionals join Mujahideen and indulge in murderous acts and nefarious anti national activities amounting to sedition. All Islamic terrorists claim themselves as Mujahideen. Therefore, most of the terrorist outfits name themselves including the word Mujahideen as a title and glorification and falsely feel elated and proud about themselves.

Indian intelligence agencies described that the Indian Mujahideen are terror activists who have been banned in the country; such as the Harkat-ul-Jihad-al-Islami (HuJI) a Bangladesh based organization and Students Islamic Movement of India (SIMI). Several bombings in past (July 25, 2008 in Bangalore and July 26th, 2008 in Ahmedabad) have been attributed to this little known organization. Several different militant groups have since taken root in Kashmir. Most noticeable of these groups are Lashkar-e-Toiba (LeT), Jaish-e-Mohammed (JeM), Jammu and Kashmir Liberation Front (JKLF) and Harkat-ul-Mujahideen (HuM). A 1996 report by Human Rights Watch estimated the number of active militants at 3,200. The Delhi bomb blasts of 2008 were claimed by this organization. The group has distributed a pamphlet in connection with Delhi Bomb blasts.

The email received during Jaipur blasts claimed that Indian Mujahideen had formed three wings — Shahbuddin Ghouri Brigade (for South India), Mahmood Gaznavi Brigade (for North India) and Shaheed Al-Zarqawi Brigade (suicide attackers) — to target various cities in the country. The names of Shabuddin Ghori and Mohammed Ghaznavi are from the medieval period. Now they are glorifying the Al Qaeda terrorist Zarqavi killed in Iraq in an American air raid. Mohammed Ghori and Mohammed Ghaznavi were rulers of Kabul who led expeditions against India during 12 century and finally managed to establish Muslim rule at Delhi in 1192 that was called slave sultanate. Ghaznavi is glorified for looting and pillaging Somanath temple several times in Gujarat (1001-1026) apart from many other shrines in India. These men are worshipped by Muslims as great warriors who subdued Hindustan in bye gone ages.

Pakistan has also named their missiles by their names. They however forget that Ghori was defeated several times by Prithviraj Chauhan the king of Thaneswar before he was defeated by treachery and killed in the battle of Tarain. Shabuddin Ghori was mean and did not reciprocate in the same way as Prithviraj Chauhan acted when Ghori was captured in earlier battles. Conduct as gentle man cost Chauhan his life and kingdom. The Mujahideen derive inspiration from the names of Ghaznavi and Ghori as Hindus derive the same from Rajput warrior king Maha Rana Pratap (1572-1597) and Maratha King and warrior Chatrapathi Rajadhi Raj Shivaji Maharaj (1630-1680) and Rani Laxmi Bai of Jhansi (Of 1857 war fame). The pamphlet distributed by the Indian Mujahideen reveal following. These are highly objectionable too:

1. Allah is the only one to be believed and there is none who can be equated to him. Naturally all others who believe other Gods are Kafirs and are to be dealt with sternly including conversion or put to sword.
2. All Hindus must accept Allah and save themselves from annihilation. This means conversion to Islam.
3. The Hindu Gods such as Ram, Krishna and Hanuman and other thousands of Gods made by clay are not going to save Hindus from getting killed by Mujahideen.
4. Hindus who believe in monkeys, pigs and naked statues would be destroyed at the hands of Mujahideen. Basically Mujahideen are critical of idol worship by Hindus that is very much opposed by Muslims.
5. It is claimed that Hindus are persecuting and suppressing Muslims in India and therefore would be slaughtered on the streets.
6. Victories of Mohammed Bin Qasim, Mohammed Ghaznavi and Mohammed Ghori are recalled to instil fear in the hearts of Hindus

7. The Mujahideen display great hatred towards Hindus of Gujarat who are held responsible for the attacks on Muslims after Godhra rail carnage some years ago. They vouch to kill the Hindus in Gujarat by conducting Jihad.
8. They are abusive of Narendra Modi who is the Chief Minister of Gujarat and give a challenge to him
9. They are critical of Police and Military in India and claim that they are Pro Hindu and watched when Muslims were killed.
10. They claim that various commissions that were formed to enquire into Gujarat riots were bogus and they did no justice.
11. Mujahidden gave a call to all Muslims in Gujarat to rise and fight Hindus and take revenge. To inspire Muslims highlight Qoranic quotes are quoted from time to time.
12. The Mujahideen are critical of Rashtriya Swayam Sewak Sangh (RSS) and Vishwa Hindu Parishad(VHP) for their alleged complicity in Gujarat riots and swear to kill them each and take revenge for the killings of Muslims.
13. The terms Democracy, secularism, equality, integrity, peace, freedom, voting, elections are hated by them and claim these words to be another fraud with Mujahideen. They do not believe in them.
14. Mujahideen have warned the governments of Andhra Pradesh, Madhya Pradesh, Maharashtra, Rajasthan and Karnataka and claimed that innocent Muslim youth are arrested and harassed in these states on the pretext of being members of SIMI. Unless this is stopped they warn that mayhem would be let loose in these states.
15. News papers such as Times of India are also warned for their columns on Islamic terrorism and for one sided articles
16. Ambanis are also warned not to construct a temple on a waqf land or else serious actions would be taken on them
17. Vilasrao Deashmukh of Maharashtra also has been warned to mend his ways
18. Special warning has been given to Hyderabad Police and AP Government for arresting and harassing Muslim youth.

In nutshell, Indian Mujahideen appear to have the agenda for taking revenge for the Gujarat riots. They harbor a grudge that the Hindu forces systematically killed Muslims in Gujarat and the government has done nothing to bring culprits to justice. They have no faith in the law enforcing agencies in India and see them as abettors of Hindu forces. They are clouded with anti Hindu tirade and try to inspire Muslims in the cause of Islam. Qoranic verses are quoted to inspire Muslims to join Jihad and save Islam. Following are relevant:-

1. "Fight them (the disbelievers), Allah will punish them by your hands and bring them to disgrace, and give you victory over them and He will heal the hearts of those who believe." (Qur'an 9:14).
2. "O you who believe! Fight those disbelievers who are near you and let them find harshness in you and know that Allah is with those who keep their duty unto Him. (Qur'an 9: 123)
3. "Go forth light armed or heavy armed and fight with your wealth and your lives in the way of Allah, that is better for you if you but knew.
4. The hosts (of the kafireen) will all be routed and will turn and flee. [Qur'an 54: 45].

It is very unfortunate that in modern times too, they are seeing Islam as the only religion that should stay around and rest all have no place in this world. The philosophy of Indian Mujahideen is no different from that of Al Qaeda and Wahabi Philosophy. The language used to exhort Muslims to wage Jihad is forceful like used by other terrorist outfits and Muslim youth naturally feel inspired at Qoranic verses that are quoted.

No doubt, Terrorism has taken deep roots in India. Now it is home bred and inspired. Deendar Anjuman, Dargah e shahdat, SIMI are the other front line active terrorist oufits in the country apart from the Kashmir based outfits. It is generally believed that government policies of appeasement and pseudo secularism practiced for creating vote banks right from the days of partition of sub continent in 1947 has done the greatest damage to the society. A section of Muslims feel alienated and Babri Maszid demolition and Gujarat riots have added fuel to the fire. Inability of Government to deal sternly with the terrorists and sympathizers and the present delay in judicial proceedings have contributed greatly to today's quagmire in which nation is stuck..Unfortunately those who are responsible to guide and protect national interests are busy in never ending scams, witch huntig, desperate acts to protect those amassing wealth abroad, ensure dynastic succession and other dilly dallying activities. Inability to hang condemned Afzal Guru the terrorist who master minded attack on Indian Parliament while in session and that of Kasab who took part in attack on Bomaby HOTELS (26/11) are the live examples and reveals the helplessness and inability of the rulers in the country. The misguided youth among Muslims fully know the weakness of the government and thus some of them are walking into terrorist activities for attaining glorification. Many are clueless and do not know that there is no coming back from it except death.

Terrorist outfits such as Lashkar-e-Toiba (LET), Jaish e Mohammed (JEM), Harkat ul Mujahideen (HUM) Jammu and Kashmir (J & K) Liberation front are mostly concentrating their activities in Jammu and Kashmir while organizations such as SIMI and the present Indian Mujahideen have fanned out in the entire country. There is a saying that it is very difficult even for God to catch a thief from within household. The sizable Muslim population in various Indian cities has also aided to spreading of these nefarious outfits. The problem becomes more complex when these terrorists look same as any normal person in India. It becomes very difficult to identify or suspect even. One never knows that the neighbor with whom he is interacting every day could be a sympathizer or directly involved in these outlawed activities. On the other hand, government is forced to go slow in investigations and follow up due to vote bank politics apart from political interference in the function of law enforcing agencies. On the whole, the scene in India appears very gloomy and unless very hard decisions are taken in this regard, situation would slip out of hand. The government occasionally repeats that a new law would be made soon to deal with terrorism. In fact Indian Penal Code is exhaustive and the provisions in the code are sufficient to deal sternly with such outfits. Most of the crimes would be treason and waging war against the country. Why go slow on such criminals? What is required is the will to enforce it truly with determination that is lacking today in the country . What we require to day is people like Sardar Vallabhai Patel the iron man of India and the first and former Deputy Prime Minister and Lal Bahadur Shastri the former Prime Minister of India and not the vacillating and color changing, wealth amassing and power hungry leaders who go around masquerading as true patriots serving the country.

THE "IDEA OF INDIA" AFTER MUMBAI

In 1947, as the British Raj prepared to devolve its former colony to the newly independent Republic of India, Jawaharlal Nehru and Mohandas Gandhi envisioned a modern, multicultural, and secular democracy whose first priority was economic progress, not ethnic communalism. Nehru and Gandhi's "idea of India" rejected the Balkanization of the subcontinent based on religious or ethnic division. Prior to and following independence, they strived to create and then preserve a unified nation.

Indian foreign policy and strategic interests, especially in relation to Pakistan, are closely linked to this founding idea. Since the partition of India and Pakistan in 1947, Pakistani founder Muhammad Ali Jinnah's "two-nation theory" of a separate, united Muslim state has inherently contradicted the "idea of India." This conflict has played out in a series of geopolitical skirmishes throughout the subcontinent.

The disputed territory of Kashmir has been at centre stage in this struggle, with each side justifying accession based on its founding theory. On the Indian side, the secession of Kashmir would be "a defeat for secularism, [which] is not acceptable if the Indian republic is to be nurtured and brought to fruition," K. Subrahmanyam, an Indian strategic analyst, writes. For Pakistan, majority-Muslim Kashmir is critical to the "two-nation theory." If India relinquishes Kashmir, then Muslim "self-determination," not secular identity, can define the division between the two rivals. And, as Stephen P. Cohen notes, the Kashmir dispute is specifically important "to those Pakistanis who focus on strategic and security issues, notably the army."

The "idea of India" has also underlined domestic policy in India since the days of Nehru and Gandhi. For example, in 1947, civil servant V. P. Menon spent two years negotiating with the leaders of five hundred princely states and chiefdoms in order to absorb them into the Indian state. (He did not succeed in Kashmir.) Since then, ethnic separatists, from the Nagas in the northeast to the Tamils in the south, have attempted to undermine the idea, but the country has responded with both military force and socioeconomic assistance in order to deter secession.

THE CHANGING THREAT TO THE "IDEA OF INDIA"

For most of India's history, dissenting parties to its founding idea—at least the ones that also pose threats of secession and violence—have metastasized in the form of separatist insurgencies. The majority of terrorist incidents in India have been the work of these insurgencies. Therefore, India's original counterterrorism strategy has been, in fact, a counterinsurgency strategy. For example, the Rashtriya Rifles, a specialized counterinsurgency force, was created to fight small-scale, low-intensity conflicts in Jammu and Kashmir, and the Indian army learned to integrate former insurgents, called*ikhwanis*, into cohorts that gather local intelligence in conflict zones. The government also provided civilian support and development assistance to insurgency areas in Punjab and Mizoram, addressing socioeconomic issues like unemployment, wealth disparities, and lack of education that exacerbate local tensions. But terrorism in India is no longer relegated to the mountains of Kashmir or the valleys of Manipur, and the culprits are not poor locals but rather well-trained urban soldiers.

Terrorism in India is no longer relegated to the mountains of Kashmir or the valleys of Manipur, and the culprits are not poor locals but rather well-trained urban soldiers.

Insurgencies employ terrorism for short-term tactical gains, but their preferred modus operandi is ideological indoctrination. Many terrorists, however, favor indiscriminate violence aimed at GENERATING feelings of insecurity and provoking harsh responses by the targeted governments. Terrorism in India has moved away from the ideological cast of insurgency. The indiscriminate nature of Indian jihadist violence today is evident in the terrorist attacks conducted over the last three years by radicalized members of the Students Islamic Movement of India (SIMI) and the Indian Mujahideen (IM), a prominent and well-networked Indian terrorist organization. In July 2006, SIMI militants detonated seven bombs on the suburban Mumbai railway system, killing two hundred commuters. Then, in 2008, the cities of Jaipur, Bangalore, Ahmedabad, and New Delhi were all sites of IM bombings whose casualties were all civilians. This is distinct from separatist operations, which tend to target security personnel. The IM and rogue members of SIMI are based domestically, and their attacks are intended to target major urban and suburban areas in order to inflict heavy civilian casualties. Not only are their motives fundamentalist and pan-Islamist, but the groups are also fueled by domestic grievances, such as ethnic riots, religious discrimination, and opposition to Hindu nationalist politics.

The IM, an umbrella organization that includes members of SIMI and other smaller groups, networks Indian terrorists across the country and organizes attacks. Its leaders, Riyaz Bhatkal and Abdul Subhan Usman Qureshi, both former engineers raised in middle-class families in Mumbai, have built a network of young radicals (including former software engineers and small businessmen) to manufacture bombs and attack India's largest cities.

Consider the July 2008 bombings in Ahmedabad. The IM prepared for these attacks in a highly coordinated, albeit decentralized, manner. Atif Amin, an IM commander, led the assault team, which planted the bombs, while a computer graphics designer, Qayamuddin Kapadia, provided safe houses and logistical support. At the same time, Bhatkal designed the bombs, and Qureshi coordinated the entire operation. A few days before their mission, three IM operatives took a train from New Delhi to Ahmedabad to conduct reconnaissance, finding unsecured wireless Internet sites for use during the bombings. Based in several cities, including Ahmedabad, Mumbai, New Delhi, and Mangalore, these terrorists used CELL PHONES, Wi-Fi, and GPS to run a sophisticated and efficient operation that was difficult to track in real time.

In an e-mail entitled "The Rise of Jihad, Revenge of Gujarat," sent by the IM following the Ahmedabad bombings, the terrorists invoke distinctly political tones in their tirade against Hindu nationalist organizations such as the Bharatiya Janata Party (BJP), the Rashtriya Swayamsevak Sangh, and the Vishwa Hindu Parishad, calling for Gujarati Muslims to take revenge for the 2002 Hindu-Muslim riots in their state. The e-mail also lashes out at counterterrorist police forces in several states for their alleged religious profiling and at the Indian government in general for its discrimination and "harassment" of Muslims. Finally, the e-mail concludes with a request "to Lashkar-e-Toiba and other organizations, for the sake of Allah, not to claim the responsibility for these attacks." Indeed, the IM and similar domestic jihadists are distinctly Indian groups with Indian goals, but they have become allies of convenience with Pakistan and Pakistani operatives.

The Pakistan Question

Indian Muslim radicals expose India's cultural and religious fissures and fault lines, just as Sikhs, Tamils, and Nagas have in the past. The terrorists attempt to redress their grievances through acts of violence and propagate the notion that minorities—especially Muslims—cannot live peacefully in the Hindu-dominated Indian democracy. This is an image that Pakistan takes advantage of for its own strategic interests in Kashmir and for Indian-Pakistani relations in general.

Just as India used counterinsurgency strategy in the past to contain domestic separatists, it will have to create a new counterterrorism strategy to deter domestic jihadists.

Many analysts argued that the three-day siege of Mumbai in November 2008 by LeT only confirmed Pakistan's internal instability and inability to control expanding jihadist threats. Even the U.S. Joint Forces Command referred to Pakistan as a possible "failed state." Quite the contrary: Pakistan's strong military, which keeps Pakistan from failing, appears to dictate the country's internal and external decision-making for its own strategic interests. In the context of the geopolitical duel between Pakistan and India, which is underlined by their conflict of founding ideas, LeT's operations and Pakistan's inaction toward them make sense. LeT is simply another operative in Pakistan's quest to corrode the idea of India, and as LeT's proxy war raises tensions on the border, the Pakistani military can also shift focus away from a difficult mission in the tribal areas of Baluchistan and the North West FRONTIER Province. Even though Pakistan fights the same Islamists at home, the benefit provided by their operations in India makes the Pakistani choice more complex than it appears. Yet, Pakistani attempts to chip away at the idea of India are nothing new.

In the late 1980s and early 1990s, Punjabi Sikh militants who were part of the Khalistan independence movement, which advocated for the creation of a separate Sikh state, engaged in a series of riots, assassinations, and bombings across India. During this time, Pakistan and its Inter-Services Intelligence (ISI) provided FUNDING, refuge, and training sites for these militants. Since then, the leader of the International Sikh Youth Federation, Lakhbir Singh Rode, who has been accused of "arms smuggling and conspiracy to attack government and political leaders in Delhi," has been allowed to live in and work from Lahore. Apart from the Sikh movement, Pakistani militants supported by the ISI have sponsored and conducted attacks in Jammu and Kashmir. LeT, for example, has conducted the majority of its operations in the disputed region, with eighteen attacks between September 2001 and October 2004.

New evidence also shows that LeT has been able to conspire with Indian separatist groups that did not previously associate with radical Islamists. In Northeast India, the United Liberation Front of Assam, the National Democratic Front of Bodoland, and other militants have worked with jihadist groups in their latest attacks. In what the Jamestown Foundation calls "ethno-Islamist" terrorism, there were, for the first time, "tell-tale signs of collaboration between ethnic-separatist militants and Muslim jihadi groups with a strong cross-border reach." After more than a decade of calm, it also appears that Pakistan has begun to renew its support for Sikh militants fighting for an independent Khalistan—this time with the support of LeT and Jaish-e-Mohammad, another Pakistan-based jihadist group.

In each of these cases, from the Khalistan movement to the Mumbai shootings, the involvement of LeT and Pakistani operatives only reflects the increasing internationalization of the jihadist threat in India. The threat is still rooted domestically, under the leadership of Indian Muslim jihadists, but both Pakistan and LeT have been able to take advantage of the vacuum in which these jihadists operate in order to pursue their own strategic goals, whether they are geopolitical gains or global Jihad. Just as India used counterinsurgency strategy in the past to contain domestic separatists, it will have to create a new counterterrorism strategy to deter domestic jihadists.

The State of Indian Muslims

The increasing radical activity of Indian Muslims—especially those of the urban middle class—poses questions: Do Indian Muslims in general buy in to the "idea of India"? Is domestic terrorism reflective of wider sentiment among the Indian *ummah*, or are these attacks merely outliers conducted by disillusioned rogues acting irrationally and excessively?

The World Values SURVEY asks subjects to respond to a series of questions about cultural and national identity, trust, and happiness. It is possible to tabulate these responses based on religion. In the case of India, not only are Indian Muslims equally as happy and proud to be Indian as Hindus, they tend to be apolitical and broadly respectful of democracy. Approximately 90 percent of Indian Muslims and Hindus express pride in being Indian, assert the importance of democracy, and are willing to fight for their country. According to the survey, Muslims are also slightly more active in religious practice (90 percent versus 80 percent) and less trusting of others (71 percent versus 61 percent) than Hindus, but they believe almost as strongly as Hindus that society should not be radically changed (85 percent to 86 percent).

Anecdotal evidence adds further confirmation of Muslim integration. Muslims play prominent roles in Indian popular culture and political life. Three of the country's most famous and widely adored Bollywood actors are Muslims named Khan (Salman Khan, Shah Rukh Khan, and Aamir Khan). The award-winning song by Muslim composer A. R. Rahman, "Jai Ho," from the blockbuster *Slumdog Millionaire* (which itself features a successful Muslim protagonist), became this year's campaign theme song for India's Congress Party. And in politics, A. P. J. Abdul Kalam was elected the first Muslim president of India by the parliament in 2002. Muslims are underrepresented in politics at the national level, but not significantly; they hold 8 percent of the seats against their national population share of 13.4 percent.

Evidence from the World Values SURVEY and examples of Muslim integration in Indian popular culture appear to support the idea that Muslims are not inherently excluded from the country's identity. Nevertheless, as a report by the Prime Minister's High Level Committee (the Sachar Commission) on the status of India's Muslims shows, there are still significant discrepancies between the socioeconomic status of Muslims and other Indians. By some measures, Muslims rank near the "untouchable" Scheduled Tribes and Scheduled Castes.

While Hindus had a literacy rate of 80.5 percent in 2004-2005, the rate for Muslims was 59.9 percent. Higher education graduation rates are also significantly disparate, with only 4.5 percent of Muslims between the ages of twenty and thirty having degrees at the tertiary level in 2004-2005, as opposed to 18.6 percent of Hindus aged twenty to thirty. As the report states, "In urban areas, Muslims are falling behind not only vis-a-vis 'All Other [Minorities],' but also Scheduled Castes and Scheduled Tribes in several states."

Despite the presence of Muslims in prominent political and cultural spaces in India, the majority of Indian political and economic power still rests in the hands of Hindus, both secular and orthodox.

Compared to the national average, a larger proportion of Indian Muslims work in the informal sector of the economy or are engaged in "small proprietary enterprises." Yet, as the Sachar Commission report notes, "the access of Muslims to bank credit... is low and inadequate," and the share of banking facilities is much lower in villages where the percentage of the Muslim population exceeds 50 percent.

Discrimination against Muslims is also evident in civil society, in which segregation continues to be the rule rather than the exception. In 2006, Muslims made up only 4.9 percent of all government employees and 3.2 percent of all civil service officers. It is also important to note the vast underrepresentation of Muslims in the Indian army: out of 1.1 million soldiers, only 29,000 (2.6 percent) are Muslims.

In addition to social rifts, the ongoing religious and political tug-of-war between certain Hindu and Muslim factions could exacerbate extremism. Three events in modern Indian history—the destruction of the Babri Mosque in 1992, the 2002 riots in Gujarat, and the 1986 Shah Bano case—have dictated these tensions. The first two events, cases of religious violence between Hindu and Muslim fanatics, are of importance because of their human toll in addition to their impact on political debate. In 1992, a group of Hindu nationalists destroyed a sixteenth-century mosque in the town of Ayodhya, claiming that the mosque was built on the birthplace of the Hindu god Ram. A riot spread following the destruction, in which two thousand Indians, mostly Muslims, were killed. In 2002, more than one thousand people perished in riots in Gujarat following an arson attack on a train of Hindu pilgrims. Once again, the majority of victims were Muslims, and the BJP-led state government was widely criticized for its failure to respond to the pogrom.

The origins of these riots still evoke debate among members of the BJP, secular Hindu politicians, and Muslims in fear of a reprisal. The Hindu-Muslim conflict also hinders political discourse by prioritizing ethnic and religious divisions over critical social and economic issues. For example, in the latest election campaign, BJP candidate Varun Gandhi—an estranged member of the Nehru-Gandhi political dynasty and grandson of former prime minister Indira Gandhi—was arrested after making disparaging remarks about Muslim parliamentary candidates and telling supporters at a rally that he would "cut the hands" of anyone who "raised a finger towards Hindus."

The other turning point, the Shah Bano case of 1986, reflects discrepancies in the legal and institutional status of Muslims versus those of other Indians. In 1986, Shah Bano, a sixty-two-year-old Muslim divorcée, filed a suit to claim alimony from her husband, claiming that she had no means to support herself and her children. While orthodox Muslims felt that alimony was unacceptable according to *sharia* law, the Supreme Court ruled in her favor, invoking the Indian Code of Criminal Procedure. Following the ruling, an organization of Muslim community leaders and intellectuals successfully lobbied the government to overrule the court's decision. The government's appeasement was derided as "pseudosecularism" by its opponents, and it set a precedent for Indian Muslims that has made room for self-imposed compartmentalization and isolation from mainstream society.

Despite the presence of Muslims in prominent political and cultural spaces in India, the majority of Indian political and economic power still rests in the hands of Hindus, both secular and orthodox. As the primary owners of the country's political and economic capital, these Hindus should be conscious of their implicit responsibility to prevent calamities like the Babri Mosque destruction and the Gujarat riots and to bolster the social and economic inclusion of Muslims in the country.

But there is also an onus on the leaders of the Indian Muslim community to reconcile Muslim identity with Indian identity and address Indian Muslims' radicalization and social segregation. The ability of external forces, regardless of their strength, to influence the Muslim community is limited, compared to the capacity of Muslims themselves to address these issues. The Shah Bano case is an example of self-imposed isolation that hinders ethnic and cultural integration and compromises the secular nature of the Indian polity, which, as the World Values SURVEY shows, is not contrary to wider Muslim sentiment.

Conclusion

There is no easy path to prevent middle-class Indian Muslims from radicalizing and attacking their fellow citizens. But before addressing the problem, the Indian government must understand the roots of domestic jihadism and its implications for India's long-term strategy. As Angel Rabasa et al. write, " t the strategic level, the Mumbai attack underscores the imperative of addressing the transnational sources of Islamist terrorism in India. How to do this is an extraordinarily difficult question that will require the reassessment of basic assumptions concerning policy toward Pakistan by members of the international community."

Nevertheless, the transnationalization of Islamist terrorism in India is rooted in the growing strength and scope of domestic Islamist terrorism, as evidenced by the increasing frequency and magnitude of attacks in urban areas of India. The attacks in Mumbai were merely one more step down a road that organizations such as the IM have been paving for more than a decade.

For more than six decades, Indian governments, despite occasional domestic pressures from the far right and left wings, have remained steadfast in their commitment to preserving the "idea of India." The threats to this idea continue to exist, but they have changed significantly. In a "post-11/26" world, preserving Nehru and Gandhi's vision of a secular and pluralistic democracy will require more than just a tough stance across the Indian-Pakistani Line of Control. It will require a reassessment of counterterrorism and counterinsurgency at home and a renewed focus toward the integration and assimilation of minorities, specifically Muslims, into the expansive definition of India.

13 SEPTEMBER 2008 DELHI BOMBINGS

The 13 September 2008 Delhi bombings were a series of five synchronised bomb blaststhat took place within a span of few minutes on Saturday, 13 September 2008 at various locations in Delhi, India. The first bomb exploded at 18:07 IST, and four other blasts followed in succession, with at least 30 people killed and over 100 injured.

Background

Three bomb attacks had already occurred the same year in India. The first of these was on 13 May in Jaipur. The series of nine blasts over a span of 15 minutes claimed 63 lives, and injured 216. The second series of nine bomb blasts took place on 25 July in Bangalore, and claimed 2 lives, while injuring 20. The next day, on 26 July in Ahmedabad, a spurt of 21 blasts killed 56 people and injured over 200. The Indian Mujahideen claimed responsibility for the Jaipur bombings through an email sent to Indian media and declared "open war" against India in retaliation for what it said were 60 years of Muslim persecution and the country's support of United States' policies, most notably the war in Afghanistan. *The Times of India* has reported that either the banned organisation Students Islamic Movement of Indiaor the militant organisation Lashkar-e-Taiba could be behind the blasts in Bangalore. Similar to the Jaipur case, after the Ahmedabad blasts, several TV channels reported that they received e-mails from the Indian Mujahideen claiming responsibility for the terror attacks.

Police say the Indian Mujahideen is an offshoot of the banned Students Islamic Movement of India, but allege that local Muslims are given training and backing from militant groups in neighbouring Pakistan and Bangladesh.

Details

Five blasts took place within a span of 31 minutes from 18:07 to 18:38 IST (12:37 to 13:08 UTC) in busy markets or commercial localities. Four bombs were defused.

The first blast took place at 18:07 at Ghaffar market (a municipal market along a stretch of Ajmal Khan Road, Karol Bagh) in which at least 20 people were injured. They were rushed to nearby RML hospital. The explosive was kept near a car, and resulted in a cylinder blast in an auto rickshaw, which was subsequently thrown up several feet into the air.

Immediately after, two explosions took place in Connaught Place in which at least 10 people were injured. Police and witnesses said that the bombs went off in dustbins in and around Connaught Place, a shopping and dining area popular with tourists and locals in the centre of the city. The first of these blasts occurred on Barakhamba Road, near Nirmal Tower and Gopal Das Bhavan at 18:34. A minute later, the second bomb exploded in the newly constructed Central Park in the centre of the Connaught Place roundabout, built above one of the main stations of the Delhi Metro. An eyewitness reportedly saw two men place the bomb in a dustbin at Central Park.

Subsequently, two explosions rocked M-Block market in Greater Kailash-I at 18:37 and 18:38 – the first near the popular Prince Paan Corner, and the other near a Levi's store. The latter damaged 10 shops.

Preliminary examination of the blast site said that low intensity ammonium nitrate tied to integrated circuits with timer devices had been used in almost all the serial blasts.

Four bombs were also defused – the first one at India Gate, the second outside Regal Cinema in Connaught Place, the third in Connaught Place, and the fourth on Parliament Street.

On the evening of 13 September 2008, IBN reported at least 30 deaths and over 100 injured. AFP reported that "Indian police (New Delhi police spokesman Rajan Bhagat) said Sunday that 20 people were killed and close to 100 injured."

Response

Police and security

Security was tightened across the national capital, with police personnel fanning out to railway and Metro stations, hospitals, bus terminals, the airport and other sensitive points like cinema halls, shopping malls and religious places. Barricades were put up on most city roads to check traffic. Several major markets, including the Sarojini Nagar market, which was targeted in the previous Diwali-eve blasts in 2005, were shut down and evacuated. Cyber-café owners were asked to keep a tab on customers.

A Central Industrial Security Force (CISF) spokesperson state that "security has already been strengthened and frisking and checking of the commuters have been stepped up. The Metro is under constant vigil". He added that extra personnel had been pressed into service to keep an eye on commuters.

Press confusion

The confusion in the aftermath of the blasts was evident in the press reports immediately following. The general consensus was that the blasts had claimed 18 lives. However, there was some disparity, with CNN claiming as low as 15, to NDTV claiming as high as 30.

There was also some controversy over blast sites and the sites where bombs were defused, most notably that where Zee News reported a bomb being defused at Central Park, while the *Outlook* Magazine stated that the park was a bomb site.

Responsibility

The Islamist "Indian Mujahideen" sent an e-mail to all major TV channels, informing them of the blasts just after the first one occurred. In the case of the bomb blasts in Jaipur, and Ahmedabad, e-mails were sent before the blasts.

Indian Mujahideen strikes back once more. Within 5 minutes from now... This time with the Message of Death, dreadfully terrorising you for your sins. And thus our promise will be fulfilled. Inshallah...Do whatever you want and stop us if you can.

The email was sent from Arbi Hindi. The email threatened nine blasts. A 13-page attached document depicts photographs of the previous blasts under the caption "our Jihad". The Delhi blasts are, according to the email, a direct reaction to the raids carried on and after the Ahmedabad blasts, and "harassments imposed by your (Indian) ATS and the police on the innocent Muslims". The document also mentions Amarnath dispute, violence against Christians in Orissa, Babri Masjid demolition and Gujarat riots.

The email was traced to Chembur, an eastern suburb of Mumbai. Mumbai's anti-Terrorism squad (ATS) confirmed that WiFi of the owner firm "Kamran Power" was hacked and used for sending the mail.

Reports claim that the Indian Mujahideen called this operation "*Operation B-A-D*", encompassing the Bangalore, Ahmedabad and Delhi Bombings. Intelligence officials had intercepted a call made "from the across the border" claiming "Operation BAD is successful", after the Ahmedabad blasts, which the Gujarat police that interpreted as Bangalore, Ahmedabad, Delhi, though the dates and specific places were not known.

Investigation

Two persons were detained from Connaught Place area soon after the blasts. Delhi Police said an 11-year-old boy had claimed to have seen the perpetrators; he informed police that the suspects, clad in black kurta-pyjamas, were seen placing bags in a dustbin. The Delhi Police soon, within three hours of the blast, arrested another person who the police suspect to be the mastermind of the blast.

Preliminary investigation by police reveal Indian Mujahideen-SIMI cell led by Abdul Subhan Qureshi alias Tauqir, having information technology background from Mumbai, to be involved. Another person named Qayamuddin is also under investigation. Four more people have also been detained and questioned.

In the morning of 19 September, the Batla House encounter took place, in which Delhi Police shot down two persons, thought to be suspects, hiding in L-18 block of Jamia Nagar, Delhi. Two others suspects were arrested while one managed to escape. Bashir alias Atif, believed to be the mastermind was one of the two killed. Inspector Mohan Chand Sharma, who was injured in the encounter, died in a hospital. He was credited with helping to have killed 35 terror suspects, 85 arrests and also the winner of 75-odd encounters, 150 medals and seven gallantry awards. Later, the intelligence team said that the arrested allegedly had links with Dubai and further questioned if they had any link with Dawood Ibrahim.

On 23 September, the police arrested five more people from Mumbai and Uttar Pradesh. All five are suspected to be part of the Indian Mujahadeen's think tank. The men were:

- Sadiq Sheikh, 31, software engineer from Mumbai
- Afzal Usmani, 32, hotelier in western suburbs of Mumbai
- Arif Sheikh, 38, electrician from Mumbra, Mumbai
- Mohammed Zakir Sheikh, 38, scrap dealer from Mumbra, Mumbai
- Mohammed Ansar Sheikh, 31, software Engineer from Mumbai

On 4 October they were sent by the judicial Chief Metropolitan Magistrate to 12 days' policy custody.

The crime branch has claimed that these are the operatives who had introduced themselves as Pakistanis to perpetrators of

11 July 2006 Mumbai train bombings. After the 2006 bombings, police had claimed that a group of SIMI activists along with five Pakistan nationals had planted bombs in seven trains.

On 11 November, the Madhya Pradesh Anti-Terror Squad (ATS) arrested Qayamuddin Kapadia, a top-ranking member of SIMI and a key conspirator and executor of the Ahmedabad attack. Police claimed that Kapadia admitted his involvement in the Ahmedabad blasts, and that he, along with Abdul Subhan Qureshi *alias* Tauqeer of Mumbai and Riaz Bhatkal of Karnataka, collaborated with the SIMI cell led by Atif to carry out the Delhi blasts. Atif was later killed in an encounter with Delhi Police.

2010 JAMA MASJID ATTACK

The 2010 Jama Masjid attack occurred on 19 September 2010 when two gunmen on a motorcycle fired at a tourist bus near Gate 3 of the Jama Masjid in Old Delhi, India and injured two Taiwanese tourists. The incident provoked fears about security for the upcoming Commonwealth Games in Delhi. About three hours later a car parked approximately 150 meters from the spot caught fire, apparently due to a minor blast.

Two bike-borne gunmen opened fire at a stationary tourist bus purportedly carrying a TV crew from Taiwan at 11:24 pm, near Gate 3 of Jama Masjid. An explosive-laden device was planted in a Maruti 800 car, parked near a transformer near the mosque. The car had approximately 20 litres of fuel in its tank, which would have caused considerable damage if it had exploded successfully, but bomb timers failed and it did not go off. There were two victims of the shootout, Zeseweiu (27) and Chiang (28), both Taiwanese citizens. Zeseweiu head was grazed by a bullet while trying to escape, while Chiang was shot in the abdomen and had to be operated on. Both were declared to be out of danger the next day when the state CM and Union Home Minister paid them a visit.

Batla House encounter link

"In the name of Allah we dedicate this attack of retribution to martyrs, Shaheed Atif Amin and Shaheed Mohammad Sajid who proudly laid down their lives valiantly fighting the idol worshippers Delhi police on this day. Surely each and every drop of their blood brought a new life in the Muslim community and this is confirmed from the fact that Indian Mujahideen have swelled unexpectedly manifold.."

Email sent to media

The attack is significant because it took place on the second anniversary of the Batla House encounteron 19 September 2008, in which Atif Amin, suspected member of the Indian Mujahideen was killed. The Indian Mujahideen had been blamed earlier for a number of terror attacks, in Delhi, Ahmedabad, Jaipur Surat and Faizabad, between 2007 and 2009. According to investigating agencies, the revival of the group was announced in an email to the media, which also elaborated on the outfits intention of avenging the death of their former members.

Investigation

Subsequent police investigations revealed that one of the timers of the cooker bomb was timed to go off exactly at 11:37 am, approximately the time when the Batla House encounter was reported to have taken place two years before on the same day.

The terror attack took place barely 200 meters away from the Jama Masjid police station, and at the time of the shooting, the cops from PCR van stationed at gate number 3 had gone to settle a family brawl nearby in the Khankhana street, in the Machli Bazar area, allowing the bikers to flee. The Guide (Vikrant K.Sharma) accompanying the T.V team took the injured inside the bus and called the police immediately, the 20 CCTVs which were installed near the Masjid, were found to be lying defunct. The cameras had been installed on 14 April 2006, after the twin blasts at the Masjid. According to the police, the terrorists were divided in two groups; the first reached the spot on a motorcycle and the second group followed them in a Maruti car, which later caught fire due to the "crudely assembled" pressure cooker bomb in it. Police detained 30 people for questioning.

Subsequent investigations revealed that the revelatory email was sent through a SIM card connection whose location was traced toBorivali. It was purchased by a man in his 20s, from a 'shop in the Dadar Truck Terminus area in Mumbai, and the police were looking for a man from Beed in Maharashtra, who had furnished a driver's license and a pan card under the name "Purva Shinde".

On 30 November 2011, the Delhi Police arrested six suspected Indian Mujahideen operatives whom they claimed to be the perpetrators of the 2010 Pune bombing, the Chinnaswamy stadium blast and the 2010 Jama Masjid attack. One Pakistani national was also reported to have been arrested.

Two of the seven people were arrested in Chennai and were identified by the Delhi Police as Mohammad Irshad Khan (age 50) and Abdul Rahman (age 19), hailing from the Madhubani district of Bihar.

Another individual – Ghayur Jamil – a student at a madarsa in Darbhanga was also arrested from Madhubani on the charge of recruiting youths from near the Indo-Nepal border for terrorist activities, Abdul Rahman was said to one such recruit. Jamil's father disputed his son's arrest and billed him as a good orator and an honest, religious man who had lost a bag containing his belongings – including his PAN card, residential proof and photos – a few days back.

In August 2013, Yasin Bhatkal co-founder of the Indian Mujahidin and his close aid Assadullah Akhtar alias Haddi were arrested byNational Investigation Agency and as per NIA, in the in interrogations they accepted that they had carried out the attack at the Masjid. As per NIA, Yasin said that he was instructed by Karachi-based IM head Riyaz Bhatkal to target the mosque as the group was upset with Imam Ahmed Bukhari for allowing *"semi-naked"* foreigners inside it.

On 19 April 2014, a special cell of Delhi Police filed its final report before a local court in Delhi against the two under various sections of the IPC including 307 (attempt to murder), 120B (criminal conspiracy) and under the provisions of Unlawful Activities (Prevention) Act and the Arms Act. The police claimed in the charge sheet that Bhatkal was instructed by Pakistan-based handlers to carry out terror attacks just before the beginning of 2010 Commonwealth Games which were held in Delhi.

JAMAAT-UL-MUJAHIDEEN BANGLADESH

Jamaat-ul-Mujahideen was an Islamist organisation operating in Bangladesh. It was founded in 1998 in Palampur in Dhaka division by Abdur Rahman and gained public prominence in 2001 when bombs and documents detailing the activities of the organization were discovered in Parbatipur in Dinajpur district. The organization was officially banned by the government of Bangladesh in February 2005 after attacks on NGOs, but struck back in mid-August when it detonated 500 bombs at 300 locations throughout Bangladesh.

The JMB was believed to have contained at least 100,000 members, and have an extensive network of organizations, including connections to legal Islamist organizations. Six of the top leaders of JMP were captured by the Rapid Action Battalion security force in 2005. On the evening of 29 March 2007, four were executed by hanging for the killing of two judges and for the August 2005 bombings.

Ideology

The JMB's aim is to replace the current state of Bangladesh with an Islamic state based on Sharia. It has explicitly stated on more than one occasion that it opposes the political system of Bangladesh and seeks to "build a society based on the Islamic model laid out in Holy Quran-Hadith." The organization follows the ideals of the Taliban of Afghanistan Its chief has been quoted as stating that "our model includes many leaders and scholars of Islam. But we will take as much (ideology) from the Taliban as we need." It opposes democracy as being in violation of Shari'a or the Islamic law.

It also opposes socialism and its avowed objective is to neutralize left-wing extremists, especially cadres of the Purba Banglar Communist Party (PBCP). JMB also is opposed to cultural functions, cinema halls, shrines and NGOs. In another leaflet it said, "We don't want Taguti [non-Islamic] law, let Qur'anic law be introduced. Law framed by humans cannot continue and only the laws of Allah will prevail."

They have claimed responsibility for several violent attacks and bombings. JMB's communiqués reveal a Salafist doctrine that is common across international radical Islamist organizations.

In a leaflet written in Bengali and Arabic found at various bombing sites of 17 August 2005 it stated:

- "We are the soldiers of Allah. We have taken up arms for the implementation of Allah's law the way the Prophet, Sahabis and heroic Mujahideen have implemented for centuries. If the government does not establish Islamic law in the country after this [third] warning and, rather, it goes to arrest any Muslim on charge of seeking Allah's laws or it resorts to repression on Alem-Ulema, the Jamaatul Mujahideen [JMB] will go for counteraction, Insha Allah."

Several captured members of the group have claimed that their targets include traditional Bangladeshi cultural and non-government organizations such as BRAC, Proshika, and Grameen Bank. Leader Abdur Rahman is alleged to have taught JMB operatives that "it's not a sin to loot valuables of Grameen Bank, BRAC, Proshika, Asa and Karitas' as they encourage women to shed Burqa (veil)."

Activities

On 20 May 2001 25 petrol bombs and documents detailing the activities of the organization were discovered and eight of its members were arrested in Parbatipur in Dinajpur district. It is believed to have been involved in an explosion of seven bombs on 13 February 2003 at one of its hideouts, having been preparing to explode them in northern Bangladeshi towns during International Mother Language Day.

On 12 January 2005, bomb blasts at two separate cultural events in Sherpur and Jamalpur districts injured 25 and 10 respectively. Bomb blasts on 15 January 2005 at Jatra performances at Bogra and Natore killed two and injured over 70 people.

On August 17, 2005, 500 small bombs at 300 locations in 50 cities and towns across Bangladesh detonated within the space of 30 minutes. Dhaka international airport, government buildings and major hotels were targeted. There were 50 injuries but only two fatalities - a child in Savar, near Dhaka, and a Rickshaw-puller in Chapai Nawabganj District - because of the small size of the bombs. Jamaat-ul-Mujahideen Bangladesh claimed responsibility for the bombings.

Blasts later in the year were more deadly "killing judges, lawyers, policemen and common people". It killed two judges in Jhalakathi in South Bangladesh on November 14, 2005.

The group has threatened journalists, with more than 55 receiving death threats between September and December 2005. Following a December 8, 2005 suicide bombing, Reuters reported the group threatened to kill women, including non-Muslims, who did not wear the veil, according to news reports posted by defenddemocracy.org.

Network

The JMB is said to be the youth front of Al Mujahideen, the parent organization that began working in the mid-1990s which remains obscure even today. Other organizations, such as Jama'atul Jihad, JMB, Jagrata Muslim Janata Bangladesh (JMJB), Harkat-ul-Jihad-al-Islami (HUJI), Hizbut Tawhid, Tawhidi Janata, Islami Jubo Shangha, Islami Shangha, Al Falah A'am Unnayan Shanstha and Shahadat-e al Hiqma are believed to be part of the Al Mujahideen network. Further, the JMB is believed to contain at least 100,000 members, and an alleged 2,000-man suicide brigade.

JMB allegedly received financial assistance from individual donors in Kuwait, UAE, Bahrain, Pakistan, Saudi Arabia and Libya. Reports have claimed that, funding of JMB by international NGOs like Kuwait based Society of the Revival of Islamic Heritage (RIHS) and Doulatul Kuwait, Saudi Arabia based Al Haramaine Islamic Institute and Rabita Al Alam Al Islami, Qatar Charitable Society and UAE-based Al Fuzaira and Khairul Ansar Al Khairia.

Some of the RIHS offices were blacklisted in 2002 by the US State Department because of alleged links with al-Qaeda. Though, these connections have not been proven. Following the blasts in August, the Bangladeshi government deported five foreign RIHS officials. Al-Haramaine was banned by the US in 2004 and its branches in Albania, Afghanistan, Bangladesh, Ethiopia and the

Netherlands were added by the UN Security Council to the Al-Qaeda and Taliban Sanctions Committee on 6 July 2004.

South Asian Terrorist Portal (SATP), *The Columbia World Dictionary of Islamism* and Defenddemocracy.org state that Jamaat-ul-Mujahideen Bangladesh "appears" to be connected with putatively non-violent, legal Islamist group or groups in Bangladesh, Defenddemocracy speculating that Jamaat-ul-Mujahideen Bangladesh is a "proxy" established by the legal Jamaat-e-Islami Bangladesh party to "push the center of gravity of the political debate towards radical Islamism" and make Jamaat-e-Islami appear more centrist. According to SATP, "many members of the JMB and JMJB have invariably been found to be cadres of the Islami Chhatra Shibir (ICS), student wing of the Jamaat-e-Islami, a partner in the ruling coalition" with the Bangladesh National Party "under Prime Minister Khaleda Zia" that came to power in 2001.

Sphere of influence

Main areas of JMB operations were:

- *Rajshahi Division:* Bogra, Sirajganj, Dinajpur, Jaipurhat, Gaibandha, Naogaon, Nator, Rajshahi, Rangpur, Tahkurgaon
- *Khulna Division:* Bagerhat, Jessore, Khulna, Meherpur, Satkhira
- *Dhaka Division:* Jamalpur, Mymensingh, Netrokona, Tangail
- *Chittagong Division:* Chandpur, Laxmipur, Chittagong

Leaders

Since its foundation, the group was led by Maulana Abdur Rahman, a.k.a. Siddiqul Islam a.k.a. Bangla Bhai, Shaykh Abdur Rahman. Six of their top men were captured by RAB security authorities in 2005. After being convicted at trial, on the evening of 29 March 2007, Abdur Rahman, Bangla Bhai, and four other leaders of the organization were executed by hanging for the killing of two judges and for countrywide bombings in 2005.

Organisation

The JMJB reportedly has a three-tier organisation. The first tier of the outfit consists of activists called *Ehsar,* who are recruited on a full-time basis and act at the behest of the higher echelons. The second tier, known as *Gayeri Ehsar*, has over 100,000 part-time activists. The third tier involves those who indirectly co-operate with the JMJB. According to JMJB leaders, the whole country has been divided into nine organisational divisions.

Khulna, Barisal, Sylhet and Chittagong have an organisational divisional office each, while Dhaka has two divisional offices and Rajshahi three. The outfit also had committees in each village and, according to media reports, villagers were being forced to join the committees. If anybody refused, he was branded as a "collaborator" of the PBCP and taken to the JMJB "trial centre".

5

New Global Threat: Transnational Salafis and Jihad

Bin Laden's death, of course, does not mark the end of the U.S. effort to prevent attacks against the United States and its citizens, as President Obama has just reminded the world. In the quest for ideas on how to go forward strategically, MEPC offers the following article by Quintan Wiktorowicz, published in the December 2001 issue of *Middle East Policy*. The author argues that the radical Islamist network of terrorists is situated within a larger transnational movement and that it would be wise for the United States to attempt to isolate the violent elements of this influential force in the Muslim world.

A new global threat to U.S. national security has emerged from the ashes of the Cold War, redefining the terrain of international contention in the twenty-first century. In the 1990s, a loose, trans-national network of radical Islamists launched a *Jihad* in an effort to drive American military forces from the Arabian Peninsula, erode American sponsorship of Israel, and undermine American patronage broader of "un-Islamic puppet regimes" throughout the Middle East. Supported by *fatwas*(religious jurisprudential opinions) militant Islamic scholars from various countries, this network has initiated devastating attacks against American military and civilian targets, including the 1993 World TRADE Centre bombing, an ambush of U.S. soldiers in Somalia, bombings of U.S. targets in Saudi Arabia, the embassy bombings in Kenya and Tanzania, and various attacks in Yemen (including an attack on the U.S.S. *Cole* in 2000). For the most part, American responses to these earlier attacks remained reserved. Law enforcement tactics combined with a series of CRUISE missile attacks in Sudan and Afghanistan in 1998 were limited in scope and duration. Concern that a broader response would engender a backlash in Arab and Muslim countries circumscribed the range of policy alternatives,and the United States carefully managed its strategy of confrontation to avoid destabilizing its allies in the Middle East. Osama bin Laden and others in the radical Islamist movement ridiculed the ineffectiveness of responses, scoffing at America's "false courage," "impotence" and "weakness" in the face of defeat

But the horrific terrorist attacks against the United States on September 11, 2001, fundamentally changed the nature of American security doctrine and concomitant responses to terrorism. Transnational teams of Arab Islamists hijacked four planes to use as flying suicide bombs. Two were flown into the World TRADECenter towers, one into the Pentagon, and a fourth crashed outside Pittsburgh after passengers attempted to regain control of the plane. Thousands of civilians were killed in the attacks, making it the largest loss of civilian life in a single terrorist attack anywhere in the world.

President Bush quickly decried the attacks and declared a war on terrorism that would qualitatively shift the rules of engagement and the range of policy responses. The magnitude of the carnage demanded new tactics, and the administration has moved to create a broad global campaign against terrorism that combines military action, law enforcement, intelligence operations and international cooperation. While the outlines of the new policy remain ambiguous, the targets are clearly specified by the administration: Osama bin Laden and his terrorist network. The president, Congress and the American public are preparing for a long confrontation with radical Islamists in the war on terrorism.

As the United States engages the new global threat of the twenty-first century, it is important to contextualize Bin Laden and his followers as a movement operating within a broader transnational community of Islamic activists. While it is tempting to dismiss Bin Laden and other radicals as outside the boundaries of Islam, such assertions underestimate the spiritual, ideological and human relationships that connect those who espouse a violent Jihad against the United States with more moderate elements within particular segments of the Muslim community. Charges that Bin Laden is not behaving as a "real Muslim" might provide a sense of psychological relief for Muslims and non-Muslims alike, but such charges fail to comprehend the roots of radical ideologies within less violent worldviews and value systems.

Rather than acting as an isolated cluster of deviant religious usurpers, the new global threat to U.S. security is dominated by a tendency within a broad transnational "Salafi movement." Salafis believe that over centuries of religious practice, errant Muslims introduced new practices and innovations that corrupted the pure message of Islam.

To rectify this condition, they advocate a strict return to the fundamentals of the religion and reject any behavior that was not specifically supported or enjoined by the Prophet Muhammed. The radicals responsible for the "Jihad" against the United States are inextricably linked to this worldview and share religious understandings with a broad consortium of non-violent groups within the Salafi community, even while disagreeing about the permissibility of Jihad and specific tactics in warfare, such as the use of terrorism.

This relationship makes the Salafi movement a significant, albeit largely unrecognized, actor in any war on Bin Laden and other Islamic terrorists. If the United States is to avoid radicalizing the Salafis and creating a legion of new supporters for Bin Laden, it must understand the ideology and dynamics of the movement and how Salafis might respond to U.S. action. The ideological affinity between violent tendencies and others in the Salafi community is qualitatively different from broader Muslim sympathies toward Bin Laden's cause. This creates one of the deepest potential recruitment pools for violent activists. Security policies should therefore evaluate the impact of policies on the balance between violent and non-violent elements within the Salafi community to avoid a "jihadization" of the movement.

The Salafi movement represents a transnational effort for religious purification, connecting members of an "imagined community" through a common approach to Islam. Although an accurate estimate of numbers is impossible, the Salafis constitute one of the fastest-growing Islamic movements and enjoy a global reach in virtually all countries. Even non-Salafi Islamists readily admit the scope of the Salafi movement and its effects on Islamic practice. Salafi thought has influenced the ideological orientation of many practicing Muslims and some of the most well-known Islamic organizations in the Muslim world, including the Gamiyya Islamiyya in Egypt, various branches of Islamic Jihad, the Armed Islamic Group in Algeria, and mainstream movements such as the Muslim Brotherhood. The Saudi state and its religious hierarchy are major producers and exporters of Salafi publications, missionary operations and humanitarian assistance; and the transnational organization of the movement, which incorporates a myriad of nationalities, renders it an effective and influential force in the Muslim world.

The term "salafi" derives from the Arabic *salaf*, which means "to precede." In the Islamic lexicon, salaf refers to the Companions of the Prophet Muhammad and generally includes the first three generations of Muslims who learned about Islam directly from the messenger of God or those who knew him. Because of this connection to the Prophet and the divine revelations, Salafis believe that the Companions enjoyed a pure understanding of the religion. Subsequent understandings, they argue, were sullied and distorted by the introduction of innovations (*bida*) and the development of schisms in the Muslim community, which pulled the community of the faithful away from the straight path of Islam. Deviations occurred with the passage of time and were reinforced by the syncretic incorporation of local customs as Islam spread to other cultural settings outside the Arabian peninsula. Popular practices such as celebrating the Prophet's birthday, visiting the tombs of saints, and various Sufi rituals are decried as un-Islamic deviations that threaten the purity of the message as revealed by the Prophet. The goal of the Salafi movement is to eradicate these innovations by returning to the pure form of Islam practiced by the Prophet and his Companions.

To foster this purification, all decisions and actions in life must be based upon direct evidence from the sources of the religion: the Quran and the Sunnah (path or traditions of the Prophet Muhammed). Salafis have therefore developed a *manhaj* or method for determining proper religious interpretations based upon the Quran, the Sunnah, and the example of the Companions. This includes searching for evidence in authentic *hadiths* (the written record of the Prophet's Sunnah), as detailed by the Companions; a rejection of popular practices not explicitly outlined in the Quran or Sunnah; emphasis on worshiping only God (*tawhid*); and a rejection of the four separate schools of Islamic jurisprudence (*mathhabs*) that divide Muslims, since there can only be one right religious answer and ruling – that which is according to God as outlined in the sources of the religion. In pursuing this approach, Salafis hope to construct a transnational community of true believers whose immutable adherence to the faith will be rewarded with salvation. Those who follow this manhaj are considered Salafis. The Salafi approach has clashed with a number of other Islamic sects, which are often decried as un-Islamic. Sufis, in particular, have incurred the wrath of Salafi purists, who argue that popular Sufi practices and rituals constitute heresy. In particular, the use of saints as intermediaries in prayer is condemned as ascribing partners to God in worship (*shirk*), an act vehemently prohibited in the Quran. Salafis argue that the Prophet did not sanction these behaviors and consequently have devoted much of their collective energy combating Sufism and other sects viewed as deviating from the straight path of Islam. Disagreements between Salafis and Sufis over such issues have led to discursive conflicts through publications, cassettes, the internet and missionary activities. At times these confrontations have led to violent Salafi attacks against Sufi mosques, leaders and followers. Salafi missionary activities, especially in Central Asia where Sufism is prevalent, have frequently met with resistance by local religious authorities, who view Salafi puritanicalism as antithetical to local understandings, often labeling it Wahhabism to connote its foreign Saudi origins.

Because of a sense of certainty in the search for religious truth, as outlined by evidence in the Quran and Sunnah, there is little attempt to bridge differences with other Islamic sects and groups. Nor is there any ecumenical tendency within the Salafi movement. Instead, Salafis believe that there is only one accurate religious truth as revealed by the Prophet Muhammad, and any differences of interpretation are considered deviations from Islam. Because Salafis believe they approximate the practices endorsed by the Prophet, they believe they are the only group that will be saved on Judgment Day. This is based on various hadiths, including: "And this Ummah [Muslim community] will divide into 73 sects all of which except one will go to Hell, and they [the saved sect] are those who are upon what I and my Companions are upon." As a result, the Salafi movement presents a forceful front of missionary appeal without adopting ideas from other sects, groups or movements. This certainty and uncompromising stance have led others in the Muslim community to label Salafis as stubborn radicals.

This ideational orientation constitutes the foundation for the religious beliefs and understandings of Bin Laden and other Salafis who espouse violence in the name of Islam. These "jihadi" Salafis identify themselves as adherents to the Salafi manhaj and use well-known Salafi identity markers such as *Ahl al-Hadith* (People of Hadith), *taifat al-mansura* (the Aided Group), *al-firqa al-najiyya* (the Saved Sect), and "those who follow the creed or way of the Sunnah and Jamaa." As a result, the arguments supporting the use of violence conscientiously implement the Salafi manhaj and devote considerable effort to locating the religious evidence needed to legitimize particular conflicts, actions and decisions. In his 1996 "Declaration of War" against the United States, for example, Bin Laden carefully constructs his legitimation of violence through the use of the Quran and authentic hadiths, citing pieces of evidence according to the Salafi manhaj and praising publications by other well-known Salafis, such as Safar al-Hawali, a Saudi religious scholar known for his opposition to the U.S. military presence in Saudi Arabia. Such careful presentation of evidence is ubiquitous in jihadi Salafi publications and statements.

Yet despite a broad base of agreement between jihadi Salafis and others in the movement, there are important points of disagreement. Most important, a vitriolic conflict over the permissibility of Jihad has fractured the movement since the conclusion of the war against the Soviet Union in Afghanistan. The Afghan experience radicalized Arab Salafi *mujahidin* (holy fighters) who attempted to export the religious justification for war to new contexts and enemies. Reform-oriented Salafis, on the other hand, mobilized to condemn broader military actions by Muslim fighters. Instead, reformists propose a focused effort to promote Salafi thought before launching a Jihad, which would come at a much later point. How U.S. actions influence this debate could have serious consequences for the war on terrorism.

Prior to the war in Afghanistan, there was very little discussion in the Muslim world about the contemporary use of violence and Jihad in Islam. Certainly small radical groups, such as Islamic Jihad, produced material that justified assassination and other forms of violence, but these justifications were rejected by most Islamists and remained limited in number and reach. The war in Afghanistan, however, led both states (e.g. Saudi Arabia) and individual Islamists to focus more extensively on religious justification for a contemporary war to facilitate Muslim support and volunteers to combat the Soviet Union.

During the initial stages of the war, the small Arab contingency that went to fight encountered difficulty soliciting volunteers from the Middle East. At least in part, this was due to a strong belief that any military efforts should first be directed toward combating the Israeli presence in the Palestinian territories and Jerusalem. Other radicals wanted first to focus on fighting incumbent Arab regimes. This was compounded by the fact that because classical Muslim debates on warfare had predominantly focused on *jus in bello*(legitimate means in warfare) rather than *jus ad bellum* (grounds for warfare), there were few recent publications about the religious justification for a contemporary war such as the one in Afghanistan.

The call to "join the caravan" in Afghanistan, however, grew through the financial support of Gulf countries and the efforts of "Arab Afghans" who believed the war was a religious obligation. Organizations based in Saudi Arabia and Kuwait, in particular, championed the call to arms and funded an array of *madrasas*(religious schools) and training camps in Pakistan for Arab volunteers. This included support for local organizations, such as Ahl-i-Hadith in Pakistan and Afghanistan, which set up an array of Salafioriented madrasas and actively recruited Salafi fighters from Gulf countries. These local spiritual and military training centers helped sponsor the Salafi manhaj among newly recruited Arab volunteers, creating socializing institutions that heavily influenced the religious understanding of thousands of Arab volunteers from non-Gulf countries, especially Algeria and Egypt, who eventually returned to their home countries indoctrinated in Salafi thought and determined to lead Muslim uprisings against Arab regimes. The spread of Salafi thought through local religious institutions was reinforced by the participation of Saudi-based Salafi mujahidin, who comprised the largest national grouping of Arab fighters in the war. Salafi organizations and groups, such as Abu Sayyaf and Jamaat al-Dawa, used their ideological affinity with Gulf contributors to raise millions of dollars for Salafi operations. The underlying religious justification for Arab participation in the war was constructed by Abdullah Azzam, a Palestinian graduate of al-Azhar University, who resurrected the call to Jihad that attracted thousands of volunteers from the Middle East. Salafi jihadis view Azzam as a cornerstone of the contemporary Jihad movement; his writings have heavily influenced conceptions of jus ad bellum and the obligations of Jihad among Salafis. His ideational influence was supported by his strategic location in the international networks that supported the mujahidin, a position that was augmented by his leadership at the Islamic Coordination Council in Peshawar, which provided social services for the mujahidin and served as the dispatcher for Arab volunteers. Azzam was eventually assassinated by a car bomb in Peshawar in 1989 and is considered a martyr in the Jihad movement.

In his legitimation for a Jihad in Afghanistan, Azzam outlined two kinds of jihads against the unbelievers. The first is an offensive attack in enemy territory when the enemy is not gathering to attack Muslims, with the minimum goal of establishing strong borders and occasionally sending armies to harass the unbelievers. According to Azzam, this is a collective responsibility (*fard kifaya*), meaning that if any one group performs the task, other Muslims are absolved of the responsibility. The second type of Jihad against unbelievers is a defensive Jihad to protect Muslim territory and populations. Under such conditions, the religious obligation is an individual obligation (*fard ayn*) incumbent upon all Muslims, equal to other religious duties, such as the five pillars of the faith. The obligation initially falls to those Muslims who are nearest the enemy. If that group cannot effectively defeat the enemy, then the obligation expands to the next closest group of Muslims. The required geographic proximity for obligatory participation expands as it becomes clear that current contingencies cannot effectively defeat the enemy. If not enough Muslims participate in the Jihad to repel the enemy, then the entire Muslim community is in sin. The Jihad in Afghanistan was clearly delineated as an invasion of Muslim territory by an unbeliever force and thus resonated with many Muslims in the Arab world.

Azzam's legitimation for Muslim participation in the Afghan war enjoyed broad support in Muslim countries, where leaders and Islamic activists alike condoned the argument for Jihad. Radical Islamists, in particular, rejoiced at the opportunity to resurrect Jihad as an essential component of religious duty. This sentiment is encapsulated in a statement by Omar Abdul Rahman, a Salafi spiritual leader currently serving a life sentence in the United States for his involvement in the 1993 World Trade Centre bombing: "When the Afghans rose and declared a Jihad – and Jihad had been dead for the longest time – I can't tell you how proud I was." Azzam's call for Jihad informs current Salafi jihadi arguments and shapes thinking about the obligation of Jihad.

This call for a defensive Jihad to protect Muslim populations continued to resonate with Salafi jihadis long after the Soviets withdrew from Afghanistan, and the Salafi Arab Afghans searched for new venues of combat. They argued that despite the liberation of Afghanistan from the Soviet Union, war in defense of Islam still remained an individual obligation since Muslim populations remained oppressed by unbelievers throughout the globe, including in the Middle East. Jihad was thus viewed as an ongoing process of Muslim liberation at a global level, what could be viewed as an obligatory "nomadic Jihad."

Shortly after the fall of Kabul in the war in Afghanistan, Arab Salafis considered a Jihad in the Philippines or Kashmir as a part of the individual responsibility to protect Muslim countries and populations, but the sense of urgency produced by ethnic cleansing in Bosnia from 1992 to 1995 redericted efforts toward the former Yuglosalv rebuplic.

Abu Abd al-Aziz (nicknamed Barbarossa because of his red beard) consulted with famous Salafi scholars, including Mohammed Nasir al-Din al-Bani, Abd al-Aziz Bin Baz and Mohammed Bin Uthman, who agreed that the war in Bosnia had become an individual obligation. Al-Aziz led a new migration of Salafi fighters into Bosnia, initially comprising nomadic jihadis based in Afghanistan and Pakistan. As Arab regimes increased repression against radical Islamists, espcially in Egypt and Algeria, the nomadic jihadis were joined by other radical Salafis who sought to escape domestic intelligence services. Still others joined the fight to enhance and practice their combat skills before returning to the Middle East.

The new Jihad was supported by Salafi missionary work, primarily funded by Saudi Arabia and other Gulf countries, which included assistance for local relgious centers to promote Salafi publications and ideology. The Travnik Islamic Centre, in particular, received funding and Islamic books and eventually recommended a booklet titled *Ideas We Have to Correct*, publsihed by the Salafi-missionary Committee for Bosnia-Herzegovinia of the Kuwait Organization for the Rebirth of Islamic Tradition

The next battle in the nomadic Jihad took place in Chechnya, embroiling the Russians in combat against Bin Laden associates and others in the Salafi global network. Although the uprising in Chechnya initially adopted an Islamic identity as a source of unification against the Russians (similar to the strategy of mobilization in the Algerian revolution against the French), Salafis soon joined the war and attempted to promote their stricter variant of Islam. Chechnya quickly became a beacon for Salafis seeking to continue the defensive Jihad, and battle-hardened Arab detachments from Afghanistan, Bosnia, Pakistan and elsewhere joined the fighting in the mid-1990s.

The rapid influx of Arab fighters challenged the hegemony of local religious leaders and created friction among different Muslim groups in Chechnya, especially as the fighting diminished. In a region where Sufi practices predominate, the Salafi ideology of the Arab mujahidin directly contradicted local understandings of Islam and fomented tensions between Chechens and their Arab allies. According to Ahmad Khadzhu Kadryov, the mufti of Chechnya-Ichkeria, "Detachments of Wahhabi [Salafi] volunteers from Arab countries came to us during the war in Chechnya. These detachments were very well armed, and for this reason our Chechens also readily joined them. Many of them [Chechens] were introduced to this teaching and began to attempt to teach us, maintaining that we were distorting Islam." Dialogue between the Chechen religious leaders and the Salafi fighters was unsuccessful, leading to factional clashes and internal conflict.

The forced Russian withdrawal from Chechnya further emboldened Salafi jihadis, who exported the revolution to neighbouring Dagestan. Reports of a Salafi presence in Dagestan had begun to emerge as early as the beginning of perestroika, when preachers from the Arab world first came to the area. This early presence was reinforced by the influx of young Dagestanis educated in Salafi-controlled madrasas, who were given cash incentives and encouraged to return to Dagestan. Later, groups of Salafis from Dagestan who fought in Chechnya returned to their homes in 1996 and made it clear that they intend to create an Islamic state. As one young Salafi from Dagestan defiantly commented, "The Chechens defeated the Russians. It is now our turn to fight for an Islamic State." This was supported by Mullah Bagauddin, the spiritual leader of the Salafi movement in Dagestan, who initially announced that Dagestan would remain in Russia, but only if Russia became an Islamic state. Growing nationalist sentiments prompted increased Russian intervention, and Salafis mobilized for Jihad under the leadership of a Jordanian Arab Afghan named Khattab, who was instrumental in the war in Chechnya. After the war, he built blood relations with Dagestanis by marrying a woman from the mountain village of Karamacki, which subsequently became a centre for Salafi activity and proclaimed itself an independent imamate in 1998. Over a series of years, Khattab and radical Salafis established a Salafi base in the central region of Dagestan that came to be widely known as "Little Chechnya."

The nomadic Jihad was expanded to a variety of other countries and regions as well, including Uzbekistan, Tajikistan, the Philippines, Macedonia, Western China and Kosovo. In effect, wherever Salafis identified an oppressed Muslim population, the Jihad became an individual obligation. There were certainly priorities, such as Bosnia and Chechnya, but the Salafi jihadi movement spawned myriad radical groups intent on defending the Muslim community through violence in multiple geographic locations. Azzam's original call to defend the Muslim community in Afghanistan was adopted to extend the Jihad indefinitely, moving the nomadic Jihad into new countries to face infidel oppression. This, in turn, created a vast international network of Salafi jihadis, many of whom joined Bin Laden and al-Qaeda.

While large contingencies of Salafis joined the nomadic Jihad, a substantial portion of Arab Afghans returned to their home countries in the 1990s to lead Islamic revolutions against regimes in the Middle East. But unlike the resilient support for a defensive Jihad against the Soviet invasion, support for such a radical endeavor was more ambiguous since it constituted an uprising against regimes that many Muslims accepted as at least nominally Islamic. Since Islam explicitly rejects rebellions against Muslim leaders, Salafi jihadis faced a potential theological obstacle in legitimating violent actions.

Given this prohibition, Salafis had to construct a discourse demonstrating that Arab leaders and regimes were no longer Muslim, thus opening possibilities for the Jihad. To do so, they drew upon the writings of the medieval scholar Taqi al-Din Ahmad Ibn Taymiyya, whose unique contribution to Salafi thought is his elaboration of the concept of Jihad. He lived during the Crusades and the Mongol invasions, and it was the latter experience that shaped his interpretation of Jihad. As the Mongols conquered Muslim societies, they were exposed to Islam and eventually converted. The dilemma faced by Islamic scholars was whether the war against the Mongols could still be considered a Jihad or had become a war between two Muslim entities, in which case it was no longer a Jihad. In his fatwa on the Mongols, Ibn Taymiyya recognized that the Mongols practiced the pillars of the faith, but questioned whether this made them true Muslims. The dominant interpretation was that the sharia (Islamic law) considered such groups Muslim, regardless of their actions, because they fulfilled the basic Muslim obligations. Ibn Taymiyya introduced a new criterion for this evaluation. He argued that regardless of whether a person follows the basics of the faith, if an individual fails to uphold any aspect of the sharia, that person is no longer considered a Muslim. Such people become*kafirs* (unbelievers) because they embraced Islam but through actions left the faith.

Declaring regimes heretical permits the defining of leaders in the Middle East as *un-Islamic* rulers who enforce their power and control over *Muslim* societies, and thus plays to defensive understandings of Jihad. Jihadi discourse goes even further. It argues that Western influence over Arab governments through foreign assistance, International Monetary FUND loans, military connections and political alignments renders these governments "puppets" of the West and its Zionist allies in the Middle East. Arab regimes are thus considered the functional equivalent of foreign occupiers. In Algeria for example, Islamist rebels went to considerable effort to frame the government as a French surrogate intent on preventing society from fully realizing its Islamic potential. The military hierarchy, in particular, was singled out as Hizb Farancia (the Party of France). Radical Salafis decry other rulers as well, including those in Egypt and Saudi Arabia, as instruments of Western imperialism determined to undermine Muslim society. Saudi Arabia's decision to allow American troops in the kingdom during the Gulf War is considered evidence of such connections. Even the Yemeni government, which had for a long time distanced itself from strong relations with the West, was charged with acting as a tool of American interests when it allowed U.S. forces to operate in Yemen in the 1990s.

In issuing these serious charges, jihadi Salafis have decentralized *takfir* (declaring someone an apostate). Whereas in the past, decisions about whether someone had left Islam were predominantly centralized in religious authorities and sharia courts often tied to the state, radical Salafis have adopted takfir as a flexible weapon to use against an assortment of individuals, institutions and regimes deemed un-Islamic by Salafi standards. The ambiguity in such standards is that it is unclear where the threshold for Jihad lies. Some radical groups argue that any single transgression can constitute apostasy and thus employ takfir with reckless abandon, even while Salafis themselves struggle to emulate the pristine model of the Prophet. Under such circumstances, takfir becomes a blanket weapon selectively wielded to legitimize attacks against those deemed obstacles to Salafi thought and activism. In addition, individual Salafi groups, some with little expertise in the study of the hadith, have adapted the defensive legitimation of Jihad without the sufficient evidence demanded by the Salafi manhaj.

The decentralization of takfir and the attendant consequences for violence became readily apparent during the civil war that plagued Algeria in the 1990s. The initial call to Jihad was launched in response to the cancellation of election results in January 1992 as the Islamic Salvation Front (FIS) was poised to control Parliament. The subsequent crackdown on the Islamic movement and repression of Islamist leaders and grass-roots activities were framed as a war against Islam by a French surrogate in Algeria; and various groups and tendencies within the movement mobilized for what was viewed as a defensive Jihad directed against the incumbent regime.

The shared understanding about legitimate targets, however, quickly disintegrated with the emergence of the Armed Islamic Group (GIA), which quickly distinguished itself from other Islamic groups through its willingness to use extreme forms of violence. While the GIA initially included both jihadi Salafis and Algerianists (more nationalist-oriented Islamic groups) in an attempt to foster a unified front against the regime, cooperation between the two quickly disintegrated over doctrinal issues. In 1994, Salafis in the GIA moved against the Algerianists, killing 140, including prominent Islamist figures such as Muhammad al-Said and Abd al-Razzak Radjam. The carnage consolidated the dominance of the

Salafi tendency within the loose organizational structure of the GIA, which, in reality, was an amalgamation of Salafi groups with varying levels of doctrinal adherence.

The decentralization of takfir led a number of GIA groups to frame civilian populations as legitimate targets in the Jihad, leading to massacres during the mid-1990s. In 1996, Antar Zouabri became the emir of the GIA and inaugurated his new leadership with a fatwa that condemned anyone who did not directly assist the GIA. In a distorted adoption of the "defensive" Jihad argument, Zouabri claimed that ordinary villagers were tacitly supporting the regime and thus an offensive against Islam. The GIA argued that such behavior made them apostates and thus sharia-sanctioned targets of Jihad. Ibn Taymiyya's argument was thus extended to include a defense against a population viewed as un-Islamic because it did not actively rise up in support of the GIA. Often GIA factions killed entire villages with machetes and other handheld weapons; the massacres are estimated to have killed tens of thousands of innocent civilians.

Other civilian targets of the GIA Jihad included the media, schools and foreign nationals. The media was framed as merely an extension of the regime and thus an offensive tool to repress Islam. In a communiqué in 1995, the GIA clearly articulated this view: "The rotten apostate regime did not stop using the mercenary media to cover its crimes and rationalize its aggression. This has turned all written, seen and heard media outlets into a tool of aggression spreading lies and rumors." Similar criteria were used to justify attacks against schools. Since most schools in Algeria are controlled by the state, the GIA reasoned that they were un-Islamic institutions designed to support an unbeliever regime. The GIA claimed that "according to the sharia, one is not allowed to work in establishments which belong to the government or its allies," especially schools where the curriculum is "contrary to Islam." In the last two months of 1994, 30 school teachers and school directors were killed and 538 schools suffered arson attacks. By the end of 1994, GIA factions had assassinated 142 teachers. For their part, foreign nationals were viewed as agents sent to undermine the Jihad and Islam. Missionaries were killed by GIA factions, including seven French Trappist monks, who were beheaded in 1996 in a brutal display of violence. In all of these cases, GIA factions paid lip service to the defensive legitimation, as adapted from the call to arms in Afghanistan.

Despite condemnations from other Salafi jihadis who charged that factions of the GIA had transgressed and misapplied Islamic principles in massacring civilians, the decentralization of takfir led ultra-violent GIA factions to continue the reign of terror. Omar Abu Qatadeh (a former spiritual guide for the GIA living in the United Kingdom), Muhammed Mustafa al-Muqri (identified as the leading candidate to succeed Omar Abd al-Rahman as spiritual leader of the Gamiyya Islamiyya in Egypt), and other jihadi Salafi personalities withdrew their support for the group once the scope of violence became clear. Even Osama bin Laden allegedly decried the actions, preferring instead to support a new Salafi movement founded by former GIA commander Hassan Hattab called "the Salafi Group for Call and Combat." In May 1998, Qamar al-Din Kharban, leader of the Algerian Afghans, received support from Bin Laden for FUNDS and networks in Europe to help consolidate Hattab's faction in an effort to distance the mujahidin from the GIA while still continuing the Jihad. At a trial in Tizi Ouzou, Muhammad Barashid, an emir close to Hattab, claimed that Bin Laden promised logistical and financial support for the new movement since the GIA had "strayed," and it is rumored that Bin Laden suggested the name for the new Salafi group.

Differences over takfir and proper conduct in warfare among Salafi jihadis in Algeria accelerated at the end of the 1990s, leading to spin-off movements and splinter groups. Divergences over the permissibility of killing civilians, in particular, led to serious intra-Salafi clashes, with various groups charging others with heresy. Takfir was thus utilized even *within* the Salafi movement to decry groups with divergent views of Jihad. In addition to Hattab's new movement, other Salafibased groups emerged to combat the GIA as heretics, including the "Islamic Movement for Spreading the Faith and Holy War" and the "Faithful to the Oath." These groups promised to continue a legitimate defensive Jihad against the regime while concurrently combating the GIA and its atrocities.

The Jihad at home, which was initially sponsored by a unified assault on the regime, was derailed by the decentralization of takfir, leading to violence against broader publics and within the Salafi jihadi community itself.

Although the Algerian civil war is a stark case of Salafi violence and the decentralization of takfir, it is certainly not the only example of a "Jihad at home." In Yemen, for example, Salafis operating in Aden launched a violent struggle against the regime and "un-Islamic behaviors" in society. This included an attempt to impose control over the city and an attack on shrines at the Hashemite mosque in 1994 as well as an assortment of other violent clashes with government troops, especially in 1998. In Libya, former Afghan Arab fighters announced the formation of the Militant Islamic Group, allegedly a Salafi-based group operating in the northeastern and northwestern parts of Libya that reportedly clashed with Qaddafi's forces during the 1990s. In Jordan, several violent Salafi groups emerged in the late 1980s and throughout the 1990s, including groups linked to internationally renowned jihadi Salafis such as Osama bin Laden, Abu Qatadeh and Abu Muhammad al-Maqdisi, a Palestinian living in Jordan who served as a spiritual inspiration for the November 1995 bombing in Riyadh, Saudi Arabia, that killed five Americans and two Indian nationals. And in Egypt, the Salafi-inspired Gamiyya Islamiyya waged a low-intensity conflict against the Mubarak regime throughout the 1990s, a conflict that claimed more than 1,300 lives.

Despite the increasing popularity of rhetoric condoning a nomadic Jihad or a Jihad at home against un-Islamic regimes, the transnational Salafi movement is not unified in its view of violence. Within the Salafi community there are strong dissenting voices that represent a counter-discourse of Jihad that is related to jihadi thought in its sources of inspiration but differs in emphasis and interpretation. These differences represent an internal battle over the discourse of Jihad and legitimate warfare as each side mobilizes rhetoric, evidence and scholars on behalf of its cause.

For reformist Salafis, there is great concern that the Muslim community is not ready to engage in Jihad, either against incumbent Arab regimes or the United States. It is not that Jihad is rejected as a tactic of religious transformation; rather, reformists believe that several prior phases are necessary before a Jihad is permissible. In the reformist interpretation, religious transformation requires an evolutionary process of stages in which Jihad builds upon platforms of the sequence.

The central component of the reformist counter-discourse on Jihad is that unless Muslims follow the straight path of Islam and the Salafi manhaj, they will be unable to engage in a successful Jihad, since God rewards only the true believers. A lack of effective Salafi propagation and concomitant divisions within the Muslim community creates weakness that will prevent a successful Jihad against Western countries led by the United States. Any premature movement toward the use of violence is therefore doomed to fail. In fact, a few well-known reformists have recently used Afghanistan as an example of failure, not success. They argue that after the Soviets were expelled, the Muslims fell into disarray, factional clashes and rifts in a civil war that reflected divisions and a lack of unity through the Salafi manhaj. Afghanistan was therefore spiritually unprepared to engage in a Jihad.

The weakness and inability to engage in an effective Jihad stems from several sources. First, reformist Salafis believe that the Muslim community remains divided, weak and apart from the Salafi manhaj. As a result, they cannot prepare for Jihad properly because they lack the spiritual preparation. In a debate between Muhammad Nasir al-Din al-Bani (d. 1999), one of the best-known and respected reformist Salafis, and a member of the Egyptian Islamic Jihad, al-Bani complained, "We notice the mujahids [those who actively take part in a Jihad] call for whatever of the Muslims to join the fight, and when they go to fight, they find disagreements among themselves in matters of their faith and the basics of Islam. How do these people get ready for Jihad when they are yet to understand what is obligatory on them of*aqida* [articles of faith]?" Reformists believe that only when Muslims agree on the true faith, as understood in Salafi doctrine, will unity in Jihad endure and Muslims remain united. It is only at such a point that triumph becomes an inevitable reward from God to the community of the faithful.

Given the current context of unbelief, deviant religious practices and weakness, the reformists believe that the first necessary stage is *tarbiya* (education and cultivation to encourage proper Muslim practices) and*tasfiya* (purification). Change thus begins at the level of individual and personal transformation without the use of violence. The hope is that religious change will transform society through individuals who adopt the Salafi manhaj. As Ali Hasan al-Halabi, a former student of al-Bani, argues: "[I]f the Muslims desire good, unity and establishment upon the earth, then they should make their manners and behaviors like that of the Salaf of this *ummah* and begin by changing themselves. However, he who is unable to change even himself, will not be able to change his family, not to mention changing the *ummah*."

The reformists draw analogies to the early stages of divine revelation when the focus of the Islamic mission was propagation rather than Jihad. Today's society is likened to the early community of Muslims who were surrounded by remnants of *jahiliyya* (period of ignorance). During this initial period, Muhammad spent most of his time in preaching and *dawa* (calling people to Islam), rather than fighting. As al-Bani argues, "History repeats itself. Everybody claims that the Prophet is their role model. Our Prophet spent the first half of his message making dawa, and he did not start it with Jihad." Instead of waging war, Muslims should use the early model of the Prophet "and train the people to understand the correct Salafi doctrine, which is void of myths and heresies, and to teach them good morals, so that we can emerge with a broad base that embellishes this religion for human beings." Jihad is thus viewed as the final stage after the Muslim community is unified and strong, certainly not conditions that prevail today.

The second source of opposition to the use of violence among reformists derives from a belief that a premature Jihad launched before the purification of the Muslim community will engender harsh responses that could make even basic propagation difficult, a condition that is considered *haram* (religiously forbidden) by many Muslims. The necessity of engaging in actions that provide more good than harm derives from a general acceptance of the medieval Salafi scholar Ibn Qayyim al-Jawziyya and his four levels of forbidding evil. According to al-Jawziyya, there are four possible consequences of any action: 1) the evil is replaced with something good; 2) the evil is diminished without ending completely; 3) the evil is replaced by an equivalent evil; and 4) the evil is replaced by an even greater evil. The first two are considered religiously acceptable, the third involves *ijtihad*(the exercise of independent judgment), and the fourth is forbidden. Reformist Salafis believe that the use of violence will prompt a pernicious response from state authorities, who would limit the capacity of the movement to promote its manhaj. As Salim al-Hilali, an internationally renowned reformist Salafi, argues, Muslims "should not say the state is un-Islamic and change it with force. Otherwise the mosques would be closed and scholars would be put in prison. Change in Islam must be for the better." Another Salafi scholar argues that, "if you cannot achieve your objectives through Jihad, then it is haram."

It is not that the reformist Salafis reject Jihad; quite the contrary. They argue that in certain contexts it is a religious obligation. However, the time is not yet right and the movement must focus first on more basic stages of religious propagation and purification. As a result, reformists have vehemently denounced the use of violence. The Saudi Salafi scholar Muhammad al-Uthaymin (d. 2001) decries the use of unrest: "Let those who riot know that they only serve the enemies of Islam; the matter cannot be handled by uprising and excitement, but rather by wisdom." Muhammad Nasir al-Din al-Bani warns, "The way to salvation is not, as some people imagine, to rise with arms against the rulers and to conduct military coups. In addition to being among contemporary bidahs (innovations), such actions disregard texts of Islam, among which is the command to change ourselves. Furthermore, it is imperative to establish the basis upon which the building will stand." Ali Hasan al-Halabi adds, "Anyone who examines the past and present of Islam would clearly see that excessiveness has brought for the Ummah disasters, bloodshed, eviction and harm that cannot be known to the full extent except by Allah. It suffices in this regard to remember the turmoils of the Khawaarij and the advocates of takfir from past to present" The reference to the Khawaarij, a sect that fomented rebellion and assassinated important leaders during the early years of Islam, is intended to equate the jihadis with what is generally viewed by many Muslims as a heretical group that undermined the stability of the Muslim world.

The reformists are well represented within Salafi communities in a variety of country settings. In Yemen, for example, Shaykh Muqbil Bin-Hadi al-Wadii runs an assortment of reform-oriented institutions and organizations designed to promote the Salafi manhaj. Al-Wadii learned about Salafi thought for fifteen years while in Saudi Arabia, before he was deported to Yemen in the early 1980s for alleged links to radical Islamists who seized the Grand Mosque in 1979. He currently supervises major Salafi missionary centers in Sanaa, including the Damaj Centre, Maaber Centre, Mahreb Centre, al-Hudeida Centre and al-Khair mosque, all officially supported by the Holy Mosque Establishment, a charitable organization in Saudi Arabia.

While there have been some rumors about a connection with Bin Laden, al-Wadii has adamantly opposed the use of violence. In particular, he actively condemns the use of violence by the Islamic Army of Aden-Abayan, which is responsible for attacks on the government and society and is rumored to have connections to attacks against U.S. forces in Yemen,including the attack against the U.S.S.*Cole*. In 2000, al-Wadii publicly distanced himself from such actions: "We have even condemned these groups and called it the movements of corruption, not Jihad. We always disapprove of any violent actions to spread Islam. Islam is a religion of peace and harmony, and such violence should never be thought of as part of Islam." Thousands of Salafi students flock to Yemen every year to learn about Salafi thought at these institutions. His reformist orientation has attracted more than 100,000 students over the past twenty years, but he has also incurred the wrath of the jihadis, who have allegedly attempted to assassinate him several times.

Reformists are also active in other Middle Eastern countries as well. In Jordan, prominent reformists such as Muhammad Abu Shaqra, Ali Hasan al-Halabi, Salim al-Hilali and Mashhur Hasan Salman enjoy substantial followings in the Salafi community. Despite the emergence of more radical Salafi groups in the 1980s and 1990s, such as the "Reformation and Challenge Group," the "Oath of Loyalty to the Imam," and an informal network of radicals affiliated with Bin Laden who were tried for attempted bombings during millennium celebrations, the reformists dominate the landscape of discursive contention. These high-profile Salafis consistently condemn violence and have successfully directed most Jordanian Salafis away from the course of Jihad. Prominent reformist Salafis also operate in Kuwait and Saudi Arabia, where they staff the state religious hierarchy.

In some cases reformist Salafis have even participated in democratic elections, indicating a strong inclination to work within the system. In Kuwait, in particular, a number of Salafis from the Society for the Revival of Islamic Heritage hold seats in Parliament, and the movement has shown strong support for participating in political life. In Egypt, jihadis-cum-reformists from the Gamiyya Islamiyya and Islamic Jihad formed the Sharia party and the Islah party to remold the movement for Jihad around party politics. Although the regime has not issued a permit for the parties, and the Gamiyya Islamiyya leadership called for an election boycott, Sheikh Muhammad Ali Suleiman from the Gamiyya ran for Parliament in 2000. And in Jordan, a few Salafis indicated an intention to run for Parliament, and one won a seat in the Chamber of Deputies in 1997. While most reformists continue to condemn democracy as antithetical to Islam, at least a few have expressed interest in working for reform through democratic institutions.

Despite the appeal of the jihadis to wage war against un-Islamic Arab regimes and those who oppress Muslim populations, the ubiquity of the reformist Salafis and their message of religious transformation do have a transnational impact. Members of the GIA in Algeria, for example, have claimed that their surrender was strongly influenced by prominent reformists who argued that the Jihad in Algeria was no longer a true Jihad. While much of this is due to the work of the Algerian reformist Alid Cherifi (alias Abu Abd al-Bari), who has encouraged widespread defections and surrenders – through informal contacts, cassettes, discussions with Salafi fighters, and lectures at the University of Algiers and Fath al-Imam Mosque – internationally recognized figures outside

Algeria have also had an impact. One Salafi fighter recalled the following influence: "I was sitting in the mountain and warplanes were dropping their bombs but that did not move me. At the time, I was leaning against something with my weapon beside me and I was listening to a tape by Shaykh Muhammad al-Salih Bin al-Uthaymayn. When I heard him say that this is not Jihad, that did to me a great deal more than a bomb dropping from the sky." The power of ideational influences by reputable scholars is echoed by a nineteen-year-old from the GIA who summarized his decision to surrender: "By God, I did not return because of the use of force of arms but because of the words of the clergymen and religious conviction." The resonance of such messages is reflected by the agitation they produced among the GIA leadership, which decried Uthaymayn and other reformists as traitors.

In a similar effect, the more reform-oriented statements by the historic leadership of the Gamiyya Islamiyya issued from the Turah prison in Egypt on July 5, 1997, helped provide the foundations of a cease-fire initiated in the late 1990s. The turning point in the low-intensity conflict between the Gamiyya Islamiyya and the Mubarak regime occurred on November 17, 1997, when, with the approval of the external military leaders abroad and Rifai Ahmed Taha, a faction of al-Shahid Talat Hamam (the military wing of the Gamiyya Islamiyya) massacred 58 tourists and four Egyptians outside the Queen Hatshepsut temple in Luxor, raising the specter of an Algerian-style conflict. The Egyptian public was stunned by the actions and condemnations were swift; leaders in the Gamiyya denounced the attack and attempted to distance themselves from the atrocities. The massacres hardly looked like a defensive Jihad, and the Gamiyya leadership in prison accelerated its new direction toward reform by once again calling for a cease-fire and a reevaluation of the group's strategies. It took until March 1999 for the movement's military leadership abroad, which has direct ties to Bin Laden and al-Qaeda, to finally agree to support the initiative. This included the support of top al-Qaeda lieutenants from Egypt, such as Ayman al-Zawahiri and Rifai Ahmed Taha. The impact of a new, more reform-oriented argument is represented by a virtual end to Islamist-sponsored violence in Egypt after 1997.

It is not clear whether such influences are systemic, but the Algerian and Egyptian cases and interviews I have conducted with both reformist and jihadi Salafis in Jordan indicate that it can have a substantial impact on perceptions about the legitimacy of violence in a particular context. The ability of reformists to mobilize symbolic and material resources to combat jihadi arguments indicates possible influence on the course of violent Islamic contention.

The difference between the jihadi and reformist factions of the transnational Salafi movement is not a disagreement over whether Jihad is needed, but rather the timing of any war. Even prominent Salafi reformists, such as the late Muhammad Nasir al-Din al-Bani, have agreed that current conditions make Jihad an individual obligation. But the factions disagree as to whether that obligation must be fulfilled immediately or after a great deal of spiritual preparation. Reformists argue that Salafis must first build the base of religious understanding before the *umma* (Muslim community) is prepared to wage Jihad. Where reformists sanction Jihad, it is only under extreme circumstances, such as the Soviet invasion of Afghanistan or the massacre of Muslims in Bosnia, when urgent conditions and necessity may drive reformists to accept Jihad. On the other hand, jihadis believe that Salafis should pursue all options at once. Propagation is important, but should temporally coincide with Jihad, which must be waged wherever Muslims are oppressed. Given the proximity of these perspectives, rooted in the Salafi manhaj and perceptions of current conditions, the U.S. response to the September 11 attacks should consider the ramifications not only in the Muslim world, but more specifically within the Salafi movement as well, since it constitutes the strongest potential recruitment base for Bin Laden and other radicals.

In Salafi circles, there is a great deal of reformist appreciation for Bin Laden's arguments legitimating an attack against the United States. Even though reformists may disagree with civilian targeting, there is a shared understanding about the defensive nature of Jihad, rooted in the earlier Afghan experience, that seems pertinent today to many Salafis; and in his fatwas and various public statements, Bin Laden is careful to couch the Jihad as a defense of Islam in the face of American aggression. In an interview with *Nidaul Islam*, for example, Bin Laden clearly takes this position: "The evidence overwhelmingly shows America and Israel killing the weaker men, women, and children in the Muslim world and elsewhere." This argument is common in other Bin Laden statements as well, and the supposed unwillingness of the United States to distinguish between civilians and military targets is considered justification for a proportional response against American civilians. Bin Laden cites several pieces of "evidence" of this "state terrorism," including atomic bombs in Japan, massacres in Lebanon by Israel (as an arm of the United States), the deaths of hundreds of thousands of Iraqis because of sanctions and military operations, the withholding of arms from Muslims in Bosnia, rendering them vulnerable to Serbian rapes and massacres, and "the occupation of the two sacred mosques in Saudi Arabia." It is the last that has driven Bin Laden since the Gulf War, when he began agitating against the decision to allow American troops into the holy land. For Bin Laden, this affront alone constitutes the grounds for Jihad. But he is careful to accumulate a list of aggressions that would justify a defensive Jihad and garner broader support among Salafis and the Muslim world in general. This is combined with an argument that the American military and Defense Department are controlled by Jewish interests intent on destroying Islam.

Because Salafis are already predisposed to accept the "Afghanistan legitimation" first constructed by Abdullah Azzam, they will likely frame any debates about the permissibility of Jihad against the United States within this framework. As a result, highly visible American military action may inadvertently provide empirical credibility for jihadi framings and tip the balance of power within the Salafi movement away from the reformist counter-discourse. If this were indeed the case, it would radicalize the transnational Salafi movement and undermine the U.S. policy goal of eradicating terrorism by creating a new legion of jihadi supporters that expands the terrorist network and its base of support.

This precarious balance is further complicated by the fact that the nomadic Jihad had already dramatically steered toward the

United States prior to September 11. In the aftermath of the Algerian civil war and the Egyptian conflict, radical Salafis, especially those living abroad in Pakistan and Afghanistan, agreed to reorient the Jihad away from incumbent Arab regimes toward the real power behind the throne – the United States. Whereas earlier discourse among many jihadis fighting "the war at home" focused on an understanding that one must fight "the enemy near" before focusing on the "enemy afar," the failure of violence and unacceptable divergences in the conflicts led many toward a new strategy. The current argument is that only by first attacking the United States (and Israel), can Salafis eventually topple their own regimes. Thus Salafis believe that if the United States withdrew its support of the Egyptian regime, Mubarak would fall, leaving a power vacuum that would usher in a new Islamic (Salafi) government. And although jihadis share concerns with the reformists that such actions will provoke serious repression, there is a belief that inaction creates a greater evil.

As a result, even before the massive attack against the United States on September 11, the direction and machinations of Jihad were already moving toward the only remaining superpower. Radical Salafis had already declared their intent by attacking the marines in Somalia in 1993. This was followed by a formal statement of aggression by Bin Laden and others through a fatwa in 1996. The September 11 attacks were a reminder that the Salafi jihadis had already declared war on the United States nearly a decade earlier.

While Americans are still reeling from the attacks against the World TRADE Centre and the Pentagon, the impulse to respond with military might should be tempered by reflection about how our response will affect strategic objectives. Certainly the United States seeks to punish those responisble and to provide a visible consequence for terrorism, but this must be weighed against the possible impact of responses on the Salafi movement as a whole and on future terrorism. If the United States wishes to avoid a radicalization of groups already predisposed to Bin laden through common religious understanding, it must fully explore how the U.S. action will influence the balance between reformists and jihadis. This will determine the future direction of the transnational Salafi movement, and thus the ability of the United States to effectively combat the new global threat of the twenty-first century.

THE MEANING OF THE CONCEPT OF "JIHAD"

Another concept that deserves clarification due in the context of our discussion is that of "jihad". The exact meaning of "Jihad" is "effort". Thus, in Islam, "to carry out jihad" is "to show effort, to struggle". The Prophet Muhammad explained that "the greatest jihad is the one a person carries out against his lower soul". What is meant by "lower soul" here is selfish desires and ambitions.

Assessed from the Qur'anic point of view, the word "jihad" can also mean a struggle carried out on intellectual grounds against those who oppress people, treat them unjustly, subject them to torture and cruelty and violate legitimate human rights. The purpose of this struggle is to bring about justice, peace and equality. Apart from these ideological and spiritual meanings, struggle in the physical sense is also considered as "jihad". However, as explained above, this has to be a struggle carried out solely for defensive purposes. The use of the concept of "jihad" for acts of aggression against innocent people, that is for terror, would be unjust and a great distortion of the true meaning of the term.

Killing Oneself, In Other Words Committing Suicide, is Forbidden in the Qur'an

Another important matter that arose in the wake of the latest terrorist assaults against the United States is that of suicide attacks. Some people who are ill-informed on Islam have made utterly erroneous statements to the effect that this religion of peace allows suicide attacks, whereas in Islam killing oneself and killing other people are both prohibited. In the words, "Do not kill yourselves." (Qur'an, 4:29) God has declared suicide to be a sin. In Islam it is forbidden for anyone to kill himself or herself, for no matter what reason. The Prophet reveals suicide to be a sin in a parable, when he says that those who commit suicide will be punished:

> *Indeed, whoever (intentionally) kills himself, then certainly he will be punished in the Fire of Hell, wherein he shall dwell forever.*

As this makes clear, committing suicide, and thus carrying out suicide attacks, and causing the deaths of thousands of innocent people while doing so, is a total violation of Islamic morality. God says in the Qur'an that it is a sin to put an end to one's own life. For that reason, it is quite impossible for someone who believes in God and says he abides by the Qur'an to do such a thing. The only people who can do such things are those who have a very mistaken perception of religion, have no idea of true Qur'anic morality, fail to use their reason and conscience, are under the influence of atheist ideologies, and who have been brainwashed with feelings of hatred and revenge. Everybody must oppose such actions.

Compassion, Tolerance and Humanity in the History of Islam

To sum up the facts we have seen so far, we can say that the political doctrine of Islam (in other words, Islamic rules and principles regarding political matters) is exceedingly moderate and peace-loving. This truth is accepted by many non-Muslim historians and theologians. One of these is the British historian Karen Armstrong, a former nun and an expert on Middle East history. In her book Holy War, which examines the history of the three divine religions, she makes the following comments:

> *... The word 'Islam' comes from the same Arabic root as the word 'peace' and the Koran condemns war as an abnormal state of affairs opposed to God's will... Islam does not justify a total aggressive war of extermination... Islam recognises that war is inevitable and sometimes a positive duty in order to end oppression and suffering. The Koran teaches that war must be limited and be conducted in as humane a way as possible. Mohammad had to fight not only the Meccans but also the Jewish tribes in the area and Christian tribes in Syria who planned on offensive against him in alliance with the Jews. Yet this did not make Mohammed denounce the People of the Book. His Muslims were forced to defend themselves but they were not fighting a 'holy war' against the religion of their enemies. When Mohammad sent his freedman Zaid against the Christians at the head of a Muslim army, he told them to fight in the cause of God bravely*

but humanely. They must not molest priests, monks and nuns nor the weak and helpless people who were unable to fight. There must be no massacre of civilians nor should they cut down a single tree nor pull down any building.

After the death of the Prophet, the Caliphs who succeeded him were also very sensitive in exercising justice. In conquered countries, both the indigenous people and the newcomers led their lives in peace and security. Abu Bakr, the first Caliph, demanded his people adopt just and tolerant attitudes in these lands. All these attitudes were in compliance with the values of the Qur'an. Abu Bakr gave the following command to his army before the first Syrian expedition:

Stop, O people that I may give you ten rules to keep by heart: Do not commit treachery, nor depart from the right path. You must not mutilate, neither kill a child or aged man or woman. Do not destroy a palm tree, nor burn it with fire and do not cut any fruitful tree. You msut not slay any of the flock or herds or the camels, save for your subsistence. You are likely to pass by people who have devoted their lives to monastic services; leave them to that to which they have devoted their lives. You are likely, likewise, to find people who will present to you meals of many kinds. You may eat; but do no forget to mention the name of Allah.

Umar ibn al-Khattab, who succeeded Abu Bakr, was famous for the way he exercised justice and made contracts with the indigenous people of the conquered countries. Each one of these contracts proved to be an example of tolerance and justice. For instance, in his declaration granting protection to Christians in Jerusalem and Lod, he ensured that churches would not be demolished and guaranteed that Muslims would not worship in churches in groups. Umar granted the same conditions to the Christians of Bethlehem. During the conquest of Medain, the declaration of protection given to the Nestorian Patriarch Yeshuyab III (650 - 660 AD) again guaranteed that churches would not be demolished and that no building would be converted into a house or a mosque. The letter written by the patriarch to the bishop of Fars (Persia) after the conquest is most striking, in the sense that it depicts the tolerance and compassion shown by Muslim rulers to the Book of People in the words of a Christian:

They [Abbasids] have not attacked the Christian religion, but rather they have commended our faith, honored our priests... and conferred benefits on churches and monasteries.

All these are very important examples revealing the understanding of justice and tolerance of true believers. In a verse God commands the following:

God commands you to return to their owners the things you hold on trust and, when you judge between people, to judge with justice. How excellent is what God exhorts you to do! God is All-Hearing, All-Seeing. (Qur'an, 4:58)

Canon Taylor, one of the mission leaders of the Anglican Church, expresses the beauty revealed by the Islamic morality in one of his speeches as follows:

It [Islam] brought out the fundamental dogmas of religion – the unity and greatness of God, that He is merciful and righteous, that He claims obedience to His will, resignation and faith. It proclaimed the responsibility of man, a future life, a Day of Judgment, and stern retribution to fall upon the wicked; and enforced the duties of prayer, almsgiving, fasting and benevolence. It thrust aside the artificial virtues, the religious frauds and follies, the perverted moral sentiments, and the verbal subtleties of theological disputants... It gave hope to the slave, brotherhood to mankind, and recognition to the fundamental facts of human nature.

The false assertion that people in conquered countries converted to Islam under threat has also been disproved by Western researchers, and the justice and tolerant attitude of Muslims has been confirmed. L.Browne, a Western researcher, expresses this situation in the following words:

Incidentally these well-established facts dispose of the idea so widely fostered in Christian writings that the Muslims, wherever they went, forced people to accept Islam at the point of the sword.

In his book The Prospects of Islam, Browne goes on to say that the real motive behind the Muslims' conquests was the brotherhood of Islam. The vast majority of Muslim administrators who have reigned over the Muslim lands throughout history continued to treat the members of other religions with the utmost tolerance and respect. Within the borders of all Islamic states, both Jews and Christians lived in safety and enjoyed freedom.

Georgetown University's Professor of Religion and International Relations John L. Esposito describes how Jews and Christians who came under the administration of Muslim states met with enormous tolerance:

> *Muslim armies proved to be formidable conquerors and effective rulers, builders rather than destroyers. They replaced the indigenous rulers and armies of the conquered countries, but preserved much of their government, bureaucracy, and culture. For many in the conquered territories, it was no more than an exchange of masters, one that brought peace to peoples demoralized and disaffected by the casualties and heavy taxation that resulted from the years of Byzantine-Persian warfare. Local communities were free to continue to follow their own way of life in internal, domestic affairs. In many ways, local populations found Muslim rule more flexible and tolerant than that of Byzantium and Persia. Religious communities were free to practise their faith-to worship and be governed by their religious leaders and laws in such areas marriage, divorce, and inheritance. In exchange, they were required to pay tribute, a poll tax (jizya) that entitled them to from Muslim protection from outside aggression and exempted them from military service. They were therefore called the "protected ones" (dhimmmi). In effect, this often meant lower taxes, grater local autonomy, rule by fellow Semites with closer linguistic and cultural ties than the hellenized, Greco-Roman elites of Byzantium, and greater religious freedom for Jews and indigenous Christians. Most of the Christian churches, such as the Nestorians, Monophysites, Jacobites, and Copts, had been persecuted as heretics and schismatics by Christian orthodoxy. For these reasons, some Jewish and Christian communities aided the invading armies, regarding them as less oppressive than their imperial masters. In many ways, the conquests brought a Pax Islamica to an embattled area.*

Another "Pax Islamica" brought by Islam was to women, a segment of society that was tremendously abused in the pre-Islamic times. Professor Bernard Lewis, known to be one of the greatest Western experts on the Middle East, makes the following comment:

> *In general, the advent of Islam brought an enormous improvement in the position of women in ancient Arabia, endowing them with property and some other rights, and giving them a measure of protection against ill treatment by their husbands or owners. The killing of female infants, sanctioned by custom in Pagan Arabia, was outlawed by Islam. But the position of women remained poor, and worsened when, in this as in so many other respects, the original message of Islam lost its impetus and was modified under the influence of pre-existing attitudes and customs.*

The reign of the Seljuk Turks and that of the Ottoman Empire were also marked by the just and tolerant outlook of Islam. In his book, *The Spread of Islam in the World,* Sir Thomas Arnold, the British researcher, explains the Christians' willingness to come under Seljuk rule because of this attitude:

> *This same sense of security of religious life under Muslim rule led many of the Christians of Asia Minor, also, about the same time, to welcome the advent of the Saljuq Turks as their deliverers... In the reign of Michael VIII (1261-1282), the Turks were often invited to take possession of the smaller towns in the interior of Asia Minor by the inhabitants, that they might escape from the tyranny of the empire; and both rich and poor often emigrated into Turkish dominions.*

Malik Shah, the ruler of the Islamic Seljuk Empire during its brightest age, approached the people in the conquered lands with great tolerance and compassion and thus was remembered with respect and love by them. All objective historians refer to the justice and tolerance of Malik Shah in their works. His tolerance also kindled feelings of love towards him in the hearts of the People of the Book. For this reason, unprecedented in history, many cities came under Malik Shah's rule of their own free will. Sir Thomas Arnold also mentions Odo de Diogilo, a monk of St. Denis, who participated in the Second Crusade as the private chaplain of Louis VII, refers in his memoirs to the justice administered by Muslims regardless of the subjects' religious affiliation. Based on the graphic account of Odo de Diogilo, Sir Thomas Arnold writes:

> *The situation of the survivors would have been utterly hopeless, had not the sight of their misery melted the hearts of the Muhammadans to pity. They tended the sick and relieved the poor and starving with open-handed liberality. Some even bought up the French money which the Greeks had got out of the pilgrims by force or cunning, and lavishly distributed it among the needy. So great was the contrast between the kind treatment the pilgrims received from the unbelievers and the cruelty of their fellow-Christians, the Greeks, who imposed forced labour upon them, beat them, and robbed them of what little they had left, that many of them voluntarily embraced the faith of their deliverers. As the old chronicler [Odo de Diogilo] says: "Avoiding their co-religionists who had been so cruel to them, they went in safety among the infidels who had compassion upon them, and, as we heard, more than three thousand joined themselves to the Turks when they retired."*

These statements by historians reveal that Muslim administrators who truly adopted the morality of the Islam always ruled with tolerance, compassion and justice. Likewise, the history of the Ottoman Empire which ruled lands on three continents for centuries abounds with examples of tolerance.

The way the Jews settled in Ottoman lands during the time of Sultan Beyazid II, after being subjected to massacre and exile in the Catholic kingdoms of Spain and Portugal, is a fine example of the tolerance that Islamic morality brings with it.

The Catholic monarchs who ruled much of Spain at the time brought grave pressure to bear on the Jews who had formerly lived in peace under Muslim rule in Andalusia. While Muslims, Christians and Jews were able to live side by side in peace in Andalusia, the Catholic monarchs tried to force the whole country to become Christian, and declared war on the Muslims while oppressing the Jews. As a result, the last Muslim ruler in the Granada region of southern Spain was overthrown in 1492. Muslims were subjected to terrible slaughter, and those Jews who refused to change their religion were sent into exile.

One group of these Jews without a homeland sought shelter in the Ottoman Empire, and the state allowed them to do so. The Ottoman fleet, under the command of Kemal Reis, brought the exiled Jews, and those Muslims who had survived the slaughter, to the land of the Ottomans.

Sultan Beyazid II has gone down in history as a most pious believer, and in the spring of 1492 he settled these wronged Jews who had been expelled from Spain in certain parts of his empire, around Edirne, and Thessalonica in present-day Greece. Most of the 25,000 Turkish Jews living in Turkey today are the ancestors of those Spanish Jews. They have adapted their religion and customs, which they brought from Spain some 500 years ago, to the conditions in Turkey, and continue to live most comfortably with their own schools, hospitals, old people's homes, cultural associations and newspapers. In the same way that they have traders and businessmen, they also have representatives in numerous professions, from technical subjects to advertising, with increasingly developing intellectual circles. While Jewish communities in many countries in Europe have for centuries been exposed to the fear of anti-Semitic racist attacks, those in Turkey have lived in peace and security. This example alone is enough to demonstrate the tolerance that Islam brings with it and its understanding of justice.

The compassion and tolerance exhibited by Sultan Beyazid II applied to all the Ottoman sultans. When Sultan Mehmet the Conqueror captured Constantinople, he allowed the Christians and the Jews to live freely there. André Miquel, who is known for the valuable works he has written about the just and tolerant practices of Muslims and the world of Islam, says:

> *Christians lived under a very well-administered government which they were unable to find in the time of the Byzantine and Latin states. They at no time saw any systematic oppression. On the contrary, the empire, and Constantinople in particular, became a shelter for those Spanish Jews who had been tortured. There was no forced imposition of Islam anywhere.*

As is clear from these facts, Muslims have at no time in history been oppressive. On the contrary, they have brought peace and security to all nations and beliefs wherever they have gone. They have abided by God's verse which says: "Worship God and do not associate anything with Him. Be good to your parents and relatives and to orphans and the very poor, and to neighbours who are related to you and neighbours who are not related to you, and to companions and travellers and your slaves. God does not love anyone vain or boastful." (Qur'an, 4:36) and have behaved well to all people. In short, friendship, brotherhood, peace and love are the bases of Qur'anic morality, and it is to these superior virtues that Muslims try to adhere.

A GLOBAL VENTURE TO COUNTER VIOLENT EXTREMISM

The rise of Islamist radicalism continues to threaten U.S. interests in the greater Middle East. Last year's attacks on U.S. embassies, instability in the aftermath of the Arab uprisings, and an increase in political activism among Salafist movements are all cause for concern. In Pakistan, extremist networks use U.S. drone strikes and the killing of Osama bin Laden to rally people to their cause. Although Muslim organizations in the Middle East, Pakistan, Indonesia, and Europe have had some success countering violent extremism (CVE), these groups desperately need FINANCIAL assistance to continue their work. The United States should address this funding gap. By using the existing Global Counterterrorism Forum (GCTF), founded by the U.S. State Department in conjunction with Muslim-majority governments (including Pakistan, Saudi Arabia, and Turkey), the United States is now ideally situated to create a long-term funding mechanism, or "global venture," that consolidates existing programs and seeds new initiatives. Done properly, within eight to ten years al-Qaeda's theology and ideology can become as unattractive among young Muslims as communism became to East Germans.

The Problem

Al-Qaeda and its ideological affiliates do not operate in a vacuum; rather, they feed off of ideas that have proliferated in Muslim communities over decades. A combination of religious literalism and conspiracist politics is at the core of their anti-Western ideology. These ideas include the beliefs that democracy is man-made and only extremist understandings of God's law should be enforced; that violent Jihad is a Muslim obligation until "God's law" is manifest; that those who die pursuing it, including suicide bombers, are martyrs; and that the greatest obstacle to Islam's dominance is the modern West, led by the United States. Killing Americans, therefore, weakens an enemy that oppresses Muslims. Unless such ideas are challenged and discredited, extremist groups will continue to regenerate no matter how many terrorists are killed.

Developing Alternative Narratives

Organizations in the Middle East, Pakistan, and elsewhere are leading the way in advocating counternarratives to extremist messaging. Organizations like Khudi, a Pakistan-based campus network, use Muslim history to argue against radicals who twist the meaning of the word *umma* into a "nation united against infidels" (its correct, historical meaning is "community"). The Radical Middle Way, a Muslim organization based in London, holds public "question time" events with clerics from Egypt's prestigious al-Azhar seminary who use scripture to undermine the belief that suicide bombers are martyrs and to support democracy within an Islamic framework. Activists in Saudi Arabia and Egypt are using social media to challenge conspiracy theories and a pervasive sense of victimhood vis-a-vis the West. They work in hubs of extremist recruitment—mosques, community centers, universities, prisons, and websites—and target vulnerable youth with innovative programming.

Building on these and like-minded organizations and activists, CVE efforts must focus on:

- Educating Muslim thought leaders in mosques and on university campuses through workshops and testimonies from former radicals about why Islamist hard-liners threaten Muslim communities. In 2009, al-Qaeda and its affiliates killed more Muslims than non-Muslims. Muslims need to reclaim their faith because Islamist extremism endangers the very fabric of mainstream, moderate Islam.

- Providing FINANCIAL support to moderates for establishing alternative satellite television channels across the Middle East. A region with bulging youth populations, high unemployment, low rates of reading books, and mass popularity of satellite television means radical clerics often provide unchallenged guidance on questions of religion and politics.
- Supporting the publication and dissemination of reading materials on normative Islam. Those looking for religious literature in the Middle East are often exposed to glossy publications from Gulf countries that promote a literalist, radical reading of Islam. Alternative and mainstream material exists in Egypt, Turkey, and Pakistan, but requires translation and targeted distribution on campuses, in bookshops, and in mosques.
- Initiating the around-the-clock presence of a professional, well-informed network of web-savvy Muslims who are active in Arab and Muslim chat rooms and on social media, refuting al-Qaeda propaganda with factual and scriptural arguments. The purpose is not to dissuade jihadis (that would be a bonus), but to ensure virtual audiences do not assume that extreme narratives are unchallenged and hence preponderant.
- Puncturing the popular perception that the United States is at war with Islam and Muslims by inviting religious leaders annually as guests of the U.S. Congress during the president's state of the union address. This respectful, high-visibility presence would generate Arab and Muslim media coverage that further dents anti-Americanism.

PIONEERING A GLOBAL VENTURE

A cornerstone of the Obama administration's counterterrorism and CVE strategy is the Global Counterterrorism Forum. Launched in 2011, this effort has rightly identified the need for governments and experts to coordinate and share effective CVE strategies. The forum has inspired the creation of the Centre of Excellence for Countering Violent Extremism in Abu Dhabi, an institution focusing on training, research, and dialogue between nongovernmental organizations (NGOs) and governments that counter extremism. Building on these efforts by establishing a CVE global FUND is a natural next step for the GCTF.

A global venture that identifies and funds counterradicalization projects in strategically important countries would be a first step in reversing the grip of the al-Qaeda narrative. Worthy efforts have been undertaken in the past, such as the State Department's public diplomacy initiatives and the appointment of a U.S. special representative to Muslim communities, but they have come up short by failing to address the ongoing FUNDINGcrisis among anti-extremism organizations. A global venture, however, would build on existing efforts and financially strengthen Muslim civil society against extremism. The money to seed this project should come from a wide variety of individuals, organizations, and governments that share an interest in countering extremism. Public and private funding is readily available in Turkey and Gulf countries, from Muslim American communities, and from Western development and philanthropic organizations. Rooting this venture in a diverse network of partners would bolster the program's appeal while heading off the al-Qaeda allegation that it is an American plot.

Garnering support to combat radicalism under the umbrella of a global venture will require a centralized effort from a body that can lend the venture prestige, direction, and continuity. Based on existing American and Turkish cooperation at the GCTF, the United States should encourage Turkey to take the lead in establishing the global venture (the two currently lead the coordinating committee).

A GLOBAL VENTURE IN PRACTICE

Initially, the GCTF should convene an international conference of high-profile Muslim and non-Muslim philanthropists, imams, thinkers, community leaders, and government officials to define objectives and elect an oversight board from within their ranks. They may wish to name the FUND after a prominent Muslim historical figure to make it appeal to religious activists. Washington should encourage American philanthropies to advise the GCTF board on how to raise money and staff the venture.

The venture should be headquartered in Istanbul or a Gulf capital, locating it centrally in terms of both physical and religious geography. Based on interest levels from potential donors, FUNDING levels for analogous ventures in the past, and absorptive capacity of future grantees, the global fund would require at least $300 million and a ten-year commitment by major donors at the outset to ensure the venture is sustainable and deeply rooted. Private and/or government-funded organizations could apply for grants of various sizes depending on the scope and activities of their proposed projects. With support, these organizations could organize youth camps, create social network–based websites to educate youth, provide speaking platforms for moderate imams, disseminate publications on Muslim campuses, offer scholarship opportunities, and create exchange programs for students to learn firsthand about Western government and society.

To ensure funds reach the right people, applicant organizations would need to demonstrate a commitment to religious pluralism, human rights, democracy, and nonviolence. Project proposals would require letters of support from groups credibly doing similar work on the ground or GCTF founding-member governments. Monitoring and evaluation would be central to the venture's mission, and therefore a robust staff will be needed to work with experts assigned to measure the success of funded programs and determine their eligibility for future FUNDING. Existing philanthropies could be enlisted to advise on best practices.

Through sustained FUNDING of existing efforts and supporting new initiatives in mosques, on campuses and satellite television, and through publications and online media, a global venture can target audiences through multiple avenues, maximizing efforts to discredit radical narratives.

6

The Role of Palestinians in the Transnational Jihad Movement

What is the relationship between the Palestinian issue and the al-Qaida phenomenon? To what extent did the Israeli-Palestinian conflict fuel the rise of transnational jihadism and do events in the West Bank and Gaza motivate non-Palestinian jihads today? Are there any relevant connections between Sams and al-Qaida? In short, what are the link-ages between nationalist and transnational varieties of militant Islamism? These connections are important to study because they can shed light on the causes of transnational jihadism as well as the conditions under which ethno-religious conflicts produce violent spillover effects.

This special issue explores the Palestine-al-Qaida connection through a particular lens, namely, biographies of prominent Jihad ideologues who chose transnationalism despite being Palestinian. It assesses the specific proposition that the Israeli-Palestinian conflict has fuelled jihadism by producing diaspora activists predisposed to transnational militancy. The purpose of this introductory article is to situate our inquiry

The term "al-Qaida", unless otherwise specified, is used to denote both the Pakistan-based core organization ("al-Qaida Central") and its various affiliates such as al-Qaida on the Arabian Peninsula and al-Qaida in the Islamic Maghreb. The term in the broader literature on Islamism and political violence and to provide relevant historical background information for the articles that follow.

MOTIVATION: A CONNECTION UNEXPLORED

The idea for this project grew out of the observation that the relationship between Palestinian Islamism and transnational jihadism remains understudied despite figuring prominently in informal discussions about the causes of Islamist terrorism. In the years after 9/11 we both found that the issue of "al-Qaida and Palestine" regularly came up at dinner conversations or in question-and-answer sessions after public talks about jihadism. The past decade has also seen a substantial number of opinion pieces staking out various claims about the Palestine-al-Qaida connection. The issue clearly has important policy implications, both for counterterrorism and for third countries' approaches to the Israeli-Palestinian conflict.

Yet, academics have largely shied away from exploring the Palestineal-Qaida relationship systematically. A review of the literature reveals no books and only a few peer-reviewed articles that tackle the issue in depth. Of these, almost all pertain to a limited subset of descriptive topics, especially the recent bickering between Hams and al-Qaida and the fighting between Hams and Salafa grouplets in Gaza. The larger causal question of whether and how the Palestinian-Israeli conflict may have fuelled transnational jihadism has yet to be addressed head-on. Moreover, an invisible fence has long separated the academic subfields of "Palestine studies" and "Jihad studies". With a few exceptions, Middle East specialists who study al-Qaida and its affiliates have tended not to study Hamas or Palestinian Islamic Jihad, and vice versa. Each of the two subfields has made important advances in recent decades, but they have mostly not overlapped.

One reason why the intersection remains understudied seems to be its politicization. Issues such as the Hamas-al-Qaida connection or the Palestine factor in Jihad recruitment are sensitive because they can potentially affect the moral standing of the main parties to the conflict. Naturally, Palestinian activists do not want to be associated with the perpetrators of 9/11 any more than Israelis want to be blamed for the rise of global jihadism. As a result, pro-Palestinian observers—who happen to be strongly represented in the academic Middle East Studies community in the West—have tended to view inquiries into al-Qaida connections with scepticism because they might be used by Israel to smear the entire Palestinian resistance. Conversely, pro-Israeli commentators have been quick to counter suggestions that al-Qaida might be genuinely motivated by Palestine, presumably because it could lead Western governments to pressure Israel for political concessions or tactical restraint in the latter's conflict with the Palestinians. In other words, this is a thorny topic and a risky specialization, especially for untenured academics.

Another reason why the subject has not been widely studied is that it is really quite complex. The "relationship between the Palestinian issue and the al-Qaida phenomenon" is a conceptually vague formulation that encapsulates a broad range of different research questions, each of which requires separate treatment. One way to start disaggregating the notion of "relationship" is to think of ideal-type mechanisms by which events in the Palestinian theatre might affect the occurrence of transnational Islamist violence. We see at least three such ideal types of mechanisms: "organizational", "motivational", and "historical". In the first, the Palestinian conflict affects transnational jihadism through organizational links between local and international organizations. In the second,

events in Palestine create solidarity-based grievances in non-Palestinians that inspire them to take up arms. In the third, the conflict or its by-products, affected the early development of transnational jihadism at critical junctures in its history. This leads to three somewhat more specific questions: 1) What is the organizational relationship between Palestine-focused and transnational militant Islamists? 2) To what extent does the Palestinian conflict motivate transnational jihadists? And 3) what has been the effect of the Palestinian-Israeli conflict on the historical evolution of transnational Jihad networks? This is but one of several possible ways to parse the problem, but the general point is that we are dealing with a messy set of distinct questions, not a single one.

Moreover, each of these inquiries requires good data, most of which have been inaccessible in open sources until recently. To study group connections, for example, we need information about the inner workings of clandestine organizations, which is by definition hard to acquire. To analyse motivations of al-Qaida recruits we need detailed biographical data on a decent sample of non-leaders as well as a relevant control group, which is also very difficult to collect. Tracing the historical impact of the Israeli-Palestinian conflict on transnational jihadism may require primary sources from decades past that may not be available on the Internet, only through interviews and archival work. Given these obstacles it is no wonder that some of these questions have been left unanswered.

It is worth recalling that these challenges are not specific to the study of militant Islamism, and that transnational dimensions of sub-state armed conflict remain under-researched in the social sciences more generally. It is arguably only in the past decade that scholars of civil war and insurgency have begun exploring the issue in depth. Social movement scholars and some international relations specialists began studying transnationalism earlier, in the 1990s, but their empirical focus was largely on non-violent protest movements in the West. In fact, the recent upsurge in transnationalism studies has also yielded new insights into the global connections of the leftist Palestinian resistance of the 1960s and 1970s. In light of this, we should perhaps not expect to have all the answers to the questions about Palestine and transnational jihadism already, but it is time to start working on them.

What We Know

So far, the literature that does exist on the Palestine-al-Qaida connection has mostly focused on the first two problem sets (connections and motivational effects). Some preliminary answers have emerged. Studies of the Hamas-al-Qaida relationship suggest that organizational links have been very limited, and that the ideological relationship is one of competition and hostility. A rare contact point was the ideologue Abdallh Azzm, who was in touch with Hamas from

Pakistan and remains popular in Palestine, but the interaction occurred back in the 1980s, and Azzm (d. 1989) never advocated international terrorism the way al-Qaida does today. Throughout the 1990s and 2000s Hamas-al-Qaida interactions were negligible, and in recent years, the rise of Salafa groups in Gaza has brought the tension between Hamas's pragmatic Muslim Brotherhood ideology and the intransigent Salafism of the transnationalists into very sharp relief.

However, Palestinian militants and transnational jihads are not in two different worlds. They have kept a close eye on, and learned from, one another over the years. Al-Qaida, for instance, adopted some of Hamas's tactics—notably suicide bombings and the practice of recording martyrdom videos—after observing them from afar in the 1990s. Mutual sympathies and respect also exist; for example, many Hamas supporters are fiercely anti-American and have expressed respect for Usma bin Ldin, although this has not translated into military operations against Western targets. It is worth noting here that reliable polls long showed levels of Palestinian popular support for Usma bin Ldin to be among the highest in the Muslim world. In 2003 no less than 72 percent of Palestinians expressed "some" or "a lot of" confidence in the al-Qaida leader. So far it is only among the relatively small—but growing—Jihad-Salafi community in Gaza that we see explicit attempts to associate organizationally with al-Qaida and a willingness to attack Western targets in the territories. However, these groups have yet to be declared formally a part of the al-Qaida franchise by the latter's leaders.

Regarding Palestine as a motivation for al-Qaida, we know that the cause features prominently in the group's ideological statements. Top leaders Usma bin Ldin and Ayman al-'awhir have both spoken regularly and extensively about Palestine since at least the late 1980s. The claim that bin Ldin only invoked Palestine after 9/11 when it was opportune to do so is patently false. As one of us (Hegghammer) noted in 2007:

> A search for the word Palestine in a compilation of al-Qaida texts between 1990 and 2002 that I made for the Norwegian Defence Research Establishment (FFI), produces no less than 158 hits. Most al-Qaida recruitment videos, including the first such production from early 2001, include images from Palestine. In short, Palestine is all over al-Qaida's propaganda and has been so for over a

decade. Usma bin Ldin remained substantially and consistently higher in Palestine than in the six other Muslim countries polled (Egypt, Jordan Lebanon, Turkey, Pakistan and Indonesia).

Similarly, Matthew Levitt of the Washington Institute for Near East Policy noted:

Palestine has featured prominently in al-Qaeda's statements and propaganda from the early outset of the group's founding. In fact, nearly every public statement made by Usama bin Ladin since 1990 has mentioned the Palestinian cause, often represented through references to the al-Aqsa Mosque in Jerusalem that strike both religious and political chords among Muslims and Arabs worldwide.

The list of quotes by al-Qaida leaders and Jihad ideologues on Palestine is too long to include here, so we shall content ourselves with a few key observations. One is that al-Qaida's arguably most important ideological statement, the "Declaration of the World Islamic Front for Jihad against the Jews and the Crusaders" (February 1998), lists Palestine as number three on a list of reasons why Jihad against America is justified (after the US military presence in Saudi Arabia and the sanctions regime against Iraq).

Another is that al-Qaida's favoured term for its enemy— "*the Jews* [our emphasis] and the Crusaders" (and variants thereof)— implicates Israel. Yet another observation is that the mastermind of 9/11, Khalid Sheikh Mohammed, cited American support for Israel as his principal motivation for undertaking the attack. Furthermore, his nephew Ramzi Yousef, who masterminded the first World Trade Centre bombing in February 1993, also appears to have been motivated by the

Israeli-Palestinian issue. Yousef later said he chose New York City because of its large Jewish population, and in letters sent to newspapers before the attack he stated three demands, the first two of which were an end to all US aid to Israel and an end to US diplomatic relations with Israel. Yousef was not an al-Qaida member, but he had fought in Afghanistan in the 1980s and was the nephew of Khalid Sheikh Mohammed. Of course we cannot know the true motivation of all these individuals, but there is good reason to believe that the Israeli-Palestinian conflict has loomed relatively large in their worldview.

However, the emphasis placed on Palestine has varied over time and between individuals. Global Jihad ideologues have tended to invoke the plight of the Palestinians more often in times of tension in the territories, for example during the second Palestinian intifada (2000–ca. 2005) or operation Cast Lead in Gaza (2008–2009). Moreover, quantitative content analysis has shown that bin Ldin's statements cite political grievances such as Palestine more often than religious arguments, but also that he invoked political grievances relatively more often in speeches addressed to Westerners than in speeches addressed to Muslims.

In addition, when Jihad ideologues speak about Palestine, it is not always to lament the Israeli oppression of Palestinians; it can also be to comment on internal Palestinian politics. For instance, in the largest online library of Jihad texts, *Minbar al-Tawhid wa-l-Jihd*, there are more texts devoted to criticizing Hamas than to the Israeli-Palestinian conflict as such.

Finally, we face a major analytical problem in that Palestine is only one of several political challenges invoked in al-Qaida's statements to persuade Muslims to take up arms. Measuring the motivating effect of Palestine *relative to that of other issues*—such as the Russian repression in Chechnya, the US-led invasion of Iraq, or any other of the many grievances invoked—is a difficult exercise indeed.

Some argue that targeting preferences might be a better proxy for leader motivations and point to the relatively few al-Qaida attacks on Israeli or Jewish targets as evidence that al-Qaida's brass are not particularly concerned with Palestine. It appears to be true that Jews and Israelis have not been *preferred* targets of al-Qaida, but there have been too many attacks on such targets to infer that al-Qaida and its affiliates avoid them. Even before 9/11 there were several attacks on Jewish/Israeli targets by non-Palestinian jihads of various affiliations—albeit not by core al-Qaida—such as:

- The killing of Rabbi Meir Kahane by Egyptian Islamist El Sayyid Nosair in New York in November 1990

- The car-bombing of a Jewish school in Lyon, France, in September 1995, by the Algerian GIA
- The killing of 17 Greek tourists—mistaken for Israelis—in Cairo in April 1996 by the Egyptian Islamic Group
- The "Millennium Plot" by al-Qaida linked operatives to attack Israeli and American tourists in Jordan in December 1999.
- Another important anecdote is that Richard Reid, known as the "shoe bomber" for his attempt to down a transatlantic plane in December 2001 with explosives concealed in his shoe, travelled to Israel in mid2001, reportedly to scout targets for al-Qaida.

The post-9/11 period saw even more al-Qaida-linked plots and attacks against Jewish/Israeli targets, the most prominent of which include:

- The plot by al-Qaida linked militants (the so-called "Tawhid Cell") to attack Jewish targets in Germany in the spring of 2002
- The bombing of the Ghriba synagogue on the Tunisian island of Djerba in April 2002
- The attacks on an Israeli-owned hotel and airliner in Mombasa, Kenya, in November 2002
- The bombing of a Jewish cultural centre, a Jewish cemetery and a Jewish-owned restaurant in Casablanca, Morocco, in May 2003
- The bombing of two synagogues in Istanbul, Turkey, in November 2003
- The rocket attack against Eilat in southern Israel in August 2005, claimed by al-Qaida in Iraq
- The rocket attacks against Northern Israel in October 2009 and November 2011, claimed by the "Abdallah Azzam Brigades"

Two observations are worth noting here. One is that several of these attacks were against soft Jewish targets outside Israel, i.e., relatively "lowhanging fruit" from a terrorist's perspective. Another is that the connection to al-Qaida Central is unclear or absent in several of these operations, so we do not really know the extent to which the top al-Qaida leadership prioritized them.

Thus, once again we are faced with evidence that al-Qaida leaders appear neither consumed with nor despondent to the Palestinian issue, but care about it to some intermediate extent. In the absence of rigorous quantitative studies of al-Qaida's attempted plots, we cannot say exactly how much resources al-Qaida has devoted to Jewish/Israeli targets. Even if we did, it is debatable whether targeting preferences would reveal underlying motivations. It is perfectly possible for a militant group to be concerned with a problem in one part of the world and pursue a military strategy in another. Just as al-Qaida's attacks against the United States can be interpreted as an instrumental strategy to undermine secular regimes in the Muslim world, so anti-Western targeting could reflect resentment against Western support for Israel.

As far as low-level al-Qaida recruits or sympathisers are concerned, the evidence is somewhat more suggestive of a Palestinian motivation effect, but uncertainties remain. For a start, many surveys indicate that Muslims in general feel quite strongly about the Palestinian issue. The *9/11 Report* remarked: "it is simply a fact that American policy regarding the Israeli-Palestinian conflict and American actions in Iraq are dominant staples of popular commentary across the Arab and Muslim world." More important, several studies of al-Qaida recruits have found the Palestinian issue to be a frequently declared motivation for joining. According to the *9/11 Report*, several of the plotters and operatives involved in the 9/11 attacks were preoccupied with the Palestinian issue in the years leading up to the operation. However, the issue is not mentioned by all recruits, and it is not always the sole motivation for those who do mention it. Besides, these studies tend to have many missing values, since declared motivations are not always available for every profile.

There is also some evidence to suggest a correlation between chronological variation in aggregate recruit supply and tensions in the territories. For example, the flow of recruits to al-Qaida's training camps in Afghanistan in the 1996–2001 period seems to have reached its highest level in early to mid-2001, after the outbreak of the second Palestinian intifada. Similarly, British government officials reported increased recruitment to radical Islamist networks during and after operation "Cast Lead" in Gaza. However, this evidence is sparse and not controlled against other factors.

Thus, aside from ruling out the most extreme positions—i.e., that Palestine does not matter at all, or, conversely, that it is al-Qaida's overriding motivation—the evidence is inconclusive. The picture is probably even less clear-cut today because the transnational Jihad movement is more fragmented and decentralised than it was in the 1990s and early 2000s, which makes it harder to generalise about what the typical transnational Jihad thinks about Palestine.

There is every reason to believe that the various affiliates—such as al-Qaida in the Islamic Maghreb, al-Qaida on the Arabian Peninsula, and Jabhat al-Nucra—differ with respect to the prevalent motivations of their recruits.

Another point worth noting is that some of the most prominent American advocates of the view that Palestine helps al-Qaida recruitment are former senior CIA officials and military commanders. These include Michael Scheuer (former head of the bin Ladin unit in the CIA), Bruce Riedel (veteran CIA analyst and former Deputy Secretary of Defense), Paul Pillar (former head of the CIA's Counterterrorism Centre), and General David Petraeus (former Commander of US Central Command and former Director of the CIA). It must count for something when those who have been at the forefront of the war against al-Qaida —and who have had access to better primary sources than most of us will ever see—reach this conclusion.

The bottom line is that the Palestinian cause does appear to motivate al-Qaida recruits to at least some extent. The best evidence for this is found in the now substantial number of internal documents that have been captured in raids on al-Qaida safe houses and compounds over the years. These documents tell us that leaders talked about Palestine when they thought nobody was listening. In several documents, al-Qaida leaders instruct their propagandists to highlight the Palestinian issue more often, on the grounds that it will increase popular support for al-Qaida. For example, the documents captured by US Special Forces from bin Ldin's compound in Abbottabad in the lethal raid on 1 May 2011 show that in the years before his assassination, bin Ldin wanted his lieutenants to focus more on Israel/Palestine in their statements and operations.

There are two equally valid ways to interpret these instructions: One is that bin Ldin cared so much about the Palestinian cause that he was willing to devote resources to it. The other is that bin Ldin believed potential recruits cared so much about Palestine that they might be persuaded to support or join al-Qaida on account of it. Either way, Palestine matters. The argument that al-Qaida leaders opportunistically "exploit" the Palestinian cause is an implicit admission that the same cause motivates recruits. There can only be opportunism if there is something to exploit.

OUR FOCUS: TRANSNATIONAL JIHAD IDEOLOGUES OF PALESTINIAN ORIGIN

In this special issue, we focus on the *historical* dimension of the Palestineal-Qaida connection. Specifically, we ask whether the Israeli-Palestinian conflict has fuelled transnational jihadism by producing activists predisposed—due to their exile and/or sense of grievance—to transnational militancy. Several analysts have proposed such an "agent production effect" of the Israeli-Palestinian conflict. The Israeli scholar of jihadism

Reuven Paz noted in 2002 that Palestinians appear to be overrepresented among ideologues associated with transnational forms of Islamism. Paz did not elaborate on the causal mechanism behind this overrepresentation, but listed a number of Palestinian ideologues of note, from Taq al-Dan al-Nabhn via Abdallh Azzm (the leader of the "Arab Afghan" movement) to Abk Qatda al-Filismini (the formerly UK-based radical preacher). More recently, the Lebanese journalist Hazim al-Amin has presented a more elaborate explanation for this phenomenon. In a book entitled "The Orphaned Salafi: The Palestinian Face of Global Jihad and al-Qaida" (2011), he argues that statelessness and exile led many Palestinian Islamists in the diaspora to focus on issues grander than national liberation. The Palestinian-Jordanian author Marwn Shahda has made a similar argument, though in less depth.

There is much anecdotal evidence to support this hypothesis. A good example is the diary of the former al-Qaida facilitator Zayn al-Abidin Muhammad $usayn (Abk Zubayda), a Palestinian who grew up in Saudi Arabia. In 1990—before radicalizing—he wrote "[I am a Palestinian] with no homeland, no passport and no identity... while the Jews are running loose in my country." Abk Zubayda was forced to attend university in India because only Saudi nationals were allowed to study computer science (his preferred subject) in the Kingdom. Only after arriving in India did he decide to explore jihadi training camps in Peshawar, Pakistan.

The main purpose of this special issue is to assess al-Amin's proposition that exile has made Palestinians predisposed to transnational activism. It is perhaps useful to start by surveying some of the available quantitative evidence on the presence of Palestinians in the world of transnational jihadism. In so doing, it is important to bear in mind that, numbering around 10 million, Palestinian Muslims make up no more than 0.6 % of the world's Muslim population. If transnational jihads were a cross-section of the Muslim population we should expect 1 in every 170 jihads to be of Palestinian descent.

As it happens, the available data suggests that Palestinians are not overrepresented in the movement as a whole. They are present, but not in particularly large numbers. The cross-national sample of 172 al-Qaida associates presented in Marc Sageman's book *Understanding Terrorist Networks* contains only two Palestinians. Available data on Jihad foreign fighters suggest the same. One of us (Hegghammer) collected a preliminary list of names of Arab fighters who appear in the main sources on the Afghan Jihad in the 1980s. Only 8 of around 250 named individuals in the sample are Palestinians (although the list is non-representative and potentially biased). In the so-called "Sinjar Records", which provide the self-reported national origin of 595 foreign fighters with al-Qaida in Iraq around the year 2006, there are no Palestinians. Even in the current war in Syria, which is right next door to Israel, Palestinians appear to be only slightly overrepresented among the pro-rebel foreign fighters: A recent study found that only 7 of 280 individuals hailed as fallen martyrs on Jihad websites were Palestinian. There are all kinds of problems with the above-mentioned data, but what exists suggests that Palestinians are not strongly overrepresented in transnational Jihad networks.

To be sure, al-Amin and Paz were not talking about foot soldiers. Indeed, if we look at lists of Jihad ideologues, Palestinians appear to be slightly better represented, although the numbers are less striking than al-Amin's argument seems to suggest. For example, the *Militant Ideology Atlas* produced by the Combating Terrorism Centre at West Point in 2006 included 132 ideologues, only 3 of whom we could identify as Palestinian. Another list circulated on Jihad websites in 2009 under the title "Mujahid's bookbag", includes some 53 names, four of which appear to be Palestinian. On both these lists, Saudis and Egyptians outnumber the Palestinians.

However, not all Jihad ideologues are equally influential. If we take into consideration the "weight" of the Palestinian presence in the Jihad ideological pantheon, then the picture changes completely. Palestine is represented on the above-mentioned lists with three veritable giants of Jihad ideology: Abdallh Azzm, Abk Muhammad al-Maqdisi, and Abk Qatda al-Filismini. Azzm (d. 1989) has been called the "Godfather of Jihad" due to his crucial role in bringing foreign fighters to Afghanistan in the 1980s. He also wrote several seminal works of Jihad literature that continue to be widely read today, such as *The Defence of Muslim Lands* and *Join the Caravan*. Al-Maqdisi, who lives in Jordan, is widely recognized as one of the most influential Jihad clerics alive today. Al-Filisyini is also a very prolific and influential author, and was long considered one of the most prominent Jihad clerics residing in the West. (He was based in the UK from 1993 until his deportation to Jordan in 2013.)

It is difficult to reliably quantify the influence of these figures, but one indicator is download counts from Jihad literature repositories. According to data from 2006, the 20 most accessed texts on any topic on the website *Minbar al-Tawhid wa-l-Jihd* included ten by al-Maqdisi (including the top one) and two by al-Filisyini.

Of the 20 most downloaded texts on any topic, 11 were by al-Maqdisi and one was by Azzm. Another indicator is recommendations and reading lists. We have already mentioned that these three men are among the 53 names in the "Mujahid's Bookbag". We also find them on a more exclusive list of the top five authors any budding Jihad should read. The list appears in a popular manual titled "39 Ways to Serve Jihad and Take Part in It", written in 2003 by a Saudi militant named Muhammad al-Slim, Abdallh Azzm [Palestinian-Jordanian], 2) Yksuf al-Uyayri [Saudi], 3) Abk Muhammad al-Maqdisi [Palestinian-Jordanian], 4) Abk Qatda al-Filisyini [Palestinian-Jordanian], and 5) Abd al-Qdir b. Abd al-Aziz [Egyptian]. All of this is anecdotal evidence, of course, but our basic claim—that Azzm, al-Maqdis, and al-Filisyini are prominent voices in the transnational Jihad movement—should not be particularly controversial.

Given that Palestinian ideologues have been few, but very influential, it is not possible to assess the historical effect of the Palestinian issue on the evolution of jihadism by looking merely at the overall proportion of Palestinian ideologues. Instead we need a research design that digs deep into these few individuals' biographies and traces the Palestinian factor, if any, in their trajectory toward transnationalism. That is why the four articles in this special issue are all in-depth biographical studies based on new primary sources. Each of the four main articles that make up this special issue examines a prominent Palestinian Islamist who engaged in or advocated some form of transnational militancy. Mark Sanagan first examines the early 20 century figure Izz al-Din al-Qassm (1882–1935), who is included here partly because he is a very prominent and understudied figure in the history of Palestinian Islamism, and partly because he engaged in what today we would call "foreign fighter activism" against the Italians in Libya and the French in Syria.

The biographies vary slightly in their focus and approach, reflecting author preferences and subject specificities, but all articles set out to explore the relationship between nationalism and transnationalism in the lives of these figures. Key questions include: What are the objective details of their biography relating to

Palestine? How Palestinian did (or do) they consider themselves? What was (or is) their view of the Palestinian issue and its significance relative to other problems in the world? Why did they choose transnational activism instead of a career focused narrowly on Palestine? Did they "go global" despite or because of their Palestinian heritage?

Before we let the contributors answer these questions, it may be useful to review, briefly, the history of the Palestinian resistance. Biographies constitute rather narrow windows into history, and our case studies cover partially distinct periods. Al-Qassm's prime time (1910s to 30s) was very different from that of Azzm (1960s to 80s), and even more so from that of al-Maqdisi and al-Filisyini (1990s and 2000s). The following section therefore draws out the historical lines that allow us to connect and contextualise the biographies we are about to read.

A BRIEF HISTORY OF THE PALESTINIAN STRUGGLE

The Holy Land, whose importance to several ideologues is analysed in this issue, has been a contentious place since Biblical times, whether named Canaan, *Eretz Yisrael* (the Land of Israel) or, as the Romans later called it, Palestine. The current conflict between Israelis and Palestinians can be traced back to the First World War (1914–1918) and the fall of the Ottoman Empire, which had at least nominally ruled the Middle East—including Palestine—for centuries, in the years that proceeded. The British and French colonial powers had long had a presence in the Middle East and had actually decided even before the collapse of the Ottoman Empire to carve up the region into spheres of influence in the famous Sykes-Picot Agreement (1916), drawn up by Sir Mark Sykes and Georges Picot, diplomats representing Britain and France respectively. In this agreement, Palestine fell under the British sphere of influence.

The different local actors—most importantly Zionists and Arab nationalists of various kinds—had started their quest for independence in Palestine even earlier. The Zionists, egged on by the rise of nationalist feelings across parts of Europe, persecution and anti-Semitism, and sometimes also a Biblically inspired longing for Jerusalem, had been active in Europe and the United States since the late 19th century. The Arab World, meanwhile, witnessed a similar sense of nationalist awakening and a renewed appreciation for the Arab literary and cultural heritage, although this did not always translate into direct opposition to the Ottoman Empire. The Zionists lobbied for (especially) British support for their goal of setting up a Jewish state in Palestine, which was eventually rewarded by the so-called Balfour Declaration (1917), an official British statement of support for "a Jewish national home" in Palestine, whose intent was later confirmed at the San Remo Conference (1920). In the meantime, the Arabs were also actively involved in efforts to achieve their independence. Most importantly, the Hashemite emir of Mecca, $usayn b. Al+ (c. 1853–1931), engaged in lobbying efforts of his own with the British official Sir Henry McMahon, promising to aid the allied war efforts against the Ottomans in return for Arab independence. This led to the infamous correspondence over the division of the Middle East between McMahon and $usayn in 1915, in which vague British promises were made and which caused the latter to launch the Arab Revolt against the Ottoman Empire in 1916.

The conflicting British promises to Zionists and Arabs not only contributed to the increased frustration and strife between the two rival parties in Palestine itself during the period of British rule (1917–1948), with both feeling betrayed by London, but it also pointed to a phenomenon that was to last for several decades after 1948: the relative lack of attention for what the Arabs of Palestine themselves wanted. Although the British presence and especially the huge waves of Jewish immigration were actively and repeatedly resisted by the country's Arab population, the latter seemed to play a very limited role at best in the international negotiations over their land. Instead, until the 1960s the major powers and the surrounding states were in control of what happened to Palestine.

Arab States

From the late 1940s to the late 1960s, the most important actors appropriating the question of Palestine on the diplomatic and military levels were not so much the Palestinians themselves but rather the leaders of Arab regimes. They were far from successful, however. The fact that the United Nations General Assembly voted in favour of Resolution 181, which divided British-controlled Palestine into an Arab and a Jewish state, showed that Arab diplomatic efforts ultimately came to naught. The same could be said about their military attempts to nip the newly founded state of Israel in the bud by entering the 1948 war for Palestine, which led to an increase in the territory controlled by Israel on the one hand and the Egyptian and Jordanian occupation of, respectively, the Gaza Strip and the West Bank (as they are now known) on the other.

Although the early Arab efforts to fight Israel in the 1940s clearly failed, the next decade saw several new Arab leaders rise to power whose ambitions did not stop at the borders of their own countries but who clearly also saw themselves as acting on behalf of the Palestinian cause. Foremost among them was the Egyptian President Gaml Abd al-Ncir (Nasser) (r. 1954–1970), who strove to unite the Arab world around his particular blend of Arab socialism and portrayed himself as the champion of the Palestinians as well. Through his powerful rhetoric, his staunch anti-colonialism and his pan-Arab discourse, Nasser was able to gain huge popularity in his own country and in the rest of the Arab world during his reign, and his defiance of France, Great Britain and Israel during the Suez Crisis of 1956 did nothing to diminish this. So much so, even, that historian William L. Cleveland refers to this period as "the age of Nasser". His popularity notwithstanding, the war between Israel and its Arab neighbours in 1967 led to a catastrophic defeat of the latter and caused a huge blow to Nasser's credibility and to his pan-Arab approach of the question of Palestine.

Perhaps less dramatic, but no less unsuccessful than Nasser, was the pursuit of the Hashemites, whose descendants still rule Jordan today, to represent the Palestinian cause. The precise nature of Hashemite ties with both the British and the Zionists has long been a subject of discussion. The controversies surrounding their ambivalent position towards Palestine in the first half of the 20 century include not only the correspondence between Sir Henry McMahon and $usayn b. Al+ mentioned above, but also the negotiations between the latter's son Faycal b. $usayn and the (later) first Israeli President Chaim Weizmann, as well as the deals that the first king of Jordan, Abdallh b. $usayn, tried to make with both Britain and the Zionists. Although King Abdallh (r. 1946–1951), like Nasser, managed to occupy part of Palestine in 1948, his grandson, King $usayn (r. 1953–1999), eventually lost this territory again in the same 1967 war that had so humiliated his Egyptian counterpart.

An essential difference between the Egyptian and Jordanian approach to the Palestinian cause was the latter's all-encompassing appropriation of the question of Palestine. Like Nasser, Jordan's rulers championed Palestinian rights for pan-Arab reasons of their own, but unlike the Egyptian president, they also viewed themselves as the true and sole representatives of the Palestinians for quite some time.

Several reasons accounted for this difference, such as the fact that many Palestinians had fled to Jordan during the 1948 war and that the country controlled the major part of what was left of Palestine—the West Bank, which included the historically and religiously significant old city of Jerusalem. As such, the Jordanian regime identified (or at least claimed to identify) with the Palestinian question in a way that no other non-Palestinian actor did.

Palestinian Nationalists

While the question of Palestine was a pan-Arab cause to Nasser and a national and religious issue to the Hashemite rulers of Jordan, to Palestinians themselves it was one of independence and self-determination. Although several small Palestinian guerrilla groups had been set up in the 1950s, of which Ysir Araft's nominally socialist Fata% movement was the most important, the main diplomatic vehicle used to further the Palestinian cause was the Palestine Liberation Organisation (PLO), founded in 1964. Born out of an idea to organise Palestinian resistance to Israel more formally, it enjoyed only reluctant support from some Arab leaders—notably King $usayn of Jordan, who feared the organisation would challenge his country's sovereignty over the West Bank and its inhabitants. As such, the PLO started as an Arab organisation dedicated to the Palestinian cause, rather than an organisation led by Palestinians themselves.

However, the mostly Arab character of the PLO did not last very long since the defeat of the Arab armies in the 1967 war not only dealt a blow to the rulers' credibility as champions of the Palestinian cause, but also caused them to lose the West Bank and the Gaza Strip—the only parts of Palestine still in Arab hands—to Israel. This, combined with the growing stature of Palestinian guerrilla fighters, eventually led to a "take-over" of the PLO by Palestinian groups in 1969. As such, the Arab loss in 1967 paved the way for a "Palestinisation" of the question of Palestine, which is something that the future Palestinian leader Ysir Araft seems to have realised quite well. However, the position of "true" representative of the Palestinian people remained contested for years, particularly between the PLO on the one hand and the Jordanian King $usayn on the other. It was not until the Palestinian intifada (1987–1992) began that the latter fully realised the important political standing of the PLO versus his own increasingly weak claims to Palestinian leadership, causing him to sever all administrative and financial ties between Jordan and the West Bank in 1988. From that year onwards, the Palestinian cause was represented by Palestinians.

Palestinian Islamists

Our brief overview of Arab and Palestinian appropriations of the question of Palestine seems to suggest that, at least until 1988, Islam did not play much of a role in efforts to fight Israel. Although it is correct to state that large-scale organised Islamist action against Israel did not begin until the founding of the Palestinian Islamic Jihad in 1981, Islam has played a role in the Palestinian struggle for much longer. This is not surprising given the significance of Jerusalem in particular in Islam. The Prophet Muhammad is said to have used Jerusalem as the first direction of prayer (*qibla*), before using Mecca for this purpose. Moreover, Q. 17: 1 states (in Arberry's translation): "Glory be to Him, who carried His servant by night from the Holy Mosque (*al-masjid al-harm*) to the Further Mosque (*al-masjid al-aqc*)." The so-called "night journey" by the Prophet from Mecca to Jerusalem and his related journey to heaven are both connected with this verse and have come to signify the importance of Jerusalem in Islamic tradition, as embodied by the Al-Aqc Mosque and the Dome of the Rock, which were built in the early 8th and late 7th century AD, respectively. Considering the religious significance of Jerusalem, it is not surprising that this Islamic symbolism is regularly invoked by Palestinian Islamists.

It should be emphasised from the outset that pious Palestinian Muslims engaged in political or military action on behalf of the Palestinian cause need not necessarily do so out of religious conviction. It is not at all clear, for instance, whether early Palestinian Muslim scholars involved in the conflict with Israel should be seen as Islamists (i.e., as Muslims who believe their religion is also an ideology calling for political and social action), instead of simply as Palestinian nationalists who happen to be religious. In any case, the earliest well-known example of a Palestinian "Islamist" was Izz al-Din al-Qassm, a preacher from the coastal town of Haifa who is said to have started a revolt against the British in northern Palestine in the early 1930s. His death at the hands of the British in Jenin in 1935 caused huge crowds to attend his funeral, followed by a nation-wide strike several months later that, in turn, led to the Palestinian revolt of 1936–1939, suggesting that his ideals struck a chord among many Palestinians.

Another important Palestinian Muslim leader involved in the conflict was the erstwhile critic of al-Qassm, Muhammad Amin al-husayni (1895–1974), better known as al-Hajj Amin. A member of the prominent Jerusalemite al-husayni family, of which Ysir Araft was also part, al-Hajj Amin was closely involved in both dealing with the British and prominent Palestinian representatives of the day, including the rival Jerusalemite al-Nashshibi family. This wavering between two parties characterised the early part of his career as Mufti of Jerusalem, during which he became the most powerful leader of the Palestinian national movement. Although initially sceptical and reluctant to rise up against the British, the latter's ambivalent plans about Palestine and the revolt of 1936–1939 that swept through the country did not leave al-husayni untouched. He quickly became the (increasingly radical) leader of the revolt and was subsequently stripped of his duties and forced to go into exile, where he continued his efforts on behalf of Palestinian independence but ultimately had to leave it to the PLO to represent the Palestinian cause.

While al-Qassm and al-husayni can be said to have been individuals giving a more Islamic flavour to the Palestinian nationalist movement, the first half of the 20th century also witnessed a rise in organised Islamism in the form of the Muslim Brotherhood, which reached Palestine too. The organisation, founded in 1928 by the Egyptian Hasan al-Bann (1906–1949) to Islamise both state and society, came to Palestine in the 1930s, where a branch of the group was founded by alBann's son-in-law Saeed Raman in 1945. From that time onwards until 1947/1948, the Muslim Brotherhood became heavily involved in the Palestine question, even militarily. However, after the 1948 war the Palestinian Muslim Brotherhood in the West Bank became increasingly close to the Jordanian regime, much to the dismay of one of its members, Taqi al-Din al-Nabhni (1909–1977), who had studied at Al-Azhar University in Cairo. Al-Nabhni favoured a much more radical approach to Islamising state and society than the gradualism that his fellow Muslim Brothers called for and broke away from the organisation to found the Islamic Liberation Party (Hizb al-Tahrir al-Islmi) in Jerusalem in 1953. His preferred solution to the Palestinian question was not so much nationalist but rather pan-Islamist, calling for an international Islamic effort to liberate Palestine and establishing a caliphate across the Muslim world, replacing the existing regimes there. Given this revolutionary position, the Islamic Liberation Party has often been suppressed throughout its history and has only a negligible presence in many Middle Eastern countries now. Little therefore appears to be left of al-Nabhni's legacy, although the organisation has a somewhat stronger presence in Western countries such as Great Britain.

A different Palestinian Islamist movement, though one that bore some striking ideological resemblances to al-Nabhni's ideas, was the Palestinian Islamic Jihad, founded by Fatmi al-Shiqqi (1951–1995) and Abd al-Aziz Awda (b. 1950) in 1981. Both men had studied in Egypt, where they came into contact with Islamist ideas. Like al-Nabhni, they grew increasingly frustrated with the Muslim Brotherhood's gradualist approach and preferred more radical action. This idea was further stimulated after the Islamic Revolution in Iran, which showed that an Islamic movement could not only overthrow a powerful regime but could even set up an Islamic state in its stead. Also like al-Nabhni, the Palestinian Islamic Jihad saw its fight as part of a greater Islamic struggle for a caliphate across the Middle East, although it placed more emphasis on the liberation of Palestine. The organisation developed a social infrastructure through its control of mosques, its founding of student associations and its publication of several periodicals. This aided the organisation in recruiting new members, which was complemented after a few years with armed struggle against Israel. Although the Islamic Jihad played a role in the intifada as well as in the Al-Aqc intifada (2000–2005) and is a force to be reckoned with even today, it could never reach the size, strength and popularity of its main Islamist challenger: Hamas.

The Islamic Resistance Movement (Harakat al-Muqwama allslmiyya), as Hamas is officially named, was initially a branch of the Muslim Brotherhood that had enough of only Islamisation from below, which had been the Brotherhood's policy until then, and also wanted to engage in armed struggle against Israel. This desire became particularly acute when the intifada broke out in 1987, during which elements within the Brotherhood did not want to be seen standing on the sidelines while the rest of the population resisted Israeli occupation. Thus, in December 1987, Hamas was founded. The organisation grew in size and popularity, eventually becoming perhaps the biggest Palestinian group in the occupied territories in terms of popular support, encompassing the Palestinian Muslim Brotherhood in its entirety. It participated not only in the uprising that started in 1987, but also played a major role in the al-Aqc intifada and has shown itself to be a staunch opponent of the peace process between Israel and the Palestinians through suicide-bombings and rocket attacks against Israeli civilians and soldiers. Incidentally, both the group's armed wing responsible for many of these attacks and Hamas's rockets have been named after Izz al-Din al-Qassm, further underlining the latter's stature in the historical imagination of Palestinian Islamists. Since 2006, the organisation has also attained political power after winning the parliamentary elections of that year, although subsequent conflicts with Fata% have lead to a split in power between the West Bank and the Gaza Strip, with only the latter being ruled by Hamas now.

Palestine and Transnational Islamism

The ideologues and groups mentioned above are Islamist, but also strongly Palestinian in nature. Yet the Palestinian question has always been an international one. However, the internationalisation of Palestine as an Islamic cause that Islamists all over the world claim as their own is of a more recent date, although its origins can perhaps be found in the pan-Islamist actions of Hajj Amin al-husayni, dating back to 1931. To understand this international Islamisation of the Palestinian question from the 1970s onwards—coinciding with the Middle Eastern rise of Islamism in general—two trends need to be taken into account: the spread of Salafism and the war in Afghanistan (1979–1989).

The rise of Salafism, often seen by both its adherents and uninformed outsiders as a pure and unadulterated form of Islam, coincided with the rise of Islamism as a whole since the Arab loss in 1967. Salafism can be defined as the branch of Sunni Islam whose adherents try to emulate the "pious predecessors" (*al-salaf al-clih*, hence the name Salafism), especially the first three generations of Muslims, as strictly and in as many spheres of life as possible. It is a much more scriptural and uncompromising trend than the relatively accommodating and doctrinally pragmatic Muslim Brotherhood and has different historical, theological and political roots. Perhaps partly because of its image as pure and devoid of cultural innovations (*bidah*), Salafism spread across the Muslim world, abetted by the writings of important mediaeval Salafi scholars such as Ibn Taymiyya (1263–1328), Ibn Qayyim al-Jawziyya (1292–1350) and Ibn Kathir (c. 1300–1373). A major factor in the promotion of Salafism was Saudi propaganda from the 1960s onwards, spreading a message of strict, yet regime-friendly Salafism to counter Nasser's socialist rhetoric, and, after 1979, the Shiite discourse of the Islamic Revolution in Iran. This process was stimulated even further by migrant workers in the Gulf region who often adopted Salafi customs there before returning to their home countries more conservative and more (overtly) pious than they had been before. This spread of Salafism had no direct link with the Palestine question, but it did mean that Islamism increasingly became Salafi in nature. This became more relevant in combination with the conflict in Afghanistan.

After the then Soviet Union had invaded Afghanistan to support the fledgling communist government there in 1979, many newly pious Muslims felt that it was their religious duty to help defend their fellow Afghan believers from the attacks by the Soviets and decided to travel to Afghanistan to fight them. This development was sometimes encouraged by Arab regimes, who often looked upon the greater religiosity of some of their citizens with concern and were therefore glad to get rid of them or were keen to support these "Afghan Arabs" in order to portray themselves as pious rulers. As such, a gathering of radical Islamists and pious Muslims—often of a Salafi persuasion—trained, studied and sometimes even fought together in Afghanistan. Their experiences not only forged ties between many of these men but also gave them military skills and in some cases led to a cross-fertilisation of ideas.

The combination of the increasing "Salafisation" of Islamism and the strengthened ties between its adherents forged on the battlefields of Afghanistan created not only a more or less ideologically coherent discourse on "Crusaders", "imperialism" and Arab "tyrants", but also an internationally supported Islamist message on Palestine. This discourse, represented most prominently by al-Qaida, is not only strongly pro-Palestinian, as we saw earlier, but also sometimes describes the question of Palestine as integral to its actions. Ayman al-'awhir+, for instance, bin Ldin's successor as the leader of al-Qaida, recently stated in relation to the political chaos in Egypt and Syria that "Cairo and Damascus are the two gates to Jerusalem" (*bawwbat bayt al-Maqdis*). This suggests that he sees the fight for overthrowing the rulers in Muslim countries at least partly as a step towards the "liberation" of Jerusalem, a belief he has expressed before.

The Rise of Salafism in Gaza

The spread of this international and much more Salafi form of Islamism championed by al-Qaida has not left Palestinians in the occupied territories untouched either. As Hroub has pointed out, Salafism of a peaceful and apolitical kind in the West Bank can be traced back to the 1970s and is related to Saudi efforts to counter the radical Shiite rhetoric coming from Iran after the Islamic Revolution took place there in 1979. The activities of such Palestinian Salafis have focussed on studying "pure" Islam, education and missionary activities. Similar Salafi groups exist in the Gaza Strip, where their activities started even before the Islamic Revolution, partly as a result of scholars returning from their studies in Saudi Arabia, but whose ideological focus is generally the same as that of their West Bank brethren. Issues such as the fight against Israel and the "liberation of Palestine", on the other hand, are seen by many Salafis from Gaza as "political", which should be avoided.

While most Palestinian Salafis do not fight the powers that be and focus on missionary activities instead, the past few years have witnessed the emergence of a radical Salafi minority that espouses a message that is much more akin to what al-Qaida stands for and engages in different types of violence. Although some of these groups seem to be rather tribal in nature without a coherent ideology, others are clearly Salafi in nature. In the Gaza Strip, groups such as Jund Ancr Allh and the Jamaat al-Tawhid wa-l-Jihd are the most prominent of a large cluster of small like-minded "organisations" that seem to have come into existence through frustration over Hamas's supposedly compromised and watered-down Jihad against Israel on the one hand and a susceptibility to the "purity" of the Salafi message—particularly that of al-Qaida—on the other. It is therefore not surprising that these groups pair a Salafi outlook with military activities against Israel. While such attacks— mostly rockets fired at Israeli towns like Sderot—are perhaps ideologically supported by Hamas, their activities may not always fit the latter's agenda of wanting to keep quiet in the Gaza Strip or maintaining a cease-fire with Israel. For this reason and others, Hamas has clashed with such radical Salafi organisations and has tried to suppress them, even going so far as killing some of their members.

Although the radical Salafi groups in the Gaza Strip are small and relatively insignificant, their conflicts with Hamas have garnered the attention of like-minded Salafi ideologues and activists across the world who were quick to condemn Hamas for its use of violence and its crackdown. The presence of such groups also shows that the Islamist concern for Palestine has, in a way, come full circle: having transcended the national level and having been adopted by international ideologues of different backgrounds in its new and more Salafi flavour, it has returned to Palestine and has been re-appropriated by some Palestinians themselves, who now use this radical Salafism as an ideology that inspires them to attack Israel and champion the Palestinian cause.

OUTLINE AND MAIN FINDINGS

As should be clear from the historical summary, this special issue is a study of outliers. Palestinian ideologues of transnational Jihad are few in number compared to their more nationally focused counterparts in Hamas or Palestinian Islamic Jihad. The existence of a few globalists does not detract from the fundamentally local character of the Palestinian resistance movement. This is all the more true of Palestinian Islamists, who until now have operated quite strictly within Israel's borders and shunned the transnational tactics of their leftist predecessors.

Still, these exceptions—especially Azzm, al-Maqdisi, and alFilisyini—are worth studying because they played such important roles within *another* political phenomenon of high import in post-2001 international politics, namely, the transnational Jihad movement. Our intention is not to smear the Palestinian cause by unduly highlighting Palestinians with al-Qaida connections, but to figure out whether the Israeli-Palestinian conflict had anything to do with these individuals "going global". If that is the case, as Lebanese journalist $zim al-Amin and Jordanian writer Marwn Shahda have argued, it would point to an important mechanism linking the Palestinian issue with the rise of al-Qaida. Ultimately, then, this is an inquiry into the causes of transnational jihadism and the dynamics of spillover violence from ethnoreligious conflicts.

Mark Sanagan revisits the historiography on Izz al-Din al-Qassm and finds, among other things, that al-Qassm may have seen himself as less Palestinian than his contemporary Palestinian admirers would like to think. The Syrian-born al-Qassm fought for the Umma (in Syria and Libya) before he fought for Palestine, and when he did the latter, it was not for the establishment of a Palestinian nation, but for a greater Syria. One gets the impression that his Palestinian Jihad in 1935 was but one in a series of fights against colonialism, not entirely unlike modern Jihad foreign fighters who move from one conflict theatre to the next to defend their Muslim brethren from oppression. Although Sanagan rightly warns against anachronistic labelling, alQassm's career does suggest that an early precursor to today's transnational jihadism existed in the early 20th century, before the creation of the state of Israel and the vicissitudes specific to the Palestinian-Israeli conflict.

Thomas Hegghammer shows that Abdallh Azzm appears to have had stronger connections to, and feelings for, Palestine than the literature has suggested thus far. Of the four individuals studied here, Azzm spent the most time in Palestine—from birth to age 25—and he is the only one to have fought militarily against the state of Israel (in 1969–1970). Moreover, Azzam's writings suggest he saw transnational activism—including his involvement in the 1980s Afghan Jihad—as a means toward the end of liberating of his homeland. He was also on much friendlier terms with Hamas than al-Maqdisi and al-Filisyini have been. Indeed, a case can be made for the counter-factual claim that Azzm would not have ended up in Afghanistan and played the leading role he did there had he not been exiled from the West Bank in 1967. Of our four cases, Azzm provides the strongest evidence of the Israeli-Palestinian conflict having had an historical "agent production effect" on transnational jihadism.

The same is not true of Abk Muhammad al-Maqdisi. For al-Maqdisi, liberating Palestine is important, but it is less important than ensuring proper Islamic governance in the Muslim world. He supports armed struggle against Israel, but not at any price; in fact, he prefers to leave Palestine occupied by Israel than to have the PLO, Hamas, or any other non-Salafis rule it. He even says he chose his name "al-Maqdisi" (the Jerusa-lemite) only because Jerusalem was the nearest big city to the place he happened to be born (Barqa), not because he wanted to flaunt his Palestinian background.

Similarly, Abk Qatda al-Filisyini has not made the Palestinian cause the centrepiece of his career and ideological production either. Petter Nesser's rigorous content analysis of al-Filisyini's ideological production shows that al-Filisyini appears to have a slightly stronger personal connection to Palestine than al-Maqdisi, but that he too considers the establishment of "proper" Islamic governments more important.

Unlike Azzm, al-Filisyini and al-Maqdisi value doctrinal purity over political pragmatism.

Overall, our findings provide only limited support to the al-Amin hypothesis that the Israeli-Palestinian conflict produced the Jihad movement's main thinkers. It is only in the case of Azzm that we see a relatively clear Palestinian factor in the transnationalization process. Al-Maqdisi and al-Filisyini, by contrast, appear almost unaffected by their Palestinian heritage and leave the impression that, to some extent at least, they are transnational jihads who simply happen to be Palestinian.

The "Palestine effect" thus appears to be a primarily motivational mechanism. As we have seen, the organizational links between Hamas and al-Qaida are few, and, with the exception of Azzm, the overrepresentation of Palestinians among top ideologues appears to be largely coincidental. Still, it is a fact of political life in the region that many young Muslims feel strongly about Palestine and that this emotion often factors into the decision by non-Palestinian Islamists to engage in militancy.

Our narrowing down of the "Palestine effect" to a motivational phenomenon does not limit its significance for current counterterrorism policy. There is already enough evidence to suggest that the Israeli-Palestinian conflict helps new al-Qaida recruitment, although we need more research into recruit motivations to specify the effect's precise scale and dynamics.

THE ISLAMIC DOCTRINE OF JIHAD

Islam is not a religion of peace. It provides a recipe for perpetual war. It is the only major religion in the world of today that institutionalizes violence against non-Muslims, which it calls jihad (normally translated "holy war," as it is usually used in that context. The literal translation is "struggle" or "strive"). Many verses in the Qur'an exhort Muslims to wage jihad against those who reject Islam, and against Muslims who do not practice Islam to its fullest. An entire sura 8 is called al-Anfal which means "spoils of war." There is no sura called "peace." Only 56 verses in the entire Qur'an mention peace, and most of them occur in the context of the Islamic greeting of "peace be upon you." Others deal with the peace that occurs after a military battle. The most vivid and repeated themes in the Qur'an are on jihad and the punishment of hell.

The Arabic word "jihad" appears in its various forms about thirty-five times in the Qur'an: nine times in the Meccan chapters (suras), and twenty-six times in the Medinan ones. The Arabic word "qatal," means "kill" (it does not mean inner struggle against vices). It appears in its various forms, meaning "kill" or "fight," about one hundred and twenty-three times in the Qur'an: thirty-four times in the Meccan chapters (suras), and eighty-nine times in the Medinan suras. The increase of these words in the Medinan Qur'an reflects the rise of the military power of the prophet of Islam after he immigrated to Medina, though a few uses of these words are not in a military context. In sura 9, al-Tawbah of the Qur'an, thought to be one of last suras given, each of these two words appear ten times in the context of war. In fact, verses al-Tawbah 9: 111 and an-Nisa' 4: 74 each contains three words rooted in the Arabic word "qatal" (meaning to kill): "God has bought of the believers their lives and their possessions, promising them paradise in return, so they fight (from "qatal") in God's cause, and kill (from "qatal"), and are killed (from "qatal")..." (al-Tawbah 9: 111).

In contrast with that, the Holy Bible (KJV) provides 420 verses on the subject of peace. Man strove for peace since ancient times (Isaiah 52: 7). Deep inner peace is the gift of the living God. Man cannot create his own peace. "The peace of God, which surpasses all understanding, will guard your hearts and minds through Christ Jesus" (Philippians 4: 7); "Now may the Lord of peace Himself give you peace always in every way" (2 Thessalonians 3: 16; James 3: 17-18); "There is no peace," says the LORD, "for the wicked" (Isaiah 48: 22; 57: 20-21; 59: 1-4, 7-11; etc).

In fact, the whole of the Qur'an and Islam support jihad in its various forms: jihad with money, with the written and spoken word and with the sword. The verses that do not refer to jihad directly or indirectly marshal the Muslims into a militant fraternity (ummah) on the basis of a common belief system, a common set of rituals, and a common code of conduct. Jihad in any form can be practiced only when there is an organized and disciplined community to practice it. The Qur'an marshals and motivates the ummah to impose Islam on the rest of mankind by every possible means, including the sword.

The purpose of jihad is the islamization of the conquered populations either by pressuring them to convert to Islam, or by forcing them to submit to Islamic rule. The main purpose of jihad is political, not religious. It is an instrument for both the universalization of the Islamic religion, and the establishment of an imperial world state. Islamic jihad must continue until the whole world is under the rule of Islamic law. All the Sunni and Shia Islamic schools of jurisprudence command waging war against unbelievers in order to establish the rule of Islamic law over them. War is the main vehicle of Islamic religious expansion. Without the sword of Muhammad and his followers after him, Islam will not exist today. Over a thousand years of unprecedented military expansion, the Islamic armies invaded vast territories in the Middle East, North Africa and even Europe. Muslim Arabs and Moors had controlled Spanish territory for eight hundred years, Portugal for six hundred years, Greece and Bulgaria for five hundred years, Romania and Serbia for four hundred years, Sicily for three hundred years, and Hungary for one hundred fifty years.

Authoritative Muslim historians, such as Ahmad ibn Yahya al-Baladhuri (d. 892) and al-Tabari (838-923), attest the fact that Islam was spread by the sword.

Jihad in the Qur'an, Hadith and Sharia

Violent jihad is a central Islamic doctrine. The prophet of Islam repeatedly stressed that there is nothing better and nobler for a Muslim to do than to engage in jihad warfare (Bukhari 1.2.26; Muslim 20.4642). He claimed that engaging in jihad warfare is more meritorious than prayers, fasting, pilgrimage, etc. He warned Muslims who did not participate in jihad warfare of punishment (Abu Dawud 14.2497). He taught that Muslims who fight in jihad would be rewarded with a higher level in the Islamic paradise (an-Nisa' 4: 95; Muslim 20.4645).

Muslims are called upon to proclaim Islam by subduing and conquering non-Muslims, murdering them, destroying their temples, and looting their possessions.

In general, the obligation to participate in violent jihad is a collective one. It becomes a personal imperative one for every Muslim when Muslim lands are invaded by uninvited non-Muslim forces (Reliance of the Traveler, o9.3).

The violent activities of the Muslim zealots are fully supported and encouraged by the Islamic teachings. Muhammad said: "I have been ordered to fight with the people till they say, 'None has the right to be worshipped but Allah ..." (Bukhari 4.52.196; 1.2.25; etc). Jihad is a Muslim religious duty and obligation, like pilgrimage (al-Baqarah 2: 216). Rejecting jihad amounts to rejecting a fundamental Qur'anic dogma. The Qur'an condemns Muslims who refuse to fight in jihad (al-Anfal 8: 20, 47, 49; al-Tawbah 9: 24, 39, 81-82). Some Islamist groups consider Muslims that do not participate in jihad infidels. Those who wage jihad rank highest in Islam.

References to jihad, and killing of infidels who reject Islam and of apostates who leave Islam abound in the Qur'an. It contains about 164 verses that refer to jihad warfare against non-Muslims and distributing the spoils of war. 24% of Medinan Qur'an is devoted to jihad.

"Fight against such of those to whom the Scriptures were given (Christians and Jews) as believe in neither god (the god of Islam) nor the last day, who do not forbid what god and his apostle (Muhammad) have forbidden, and do not embrace the true faith (Islam), until they pay tribute out of hand and are utterly subdued" (al-Tawbah 9: 29)

"When the forbidden months are past, then fight and slay the Pagans wherever you find them, and seize them, beleaguer them, and lie in wait for them in every stratagem; but if they repent, and establish regular prayers and practice regular charity, then open the way for them: for Allah is Oft-Forgiving, Most Merciful" (al-Tawbah 9: 5, 12, 14, 19, 20, 29, 36, 38, 39, 41, 73, 81, 86, 88, 111, 123; al-Baqarah 2: 190, 193, 216, 244; Al-Imran 3: 169; an-Nisa' 4: 47, 74, 76, 77, 84, 89, 95; al-Ma'idah 5: 33, 51; al-Anfal 8: 12-17, 39, 59-60, 65, 67, 74; al-Anbiya' 21: 44; Muhammad 47: 4-6, 35; al-Fath 48: 16; al-Hujurat 49: 15; al-Mumtahanah 60: 1, 11; as-Saff 61: 4; at-Tahrim 66: 9; etc).

The Qur'an urges Muslims to kill, even those willing to surrender (al-Anfal 8: 67). The Qur'an claims that Islam is superior to all other religions (Al-Imran 3: 85; al-Tawbah 9: 33; al-Fath 48: 28; as-Saff 61: 9; etc). The jihad warfare commands for waging offensive, aggressive and unjust wars to Islamize all the non-Muslim populations are open-ended, perpetual, global, and generic in nature. That is what motivates Islamists to terrorize and kill non-Muslims following the example of Muhammad, the architect of Islam.

To read such blood thirsty injunctions in the Qur'an, the holiest book of Islam, is shocking. It grants Muslim jihadis a license to kill in the name of the Islamic god in the Islamic jihad. Extreme hatred and bloody violence against the non-believers are built into the religion of Islam. It is a historical fact that, with the exception of some Indonesian islands, no nation has ever willingly converted to Islam. On the other hand, no nation has ever unwillingly been converted to Christianity in the first three centuries of the Christian era.

In addition, the Hadith collections of Sahih al-Bukhari and Sahih Muslim include hundreds of references to jihad warfare. A sampling of the Islamic teaching on violence is provided herein from the Hadith of Sahih al-Bukhari which is second in authority only to the Qur'an in Sunni Islam. It contains about 199 references to jihad in the sense of armed warfare against non-Muslims. Muhammad, the prophet of Islam, said:

"The example of a Mujahid in Allah's Cause— and Allah knows better who really strives in His Cause——is like a person who fasts and prays continuously. Allah guarantees that He will admit the Mujahid in His Cause into Paradise if he is killed, otherwise He will return him to his home safely with rewards and war booty" (Bukhari 4.52.46; 1.2.35);

"Nobody who dies and finds good from Allah (in the Hereafter) would wish to come back to this world even if he were given the whole world and whatever is in it, except the martyr who, on seeing the superiority of martyrdom, would like to come back to the world and get killed again (in Allah's Cause)" (Bukhari 4.52.53);

"There is no migration (after the Conquest of Mecca), but Jihad and good intentions, and when you are called for Jihad, you should immediately respond to the call" (Bukhari 4.52.42; etc).

All the four principal Sunni schools of jurisprudence, the Maliki, Hanbali, Hanafi, and Shafi'i, agree on the importance of jihad. Prominent Islamic scholars of antiquity from each of the four major schools of jurisprudence in historical Islam clearly understood the Qur'anic injunctions of jihad to command holy war. This includes al-Tabari (838-923), al-Biadawi (d. 1286), Ibn Khaldun (1332-1406), Ibn Kathir (1301-1373), Ibn Taymiyya (1263-1328), al-Ghazzali (1058-1111) who was a peaceful Sufi, etc.

Reliance of the Traveler (Undat al-Salik), the Shafi'i manual of Islamic law, devotes three sections o9, o10, o11 (eleven pages) to jihad. Making war on unbelievers is one of the responsibilities of the Muslim nation. The Islamic umma (nation) must exist in a state of perpetual war, interrupted only by temporary truces, with the non-Muslim world in order to compel either conversion to Islam, or subjugation to its rulers. When the Islamist regime is militarily weak, it reaches out for truce and peace simply in order to buy time to build up its strength (Muhammad 47: 35). Those that reject the invitation to convert to Islam are required to pay the poll tax (jizya) in humiliation and subjugation in their homelands. Should they refuse, war is to be declared against them (Muslim 19.4294; etc). In addition, Shia Islam calls for the necessity of jihad. Islam lacks any doctrine of equal coexistence. Islam lacks any doctrine of coexistence with non-Muslims in equality. In fact, peaceful coexistence as equals in a pluralistic society is not an option in Islam.

Islam divides humanity into two classes: a superior class of Muslims (Al-'Imran 3: 110; at-Tawbah 9: 33), and an inferior class of non-Muslims (infidels). There are more than four hundred verses in the Qur'an that describe the torment of hell that the god of Islam has prepared for the infidel. There are approximately seven hundred verses in more than fifty Qur'anic suras that have explicit negative references to the Jews (an-Nisa' 4: 47; al-Ma'idah 5: 13; etc.). The Qur'an dehumanizes and demonizes the non-Muslim infidels and calls them "... the vilest of animals ..." (al-Anfal 8: 55; al-A'raf 7: 179), and the vilest of all creatures (al-Bayyinah 98: 6; al-Mujadilah 58: 20). It claims that Jews were transformed into apes (al-Baqarah 2: 65 and al-A'raf 7: 166), and Jews and Christians into swine (al-Ma'idah 5: 59-60)? It likens Jews to asses (al-Jum'ah 62: 5). It tells Muslims that Jews are cursed because of their unbelief (al-Ma'idah 5: 78). Muhammad claimed that Muslims will eventually exterminate the Jews in a global holocaust. "Allah's Apostle said, The Hour will not be established until you fight with the Jews, and the stone behind which a Jew will be hiding will say, O Muslim! There is a Jew hiding behind me, so kill him" (Bukhari 4.52.177; Muslim 41.6981-5).

The Qur'an goes as far as commanding Muslims to eschew friendships with infidels, including Christians and Jews (Al-'Imran 3: 28, 118; an-Nisa' 4: 89, 101, 144; al-Ma'idah 5: 51, 82), even if they be their fathers, sons, brothers, or kin (al-Tawbah 9: 23; al-Mujadalah 58: 22). Abu Obaida, son of Garah, who was praised by the prophet of Islam, killed his own father who refused Islam. Musaab, son of Omair, never listened for his mother's cries for help and left her to die because she rejected Islam. Abu Bakr, the first guided caliph, told his father he would kill him if he refused Islam.

Traditional orthodox Islam promises the jihadist that if he dies fighting for the god of Muhammad in Islamic jihad, he is guaranteed to be rewarded with the sinful Islamic paradise of sexual promiscuity and gluttony (as-Saff 61: 10-13; ad-Dukhan 44: 51-56; at-Tur 52: 17-29; ar-Rahman 55: 46-78; al-Tawbah 9: 111; Al-Imran 3: 157-8, 169; an-Nisa' 4: 74; al-Fatir 35: 50; Muhammad 47: 6; etc). Muhammad said: "Know that Paradise is under the shades of swords" (Bukhari 4.52.73, 72, 46, 48, 53; 4.53.386). Muhammad promised these fictitious rewards, which are merely a desert mirage, in order to motivate his fighters. Unable to give them a reason to live, he gave them a reason to die.

On the other hand, should the jihadist survive and live, he gets a share from the spoils of war, which enriches him (al-Anfal 8: 41, 60). In addition, he obtains forgiveness of his sins (as-Saff 61: 11-12), and the love of the Islamic god (an-Nisa' 4: 95; al-Anfal 8: 16). According to orthodox Islamic belief, martyrdom in Islamic jihad is the only sure way a Muslim could take to avoid the horrifying torments of the grave and hell, and to get into the Islamic paradise. In fact, when a Muslim dies in jihad, his corpse is not washed or dressed in clean clothes. It goes in his coffin just as he died. The stains of blood on it are a witness for him before the Islamic god. It is a sign of honor that would prompt the angels to treat him in a special distinguished way.

The Example of the Prophet of Islam

The history of Islam to-date has been one long jihad (holy war) against non-Muslims. Muslims are exhorted to emulate Muhammad's pattern of behavior (al-Ahzab 33: 21). In the ten years that he lived in Medina (622-632 AD), Muhammad, the prophet of Islam, was the aggressor in seventy-three of seventy-five raids and conflicts he got involved in. He initiated seventy-three raids, military expeditions, full-scale military campaigns, and small assassination hit bands to kill his opponents. This adds up to more than seven slayings, raids or battles for each of the ten years he ruled in Medina in the beginning of the Islamic era. There is a lot of blood on his hands. He did not personally participate in forty-eight of those raids. He personally accompanied his Muslim fighters in twenty-seven raids. In eight of them, he was in the battlefield fighting alongside with them. Muhammad used to order his followers and commanders to kill those who disbelieved in his god, not making any distinction between combatants, and civilians.

The prophet of Islam financed his military expeditions through a variety of avenues. His economic lifeblood was the plunder usurped from defeated enemies, and the jizya tax levied on unbelievers.

The majority of the Arabs who adopted Islam and fought in the military battles of jihad did so in order to acquire booty usurped from the conquered tribes and peoples who did not submit to Islam.

The Muslim fighters have been motivated mainly by their greed for the booty of wealth and women (al-Fath 48: 19-20). Four-fifths of the booty went to them, and one-fifth to Muhammad, or to the caliph after him (al-Anfal 8: 41). That was how the god of Islam made Muhammad and his followers wealthy (ad-Duha 93: 8; al-Tawbah 9: 74; Bukhari 3.37.495). Muhammad distributed his share of the booty as he wished to close relatives, orphans, the needy, travelers, and new converts to Islam to coax them to stay in Islam (al-Tawbah 9: 60; Bukhari 4.53.373; 4.55.558; Muslim 5.2313).

Sura 8 is titled "al-Anfal," which means "the spoils of war." The entire book no. 53 of Bukhari is called "One-fifth of Booty to the Cause of Allah (Khumus)." The battle plunder included captive women and children who were sold as slaves for profit. Slave trading flourished in Arabia in the early Islamic era. The Qur'an describes the loot as "...lawful and good...," and supports pillaging and plundering infidels, enslaving their children, and placing their women in concubinage (al-Anfal 8: 69; an-Nisa' 4: 24; etc). In fact, the first Islamic raid on the peaceful Meccan merchant caravan at Nakhlah was to loot and rob the caravan. This is what motivates bandits and pirates.

The Rules of Jihad

Based on Islamic jurisprudence derived from the Qur'an, the Hadith, and classical Islamic legal opinions, the principal rules of Jihad are summarized herein. These rules are immoral and exploitative:

1. Muslims may enslave women and children of the conquered non-Muslim populations (Reliance of the Traveler, #o9.13).

Islam codifies slavery in its religious law (Sharia). Selling humans into slavery produced a lot of wealth for Muhammad and his followers. Slaying women and children is prohibited, not for mercy, but for profit. However, if a Muslim slays them, he is not censured.

2. The marriages of those women are annulled upon their capture. They may be forced to marry their Muslim masters and added to their harim (an-Nisa' 4: 24).
3. Worse off, Muslim jihadists are allowed to rape the captured female prisoners of war. Ali, Muhammad's cousin and son-in-law, did this abomination, and Muhammad defended him (Bukhari 5.59.637). Islam codifies and legalizes rape for conquering jihadist Muslim men (Muslim 8.3371, 3373-7, 3432). Islam is the only religion in the world that condones and encourages the crime of raping female captives of war as a reward to victorious Muslim soldiers for conquering the infidels.
4. Muslim jihadists are allowed to kill old men and Christian monks (Reliance of the Traveler, #o9.10), and women and children in night raids (Bukhari 4.52.256; Muslim 19.4321-4323).
5. The non-Muslim prisoners of war may be killed, enslaved, ransomed (exchanged for money or a Muslim captive), or released (al-Ahzab 33: 26; Muhammad 47: 4; Reliance of the Traveler, #o9.14).
6. Pagan Arabs were pressured to convert to Islam on pain of death. Enemy men who converted to Islam were allowed to keep their property and children (al-Tawbah 9: 5, 11, 14, 33; Bukhari 4.52.263).
7. The Muslim jihadist invaders may confiscate or destroy non-Muslim civilian property, including homes and groves (al-Ahzab 33: 27; al-Hashr 59: 5, 2; Bukhari 4.52.262, 263; Muslim 19.4324).
8. A Muslim jihadist who kills a non-Muslim in jihad gets his belongings. This is called personal booty. In addition, he gets his share from the four-fifths of the collective spoils of the battle.

9. The Muslim jihadist invaders give the people of the Book (Jews and Christians) three options (al-Tawbah 9: 29) either to convert to Islam, to keep their faith and pay the submission tax of jizya (poll tax) while living under Islamic rule, or to get killed fighting if they refused the first two options. However, Muslims can mount surprise attacks on the infidels, slay them and usurp their property. This is not censured because the victims are not Muslims, and they are not protected in the Islamic state.

Although Islam permits Jews and Christians to remain in their faiths as dhimmis under Islamic rule (second class citizens in their homelands), from the dawn of Islamic history till the present, forced conversions are widely practiced in the Islamic world. This is because Islamic teachings scorn non-Muslim infidels who are, according to Islamic culture, bound to the Islamic hell. Battle, animosity and hatred directed towards the non-Muslim infidels are part of Islamic mindset.

The Dhimma

The concept of the dhimma was first introduced by the prophet of Islam. After conquering the Jews of the oasis of Khaybar in 628, he agreed to let them continue to cultivate their oasis only if they gave him half their produce. He reserved the right to cancel out this treaty and expel the Jews whenever he liked (Bukhari 4.53.380). This type of treaty is called a "dhimma."

Peoples that came under Islamic rule and agreed to pay tribute (jizya) in return for Muslim protection are referred to as "dhimmis." They were ultimately reduced to the status of a tiny culturally derivative marginalized minority in their homelands. The only peoples that escaped Islamic dhimmitude were those who were successful in resisting and eventually, after centuries of armed struggle, defeating Islamic imperialistic jihad: the Christians of Europe and the Hindus of India.

The dhimmis (Jews, Christians, etc. under Islamic rule) were not equal to Muslims in dignity and rights. They lived in subjugation to Islamic rule. The terms of the dhimma were first articulated by the second guided caliph, Umar ibn al-Khattab

(634-644). The dhimma was an agreement imposed on conquered populations.

It required them not to build churches, monasteries, and synagogues, nor restore them. It also required them to wear clothes different from those worn by Muslims, not to acquire weapons, not to ride horses, to refrain from using church bells and from erecting crosses on top of the churches, not to proselytize Muslims, to pay the poll tax (jizya), etc.

The jizya indicated the dhimmis submission and inferiority to Islamic rule (at-Tawbah 9: 29). It led to the overall humiliation and abasement of non-Muslims. Payment of the jizya often took place in a demeaning ceremony to ensure the belittlement and humiliation of the dhimmi.

The Muslim tax-collector slapped the Christian man on the back of his neck or on his head telling him: 'O unbeliever, pay al-jizya.' This was followed by the Christian man handing him the tax money with his head bowed down and his back bent while the tax-collector held him by the beard.

The dhimmi was not allowed to marry a Muslim woman. The penalty for such marriage was death. The dhimmi was barred from public office. The history of Muslim dealings with the dhimmis is one of oppression, random massacres, avaricious greed and plunder, extortion under the threat of persecution, rape, systematic degradation and slavery.

According the Shafi'i school of Islamic Sharia, the dhimma pact is broken if the dhimmi fights the Muslims, refuses to pay the jizya, or disobeys Muslim laws. It is also broken if the dhimmi violates the dhimma's additional stipulations, if any, by having relation with a Muslim woman, leading a Muslim away from Islam, killing a Muslim, or slandering Muhammad and his god. When the dhimma is broken, the rules of the prisoners of war will apply on the dhimmi subjecting him to either death, slavery, ransoming, or release.

By denying basic human rights to non-Muslims in Islamic controlled lands, Islam has sanctioned slavery on an unprecedented scale. Jihad slavery in its various forms (slave soldiers, harem slavery, child slavery, etc.) became a powerful tool to both expansive islamization and the support of Muslim society.

The dhimma terms and requirements are codified in Islamic Sharia (Reliance of the Traveler, #o11). Under Western pressure on the weakened Ottoman Empire, the dhimmis were emancipated in the mid-nineteenth century. Although Islamic Sharia is enforced at this time only in a few countries, such as Saudi Arabia, Iran, and the Sudan, many of its elements are practiced in Islamic countries. It is surprising indeed that the dhimmi communities have survived at all despite the Islamic pressures on them throughout centuries of Islamic rule.

7

Political Destabilization in South and Central Asia: The Role of the CIA-ISI Terror Network

INTRODUCTION

Recent terror attacks in New Delhi on September 13, 2008, raise the questions of who was responsible and for what reason these attacks occurred. Terror attacks in India are not a new phenomenon, however, in their recent past, they can be largely attributed to the actions, finances, training and resources of one organization: The Pakistani Inter-Services Intelligence (ISI). These new bombings bare the same relationship with the ISI as has occurred in the past, and so it must be asked: what is the purpose of the ISI both in Central Asia as well as South Asia?

The ISI appears to play the role of a force for the destabilization of Central Asia, India and the Middle East. It acts as a Central Asian base of operations for the CIA and British Intelligence to carry out Anglo-American imperial aims.

India will be the main focus of this report, due to the escalation of organized terror and violence against it in the past few years. As India is one of the fastest-growing economies in the world, after China, its northern neighbor which also borders Central Asian countries, its place in the New World Order is yet to be set in stone. Do western, and particularly Anglo-American elites allow India to grow as China, all the while attempting to co-opt their banking system to the western banking elite, thus, making them controllable? Or, will India be destabilized and dismantled, as is the plan with the Middle East and Central Asia, in order to redraw borders to suit geopolitical imperial ambitions, creating a network of manageable territories feeding the Metropoles of the New World Order, specifically New York (Wall Street) and London (The City of London)?

BACKGROUND OF CIA, ISI COOPERATION

Both CIA and ISI earlier shared similar effort to support the Afghan and foreign mujahideen to covert-fight against Soviet forces in Afghanistan. They not only provided strategic and intelligence support for Afghan militia but also provided training, arms and funding in the 1980s. CIA had an impressive support from ISI role during the Cold War period when Pakistan received extensive military and other assistance from USA. Their relation was bitter after Soviet withdrew from Afghanistan in 1989. ISI solely engaged in the Afghan Civil War in 1990s and backed the Taliban regime. During that period, CIA was focused in Europe and Middle East and paid little attention on Pakistan and Afghanistan.

After seeing potential threat from Afghanistan, CIA agents/ informer in Pakistan and Afghanistan were at an unsurpassed level. After al-Qaeda attacked U.S. embassies in Kenya and Tanzania on August 7, 1998, CIA was a realizable frontier as well foreign policy tool for the US government. Their role increased by folds than the Cold War period. CIA's bin Laden mission began to hunting mission after they came from Sudan to Afghanistan. CIA local agent had a face-to-face with Laden and his fundamentalist supporters several times during the Taliban regime. Intelligence working on 'Bin Laden mission' had a huge investment. After increasing instances of terrorist attacks, CIA's only concern was to get hold of Laden – forget what's happening in Afghanistan.

As retaliation measures against bombings in US embassies, US forces started targeting Laden hideouts, including remote places. On August 20, 1998, about 75 cruise missiles were fired by the U.S.

at four Afghan training camps in Afghanistan from Arabian Sea through Pakistan's airspace. CIA's station in Pakistan provided the principle target list. However, Laden had left some hours before the missiles hit. US missile targeted Al Farouq training camp, Muawai camp – run by Pakistani Harkat-ul-Mujahideen to train militants, training camps in the Jarawah, the possible radical leaders' meeting point.

In the changed scenario in Afghanistan, CIA official's role became more influential. The CIA station chief in Pakistan is more powerful than its Ambassador. CIA's Pakistani station operator agent involved in tracing Bin Laden, directly informed the location in Afghanistan and provided information to the headquarters at the Counterterrorist Center. CIA directly briefed President Bill Clinton about the missile attack on their base. However, the President did not give orders to the military to strike on the Laden hideout. Following the 9/11 attacks, US demanded Taliban to handover laden and close the training camp, which the Taliban ignored. US force then launched "Operation Enduring Freedom" on 7 October 2001 which led to the downfall of Taliban regime in Afghanistan. Thereafter, CIA unit hunting Osama bin Laden dramatically increased its presence and activities in Pakistan and Afghanistan. After the Battle of Tora Bora in December 2001, laden and senior al Qaeda leaders escaped from there.

CIA has analysed that Pakistani tribal region is becoming a global hideout base for jihadist militants. The U.S. covert operations have continued in this region through pay role tribal agents. They also use local tribal leaders to fight against Taliban and other foreign fighters. Several bloody fights between tribal militants and foreign militia have been reported in remote Afghan borders. After failing their initial strategy to fight with foreign militia, CIA used several ground agents, intelligence network to trace the militia movement. However, foreign fighters gained control over tribal areas. CIA then used new approach of war and intensified drone campaign. Pakistan has described those attacks as an infringement of its sovereignty. But several air strikes have not yet gained concrete result but led to militant revenge through suicide bombings in return.

The CIA has often blamed ISI for supporting or planning several strikes and bombings against the US and western interest in Afghanistan. ISI's concern in Afghanistan has been different with that of USA. After potential strategic threat in Afghanistan, ISI joined hands with some proxy militant groups to secure their interest toll. But CIA easily traced the real channel and mentor of such hostile groups targeting the US and it's ally's interests.

Extremists' ties with ISI had alarmed the CIA. The US had repeatedly pressurized the Pakistani government to hunt down the militants. CIA has also handed over the list of Pakistani madrassas, where jihadists are fed against the US force in Afghanistan. Pakistan started several offensive operations in the tribal areas where foreign and local militia have set their safe haven. Operation was limited and eventually concluded with a peace deal. According to a US State Department data, since 2001 Pakistan has provided assistance in counter-terrorism efforts by capturing more than 600 al-Qaida members and their allies.

CIA not only faced the al-Qaida, their number one enemy, but also faced the most sophisticated insurgent group Haqqani network. The US has accused the ISI that this group has been established as its proxy force to serve Pakistani hidden interests in Afghanistan. US intelligence also accuses the Pakistani secret service of operating the Lashkar-e-Taiba to use the army's covert foreign mission. They still believe that ISI has not still abandoned to support militia. U.S. has accused Pakistan of using militants and killing of NATO troops in Afghanistan, which Pakistan denies. The US doesn't trust Pakistan's commitment to counter-terrorism efforts. Therefore, it raided the hideout of al-Qaeda chief Osama bin Laden in May 2011 and killed him. It also carries out drone strikes in the tribal area without informing the Pakistani security. According to New American Foundation data, 58 al-Qaeda and Taliban affiliated senior leaders have been killed in the CIA drone campaign in Pakistan from Afghanistan.

Who Gained the Ground?

Question remains, who achieved the strategic goal in Afghanistan? There are several players – not only USA, European Union and Pakistan but Iran, India, Saudi Arabia, and UAE to

Qatar have been playing the different roles. Afghanistan's central command has been in limbo after post 2014 because of foreign intelligence agencies' competition to get hold of the geopolitical ground.

Iran has also set of cultural, religious, political, and security relations with Afghanistan, which can be a ground to increase its influence. Tajik and Shi'a groups support Iran and are opposed to Taliban. Anti Iranian Baluchi insurgency group killed Iranian security personnel and Iran has security concern as well as Narcotics trafficking. Iran too has a strategic objective of defeating both US, Pakistan and Taliban because they do not want any other hostile force gain the ground in Afghanistan.

Islamic Revolutionary Guard Corps foreign wing 'The Quds Force' has been moving silently to the ground to secure their strategy. They have initiated an extensive covert campaign to play a key role to protect their nation's interest as well extensive influence over Afghan spies and paid informers' network. They want to seek a greater role after post 2014 Afghanistan like post US military present Iraq. Iran has certain concerns in Afghanistan because of it's geographical as well geopolitical situation.

India too has its own national security calculations, and has significantly increased its foreign intelligence agency Research and Analysis Wing (RAW) as well as its Military Intelligence (MI). Both RAW and MI have extensive influence in the government as well as in the security. India also increased its political and economic influence and launched different huge projects in Afghanistan. ISI fears Indian growing influence in Afghanistan and counter-measure strategy. New Delhi and Tehran has had close ties since the 1990s and both might continue to coordinate in the post 2014 Afghanistan. Behind the scene, both countries are actively engaged in countering Pakistani influence over Afghanistan and protect their joint interest. After concluding the fact, ISI played a double game with USA and adapted new tactics to gain the Afghan ground.

After realizing the loss of ground, ISI wants much closer relationship with CIA. On of the most recent examples are the recent prisons swap between Taliban and US government. But current overt action and open rhetoric cannot be the judgment of the final reality. This may take some more time unravel. Tehran's growing influence in Afghanistan is not favourable for its regional rival Saudi Arabia. Saudi intelligence agency General Intelligence Presidency (GIP) is also playing a role in Afghanistan. Behind the scenes, GIP continues to engage with ISI and Taliban representatives and may have been directly in touch with Taliban figures. The British Secret Intelligence Service MI6 idea is to hold talks with moderate Taliban elements and end the conflict. Other EU intelligence agencies consent with the British. All the intelligence agencies believe that fugitive senior Afghan Taliban leaders are safe in ISI protection.

How Pakistan Deals its Internal Conflict?

USA insisted Pakistan to initiate an 'all out war' against militia. However, Pakistan calculated that it will have to pay a huge price. Pakistani military is now in a difficult position to flush out militants since it faces multiple threats not only from Afghanistan but its own territory. Pakistan already faces war or conflict within its own soil. Pakistan has different categories of militia besides widely known TTP, al-Qaeda, Haqqani network but also Sunni to Shia sectarian motivated militia, anti and pro-Indian militant groups such as well sectarian and foreign militants. Sectarian conflict with Balochistan Liberation Army in southwest Pakistan is a battle of different course.

Pakistan faces dozens of major militant groups, which are of deadly and uncivilized nature. There is also a strong criminal gang and internationally organized mafia elements targeting civilians, security personnel to politicians. It is difficult to predict how some of the Pakistani secret elements cut ties with several militant groups. Pakistan military has a high profile threat of retaliation against the militants and could even spread violence in all the major Pakistani cities.

THE SEPTEMBER 13, 2008 NEW DELHI BOMBINGS: 9/13/08

The Bombings

On September 13, 2008, five blasts ripped through New Delhi within 45 minutes of each other, killing 21 people and injuring roughly 100 more. The Indian Mujahedin claimed responsibility for the bombings, sending emails to major Indian news organizations. In July, bombings took place in the western state of Gujarat, which killed 45 people, and in May in the city of Jaipur, which killed 61 people. The Indian Mujahedin also claimed responsibility for those attacks. This new wave of attacks across Indian cities was intended to "sow panic, inflict civilian casualties and, according to Indian officials, inflame tensions between Hindus and Muslims."

National elections are also approaching in India, giving the opposition Bharatiya Janata Party the opportunity to criticize "the coalition government led by the Congress Party for its inability to prevent bombings like those of Saturday," making it a "major point of vulnerability for the incumbent administration."

What is the Indian Mujahedin?

According to Indian police, the Indian Mujahedin (IM) is "an offshoot of the banned Students' Islamic Movement of India (SIMI)." In fact, it is "the hardline faction of Students Islamic Movement of India (SIMI) that broke away in 2005 to protest against the diffidence of the moderate faction about declaring a full-scale war on India." Reports also link the IM with the banned organizations, Harkat-ul-Jihad-e-Islami and Harkat-ul-Mujahedeen.

The Students Islamic Movement of India (SIMI) has reported ties with the Pakistani ISI, in having had cadres of its members being trained by the ISI to launch terror attacks in India. The ISI is also reported to have maintained contacts with SIMI in relation to their operatives traveling around the Middle East, specifically Saudi Arabia, to engage in fund raising. SIMI's reorganization was also aided by the ISI, which led to the branching out of the hardline element, the Indian Mujahedin.

Harkat-ul-Jihad-e-Islami also has extensive ties with the ISI, as the group carried out terror attacks in Hyderabad in 2007, "at the instance of Pakistan's Inter Services Intelligence." Many members of the Harkat-ul-Jihad-e-Islami were trained at ISI camps in Pakistan, and it "receives patronage and support from Pakistan's Inter-Services Intelligence." Significantly, "the group's anti-India operations are planned by the ISI, mostly from the Bangladeshi capital Dhaka."

Harkat-ul-Mujahedeen, the third terror network with extensive ties to the Indian Mujahedin, used to be known as the Harkat ul-Ansar. Harkat ul-Ansar was created by then-Pakistani General and future President Musharraf in the early 1990s, and was active in recruiting 200 Pakistanis to be trained by the ISI and sent to fight a Jihad in Bosnia, "with the full knowledge and complicity of the British and American intelligence agencies." This group also has links to those individuals associated with financing 9/11, as well as being involved with the London 7/7/bombings.

So all three terrorist groups associated with creating and having links with the Indian Mujahedin (IM) have extensive ties with the Pakistani ISI. Since these three organizations created the IM, it is essentially a creation of the ISI itself.

Who Benefits?

Two days before the bombings took place, the *Times of India* ran a story discussing US defense corporations seeking major contracts in India, including "the single largest one-time military contract in history," India's buying 126 multi-role combat aircraft (MRCA). The deal is said to be worth $10 billion, "which would not be concluded in the term of this government but by the next government." Two major US companies vying for this contract are defense giants Boeing and Lockheed Martin. India's Defense Minister A.K. Antony said that his recent meetings with US Defense Secretary Robert Gates and other Washington figures were primarily focused on "Pakistan's rapid descent into chaos and the stepped up terrorist activity by renegade elements in the country, including provocations on the border and in Kashmir."

Two days later, the attacks within India would confirm the need for a built up defense and military establishment within India. Contracts are sure to be signed.

The bombings also occurred at a time that "India is resisting renewed pressure from the West to send its troops into Afghanistan to boost the coalition troops there." More troops are needed in Afghanistan as the Taliban experience a resurgence, armed and financed by Pakistan's ISI. However, as the *Times of India* notes, "India is not about to enter this particular cauldron because its troops would fan the flames in a way that no others would do. They would draw fire from Pakistanis and India would be sucked into a battle, which would have huge implications for its internal security." Perhaps this is the idea?

The attacks also occurred just as "the US Congress is considering the approval of the US-India civil nuclear deal and days before [Indian] Prime Minister Manmohan Singh visits Washington."

THE ISI-CIA ISLAMIC TERROR NETWORKS

The Mujahideen

The ISI has long established ties with terrorist networks in the region. The ISI was used as a conduit by the CIA in 1979 to finance and arm the Afghan Mujahideen in Afghanistan in the Afghan-Soviet War of 1979 to 1989. The Mujahideen then branched off, with the active financing and support of the ISI, into both Al-Qaeda and the Taliban.

During the 1980s, many "officers from the ISI's Covert Action Division received training in the US and many covert action experts of the CIA were attached to the ISI to guide it in its operations against the Soviet troops by using the Afghan Mujahideen, Islamic fundamentalists of Pakistan and Arab volunteers." Further, the "CIA, through the ISI, promoted the smuggling of heroin into Afghanistan in order to make the Soviet troops heroin addicts. Once the Soviet troops were withdrawn in 1988, these heroin smugglers started smuggling the drugs to the West, with the complicity of the ISI."

Al-Qaeda and Yugoslavia

The ISI not only has had close ties to Al-Qaeda, but also to guerillas fighting in the disputed territory of Kashmir between India and Pakistan. The ISI's connections with Al-Qaeda were so extensive, that even on the night before 9/11, Osama bin Laden was in a hospital in Pakistan protected by Pakistani military and intelligence. The ISI also supported the wars in Bosnia, Kosovo and Macedonia throughout the 1990s, by training and sending militant Islamists into the regions to sow chaos and exacerbate ethnic tensions, leading to the break-up of Yugoslavia. All this was done with the tacit approval, support and complicity of British and American intelligence. The ISI financed its covert terrorist support through the global drug trade, especially important in Afghanistan. The ISI also supported terrorist groups in Chechnya.

The LeT

The Lashkar e Toiba (LeT) terrorist organization also works very closely with the ISI, and they work together in a "coordinated effort" in orchestrating terror attacks in Kashmir. The LeT is "funded, armed and trained by the Inter-Services Intelligence," and is linked up with Al-Qaeda, and is "the most visible manifestation" of Al-Qaeda in India. The LeT "receives considerable financial, material and other forms of assistance from the Pakistan government, routed primarily through the ISI. The ISI is the main source of LeT's funding. Saudi Arabia also provides funds." The LeT also played a part in the ISI organized "Bosnian campaign against the Serbs," which was directed above the ISI by the CIA and British intelligence.

The ISI and 9/11

The ISI may also have played a roll in 9/11 itself, as its General was in Washington in the lead up to and during the 9/11 attacks, meeting with top intelligence, State Department and Congressional officials, including CIA Director George Tenet, Deputy Secretary of State Richard Armitage, Secretary of State Colin Powell, Senator Bob Graham, Representative Porter Goss, who would go on to become CIA director, and Joseph Biden, who is now Barack Obama's running mate. The ISI's General, while meeting with all these top US officials in foreign affairs and intelligence, also happened to be the money man behind 9/11, having wired $100,000 to the lead 9/11 hijacker, Mohammed Atta.

The Liquid Bomb Plot

In August 2006 in the UK, there was a massive roundup of terrorism suspects as the British and Pakistani authorities revealed that they uncovered and prevented a massive terrorist plot to blow up several transatlantic airliners with liquid explosives. This plot is the reason for which people can no longer carry a bottle of water or any liquids through security at airports. However, following the roundups, Pakistan arrested the "lead suspect" who was said to have masterminded the whole operation, Rashid Rauf. Over a year later, Rashid Rauf escaped from Pakistani police custody, however, as it turned out, he was kidnapped by the ISI to prevent him being extradited to the UK.

As Craig Murray, former British Ambassador to Uzbekistan, wrote shortly after the plot was 'foiled', "According to John Loftus, a former Justice Department prosecutor, [bomb plot suspects] Omar Bakri and Abu Hamza, as well as the suspected mastermind of the London bombings Haroon Aswat, were all recruited by MI6 in the mid-1990s to draft up British Muslims to fight in Kosovo. American and French security sources corroborate the revelation."

Covert War Against Iran

It was revealed by the *London Telegraph* in 2007 that the US, through the CIA, was funding and arming terrorist organizations to "sow chaos" inside Iran. *ABC News* reported just over a month later that the terrorist group was a Pakistani militant group named Jundullah, which is based in the Baluchistan region of Pakistan, just across the border from Iran. Jundullah also has very close ties with Al-Qaeda. Although the US funds this Al-Qaeda-linked group, the funding is indirect, as it travels through Pakistan's ISI.

So clearly, the ISI has some troubling connections to Al-Qaeda, various other Islamic extremist groups, and British and American intelligence. Where the ISI is operational, so too, are Anglo-American ambitions.

THE 1993 BOMBAY BOMBINGS: 3/12/93

On March 12, 1993, Bombay (now called Mumbai) experienced 13 explosions in a coordinated attack, of which the most significant target was the Bombay Stock Exchange, which killed roughly 50 people. The total number of dead was 257, with roughly 1,400 other injured. Dawood Ibrahim was believed to have coordinated the attacks. Ibrahim is known for extensive ties to Osama bin

Laden and Al-Qaeda, has financed operations of the Lashkar e Toiba (LeT), and was believed to be hiding out in Pakistan. The 1993 Bombay bombings were "organised by Dawood Ibrahim under pressure from the Inter-Services Intelligence of Pakistan." In 2007, the ISI was reported to have taken Ibrahim and his top lieutenant into custody from the Pakistan-Afghan border.

THE 2006 MUMBAI BOMBINGS: 7/11/06

On July 11, 2006, Mumbai experienced another major terrorist attack, as seven bombs went off within 11 minutes of one another on trains. The total deaths reached 209 with roughly 700 others injured.

The blame for the bombings was placed on the Lashkar-e-Toiba (LeT) and local Students Islamic Movement of India (SIMI), which are closely interlinked with each other and have direct links with the ISI. A few months later, following an investigation, Mumbai police "blamed Pakistan's intelligence agency ISI for masterminding the explosions which were executed by activists of the banned Lashkar-e-Toiba and SIMI." The Mumbai Police Commissioner said that, "the attacks were planned by ISI in Pakistan and carried out by Pakistan-based militant group LeT with the help of banned Students Islamic Movement of India (SIMI)." India even shared evidence of Pakistani ISI involvement in the attacks with the United States.

The bombings led to a postponement of India-Pakistan peace talks, which were set to take place the following week. The Indian Prime Minister had said that, "a peace process with Pakistan was threatened if Islamabad did not curb 'terrorist' violence directed at India." Again, perhaps a peace in the region is not in the interests of the Anglo-Americans.

THE 2008 INDIAN EMBASSY BOMBING IN KABUL: 7/7/08

On July 7, 2008, the Indian Embassy in Kabul, Afghanistan was bombed, killing 58 people and wounding 141. Two days after, it was reported that, "The Afghanistan government and Indian Intelligence Agencies have confirmed that some elements within the ISI in collaboration with the Taliban/Al Qaeda planned and executed the attack on the Indian embassy." Further, "the ISI Station Head in Kabul, is collaborating with the Taliban to destabilise India's strategic presence in Afghanistan."

The day after the attack, the Afghan Interior Ministry said that, " was carried out in co-ordination and consultation with an active intelligence service in the region," and as the *Financial Times*reported, "Western diplomats in Islamabad warned that the Kabul bombing was likely to increase the distrust between Pakistan and Afghanistan and undermine Pakistan's relations with India, despite recent signs that a peace process between Islamabad and New Delhi was making some headway."

It was also reported that the Afghan Interior Ministry stated that, "Militants who carried out this week's suicide bomb attack on the Indian embassy in the Afghan capital received their training at camps in Pakistan."

Just weeks earlier, on June 25, 2008, "An Afghan official accused Pakistan's premier spy agency on Wednesday of organizing a recent assassination attempt on Afghan President Hamid Karzai," and that they were "sure and confident" of an ISI connection.

On July 13, "Pakistan's Inter-Services Intelligence agency (ISI) [had] been blamed by India for the bomb attack on Kabul's Indian embassy." On July 10, "The United States has said there was no evidence suggesting involvement of foreign agents in the suicide bombing on the Indian Embassy in Afghanistan."

However, on August 1, the *New York Times* reported that, "American intelligence agencies have concluded that members of Pakistan's powerful spy service helped plan the deadly July 7 bombing of India's embassy in Kabul," and that, "The conclusion was based on intercepted communications between Pakistani intelligence officers and militants who carried out the attack." Interestingly, "American officials said that the communications were intercepted before the July 7 bombing, and that the C.I.A. emissary, Stephen R. Kappes, the agency's deputy director, had been ordered to Islamabad, Pakistan's capital, even before the attack." Further, "a top Central Intelligence Agency official traveled to Pakistan this month to confront senior Pakistani officials with information about support provided by members of the ISI to militant groups."

However, given that this is not new information, and that CIA collaboration with these efforts has been widely documented, what was the real purpose of this top CIA emissary going to Islamabad?

Two days after the *New York Times* report surfaced, it was reported that, "The United States has accused Pakistan's main spy agency of deliberately undermining Nato efforts in Afghanistan by helping the Taliban and Al-Qaeda militants they are supposed to be fighting." In January, the Bush administration "sent two senior intelligence officials to Pakistan" over "concerns" that the ISI was supporting militants, and further, "Mike Mc-Connell, the director of national intelligence, and [CIA director] Hayden asked Musharraf to allow the CIA greater freedom to operate in the tribal areas." President Bush also "warned of retaliation if it continues."

Who Benefits?

In 2006, it was reported that as Hamid Karzai, President of Afghanistan, was trying to balance a relationship with Pakistan and India, "Islamabad might be feeling squeezed and do its best to undermine the renewed Afghan-Indian partnership — at great cost to Afghanistan."

As *Time Magazine* reported on the day of the Embassy bombing, "The bombing is likely to have regional ramifications, both for India's relations with the neighborhood and those of every other country supporting Afghan President Hamid Karzai." Further, "India and Pakistan have been vying for influence in Kabul for decades, and India — which for years backed the opposition Northern Alliance against the Pakistan-backed Taliban regime — came out on top after the U.S.-led invasion scattered the Taliban and installed President Karzai in power." India has also pledged $850 million in reconstruction aid for Afghanistan.

As the UK *Times* explained, India is "the only regional power committed to a new democratic Afghanistan. It was no accident that India shouldered part of the cost of the parliamentary and presidential elections. Nor should one ignore the symbolic value of the fact that India is building the new Palace of Democracy to house the Afghan parliament." Further, "The only power likely to offer Afghanistan long-term support is India. Helping Afghanistan would weaken radical Islamism and prevent Pakistan acquiring a hinterland through Afghanistan in Muslim Central Asia."

Historically, the Taliban were financed and armed by the Pakistani ISI, while India had backed the Northern Alliance during the 1990s. After the 2001 invasion and occupation of Afghanistan, the Northern Alliance was put back into power as the Taliban were deposed. This would explain why the ISI and Pakistan has again become the main supporter of the Taliban. However, in most discussion on Pakistan funding the revival of the Taliban, what is left ignored is the ISI's continued connections to British and American intelligence. For example, with the London 7/7 bombings, the mastermind was an MI6 asset and he had, along with several of the suspected bombers, connections to the Pakistani ISI.

Interestingly, keeping in mind the ISI's help in the resurgence of the Taliban, in February of 2008, it was reported that, "Britain planned to build a Taliban training camp for 2,000 fighters in southern Afghanistan, as part of a top-secret deal to make them swap sides." Further, "Afghan government officials insist it was bankrolled by the British. UK diplomats, the UN, Western officials and senior Afghan officials have all confirmed the outline of the plan, which they agree is entirely British-led, but all refused to talk about it on the record."

Conclusion

Ultimately, the benefactors of the Indian Embassy bombing in Kabul and other bombings, such as the recent New Delhi bombing in India, is not Pakistan, but is the Anglo-Americans. Pakistan ultimately will collapse as a result of these actions being taken. The ISI has long been referred to as Pakistan's "secret government" or "shadow state." It's long-standing ties and reliance upon American and British intelligence have not let up, therefore actions taken by the ISI should be viewed in the context of being a Central Asian outpost of Anglo-American covert intelligence operations.

This connection between American and British intelligence and the ISI is also corroborated by their continued cooperation in the covert opium trade in Afghanistan, whose profits are funneled into the banks of Wall Street and the City of London.

The goal in Pakistan is not to maintain stability, just as this is not the goal throughout the region of the Middle East and Central Asia. Recent events in Pakistan, such as the assassination of Benazir Bhutto, which has been linked to the ISI, should be viewed in the context as an active Anglo-American strategy of breaking up Pakistan, which will spread chaos through the region.

Pakistan's position as a strategic focal point cannot be underestimated. It borders India, Afghanistan, China and Iran. Destabilizing and ultimately breaking Pakistan up into several countries or regions will naturally spread chaos and destabilization into neighbouring countries. This is also true of Iraq on the other side of Iran, as the Anglo-American have undertaken, primarily through Iraq, a strategy of balkanizing the entire Middle East in a new imperial project.

One of the main targets in this project is Iran, for which the US and Britain have engaged in massive acts of terror and orchestrating large battles and conflicts from within the already-failed state of Iraq. The Anglo-American role as terrorist supporters and as covertly orchestrating terror attacks within Iraq is amply documented.

To imagine that these same Anglo-American intelligence and covert networks are not using their long-time conduit, the ISI, for the same purposes in Central Asia, is a stretch of the imagination and logic. It is not merely the Middle East that is the target, but Central Asia, specifically for its geographical relationship to the rising giants such as India and China. This also follows in line with Anglo-American strategies in destabilizing the Central European region, specifically the former Yugoslavia, and more recently, Georgia, largely in an effort to target Russia.

What we are seeing with Pakistan and India is an effort to drive the region into chaos. The US allowing blame to be placed on the Pakistani ISI for the Embassy bombings in Kabul has provided an excuse and basis for US military intervention in

Pakistan, which has already begun, and which threatens to plunge the region into total war and crisis. But then again, that's the idea.

STUDENTS ISLAMIC MOVEMENT OF INDIA

Students Islamic Movement of India (SIMI) is a banned Islamic student organisation that was formed in Aligarh, Uttar Pradesh, in April 1977. The stated mission of SIMI is the 'liberation of India' from Western materialistic cultural influence and to convert its Muslim society to live according to the Muslim code of conduct. This organisation is blamed byGovernment of India, to be involved in terrorism. The Supreme Court of India in 2007 described the Students Islamic Movement of India as a secessionist movement.

SIMI was banned by the Indian government in 2001, soon after the 9/11 attacks and declaration of the "War on Terror" by the U.S. government, for its alleged involvement in terrorist attacks in India. It has been labelled a terrorist organisation by the administrations in India and U.S. In August 2008, a special tribunal lifted the ban on SIMI, after a long review process. The ban was immediately (in 24 hours) reinstated by K.G. Balakrishnan, then Chief Justice, on 6 August 2008, at the special request of theCongress-led government on national security grounds. Though an appeal was submitted by SIMI leadership challenging the political ban, it has not been accepted in file by the Supreme Court.

Background

On 25 April 1977, SIMI was founded in Aligarh, in the state of Uttar Pradesh, with Mohammad Ahmadullah Siddiqi as its founding president. (Siddiqi currently serves as a Professor of English and Journalism at Western Illinois University in Macomb, IL.)

SIMI originally emerged as a student wing of the Jamaat-e-Islami Hind (JIH) in an effort to revitalise the Students Islamic Organisation (SIO) established in 1956. In 1981, SIMI activists protested against PLO leader Yasser Arafat's visit to India, and greeted him with black flags in New Delhi. Young SIMI activists viewed Arafat as a Western puppet, while the senior JIH leaders saw Arafat as a champion of the Palestinian cause. The JIH also became uncomfortable with SIMI's support of the Iranian Revolution and oriented itself towards the SIO as its student wing. When SIMI sought self governance and independence of operation from JIH, JIH declined. SIMI separated from JIH and continued as a hard line Islamic Organization..

Ideology

Its slogan is "Allah is our Lord, the Qur'an is our constitution, Muhammad is our leader, Jihad is our way and shahada is our desire". SIMI became more militant and extremist in the backdrop of communal riots and violence between Hindu and Muslim groups in the 80s and 90s. Among its various objectives, SIMI aims to counter what it perceives as the increasing moral degeneration, sexual anarchy in Indian society and the 'in sensitiveness' of a 'decadent' West. SIMI maintains that concepts of secularism, democracy and nationalism, keystones of Indian Constitution, are antithetical to Islam. They aim to restore the supremacy of Islam through the resurrection of the khilafat, emphasis on the Muslim ummah and the waging of Jihad.

Clashes with Radical Hindu Organizations

SIMI organised violent protests against the demolition of the Babri Mosque. In the nationwide violence that followed the demolitions, SIMI activists clashed against the Police and the Sangh Parivar.

Ban and Aftermath

The Government of India, by notification dated 08-02-2006 banned SIMI for the third time. SIMI was first banned on 27 September 2001 immediately following the September 11 attacks in the United States. SIMI remained banned from 27 September 2001 to 27 September 2003 during which period several prosecutions were launched against its members under the provisions of [Terrorist And Disruptive Activities Prevention Act (TADA), the Maharashtra Control of Organised Crime Act (MCOCA), and the Unlawful Activities (Prevention) Act 1967.

SIMI was banned for the third time on 8 February 2006. The second ban of SIMI dated 27 September 2003 came to an end on

27 September 2005. Therefore SIMI was in existence between 28 September 2005 and 7 February 2006 but was believed to be dysfunctional due to the fact that many of its members were demoralised or had crossed the age of 30 years; which automatically made them ineligible to continue as a member of SIMI-SIMI has an age limit of 30 years for membership. Many of its members had to fight cases registered against them by the Government.

However, on 27 July 2006, a spokesperson of the Indian Government told the Unlawful Activities (Prevention) Tribunal held in New Delhi, that contrary to notions that SIMI's activities declined following its ban, the organisation "had stepped up its subversive activities and was involved in almost all major explosions, communal violence and circulation of inflammatory material across the country."

The ban notification and the background note stated that SIMI deserved to be banned for clandestine activities and links with around 20 organisations through whom SIMI was allegedly operating. The background note clearly says that there was no violent incident in which SIMI was involved in the last 2–3 years.

To prove its case against SIMI, the Government cited several cases under the Unlawful Activities (Prevention) Act registered between 1998–2001.

The third ban on SIMI was lifted by the Delhi High Court Tribunal on 5 August 2008. "Material given by the home ministry is insufficient, so ban cannot be continued," Justice Geeta Mittal, a sitting Delhi High Court judge, said while lifting the ban. But the lifting of the ban was stayed by the supreme court of India on the next day itself(6 August 2008).

A special tribunal has upheld the ban imposed on SIMI by the Home Ministry under the Unlawful Activities (Prevention) Act, 1967. The Tribunal's head confirming the ban held that SIMI has links with Pakistan-based terror outfits and its front, the Indian Mujahideen.

Transformation into Indian Mujahideen

The exact nature of the relationship between SIMI and Indian Mujahideen (IM) is debated. Some analysts contend that IM is a militant branch of SIMI while others believe that the two groups are distinct although linked. Delhi Police sources claimed that Fasih Mahmood was one of the five men who transformed the Students Islamic Movement of India (Simi), a radical student body into a deadly Indian Mujahideen (IM).

Incidents

2006

- 30 October: Noor-ul-Hooda, a SIMI activist, was arrested by the police for his alleged involvement in the 2006 Malegaon blasts. Authorities said the bombs used in the blasts were assembled in the garage of "main conspirator" Shabbir at Malegaon. Maharashtra police claims that 2006 Malegaon blasts were the handiwork of ex-SIMI members. But later on Law enforcement agenicies decided not to oppose bail plea of Muslim youths because the role of a Hindu Radical organisation became evident when investigation progressed further

2007

- 15 February: The Supreme Court describes the banned Students Islamic Movement of India as a "secessionist movement."

2008

- 27 March: SIMI Ex-General Secretary Safdar Nagori (Mahidpur), Amil Parvez(Unhel) arrested from Indore, along with 10 alleged members of the group by Madhya PradeshState Police's Special Task Force
- 5 August: Delhi High Court Tribunal lifts ban on SIMI. The lifting of the ban was subsequently stayed by the Supreme Court of India on 6 August 2008.
- 13 September: A group calling itself the Indian Mujahideen claims responsibility for the serial blasts in New Delhi. 30 people were killed in these blasts & more than 90 injured.

2010

- 7 December: The terrorist outfit Indian Mujahideen claims responsibility for Varanasi bomb blast which claimed the life of a two-year old girl and left more than 30 people injured.

2012

Union government extended the ban imposed on SIMI by two more years.

2014

The Union government has renewed the ban on Students Islamic Movement of India (SIMI) under the Unlawful Activities (Prevention) Act for another five years.

On 18th May 2014, at Bhopal district court, alleged members who were being produced before the court shouted pro-Taliban slogans saying "Taliban zindabad" (long live Taliban) and indicated a threat to designated Prime Minister Narendra Modi with "Ab Modi ki baari hai"(It is Modi's turn now) at Bhopal district court.

THE ISI AND TERRORISM: BEHIND THE ACCUSATIONS

Pakistan's military intelligence agency, the Inter-Services Intelligence (ISI), has long faced accusations of meddling in the affairs of its neighbors. A range of officials inside and outside Pakistan have stepped up suggestions of links between the ISI and terrorist groups in recent years. In fall 2006, a leaked report by a British Defense Ministry think tank charged, "Indirectly Pakistan (through the ISI) has been supporting terrorism and extremism— whether in London on 7/7 [the July 2005 attacks on London's transit system], or in Afghanistan, or Iraq." In June 2008, Afghan officials accused Pakistan's intelligence service of plotting a failed assassination attempt on President Hamid Karzai; shortly thereafter, they implied the ISI's involvement in a July 2008 attack on the Indian embassy. Indian officials also blamed the ISI for the bombing of the Indian embassy. Pakistani officials have denied such a connection.

Numerous U.S. officials have also accused the ISI of supporting terrorist groups, even as the Pakistani government seeks increased aid from Washington with assurances of fighting militants. In a May 2009 interview with CBS' *60 Minutes*, U.S. Defense Secretary

Robert Gates said "to a certain extent, they play both sides." Gates and others suggest the ISI maintains links with groups like the Afghan Taliban as a "strategic hedge" to help Islamabad gain influence in Kabul once U.S. troops exit the region. These allegations surfaced yet again in July 2010 when WikiLeaks.org made public (*NYT*) a trove of U.S. intelligence records on the war in Afghanistan. The documents described ISI's links to militant groups fighting U.S. and international forces in Afghanistan. In April 2011 during a visit to Pakistan, U.S. Chairman of the Joint Chiefs of Staff Admiral Mike Mullen pointed to ISI's links with one such group, the Haqqani network. The May 1, 2011, killing of America's most wanted terrorist Osama bin Laden in a Pakistani military town not far from Islamabad raised new questions over army and ISI support for the al-Qaeda leader and the legitimacy of their counterterrorism efforts. Pakistan's government has repeatedly denied allegations of supporting terrorism, citing as evidence its cooperation in the U.S.-led battle against extremists in which it has taken significant losses both politically and on the battlefield.

Supporting Terrorism?

"The ISI probably would not define what they've done in the past as 'terrorism,'" saysWilliam Milam, former U.S. ambassador to Pakistan. Nevertheless, experts say the ISI has supported a number of militant groups in the disputed Kashmir region between Pakistan and India, some of which are on the U.S. State Department's Foreign Terrorist Organizations list. While Pakistan has a formidable military presence near the Indian border, some experts believe the relationship between the military and some Kashmiri groups has greatly changed with the rise of militancy within Pakistan. Shuja Nawaz, author of*Crossed Swords: Pakistan, its Army, and the Wars Within,* says the ISI "has certainly lost control" of Kashmiri militant groups. According to Nawaz, some of the groups trained by the ISI to fuel insurgency in Kashmir have been implicated in bombings and attacks within Pakistan, therefore making them army targets.

"I do not accept the thesis that the ISI is a rogue organization." —William Milam, former U.S. ambassador to Pakistan.

On Pakistan's western border with Afghanistan, the ISI supported the Taliban up to September 11, 2001, though Pakistani officials deny any current support for the group. Pakistan's government was also one of three countries, along with the United Arab Emirates and Saudi Arabia, that recognized the Taliban government in Afghanistan. The ISI's first major involvement in Afghanistan came after the Soviet invasion in 1979, when it partnered with the CIA to provide weapons, money, intelligence, and training to the mujahadeen fighting the Red Army. At the time, some voices within the United States questioned the degree to which Pakistani intelligence favored extremist and anti-American fighters. Following the Soviet withdrawal, the ISI continued its involvement in Afghanistan, first supporting resistance fighters opposed to Moscow's puppet government, and later the Taliban.

Pakistan stands accused of allowing that support to continue. Afghan President Hamid Karzai has repeatedly said Pakistan trains militants and sends them across the border. In May 2006, the British chief of staff for southern Afghanistan told the *Guardian*, "The thinking piece of the Taliban is out of Quetta in Pakistan. It's the major headquarters." Speaking at the Council on Foreign Relations in September 2006, then-president Pervez Musharraf responded to such accusations, saying, "It is the most ridiculous thought that the Taliban headquarters can be in Quetta." Nevertheless, experts generally suspect Pakistan still provides some support to the Taliban, though probably not to the extent it did in the past. "If they're giving them support, it's access back and forth [to Afghanistan] and the ability to find safe haven," says Kathy Gannon, who covered the region for decades for the Associated Press. Gannon adds that the Afghan Taliban needs Pakistan even less as a safe haven now "because [it has] gained control of more territory inside Afghanistan."

Many in the Pakistani government, including slain former prime minister Benazir Bhutto, have called the intelligence agency "a state within a state," working beyond the government's control and pursuing its own foreign policy. But Nawaz says the intelligence agency does not function independently. "It aligns itself to the power centre," and does what the government or the army asks it to do, says Nawaz.

DE-CLASSIFIED OPERATIONS OF INTER-SERVICES INTELLIGENCE

In the 1950s, the ISI's Covert Action Division was used in assisting the insurgents in India's North-East and its role was expanded in the late 1960s to assist the Sikh Home Rule Movement of London-based Charan Singh Panchi, which was subsequently transformed into the Khalistan Movement, headed by Jagjit Singh Chauhan in which many other members of the Sikh diaspora in Europe, USA and Canada joined and then demanded the separate country of Khalistan. CIA and ISI worked in tandem during the Nixon Administration in assisting the Khalistan movement in Punjab.

ISI decided to spy on the residence of Colonel Hussain Imam Mabruk who was a Military Attaché to the Embassy of Libya in Islamabad as he had made some inflammatory statements towards the military regime of Zia-ul-Haq. The spying paid off as he was seen talking with two Pakistani gentlemen who entered and left the compound suspiciously. The ISI monitored the two men and were later identified as Pakistani exiles that hated the current military regime and were Bhutto loyalists. They had received terrorist training in Libya and were ready to embark on a terrorist campaign in Pakistan to force the Army to step down from power. All members of the conspiracy were apprehended before any damage could be done.

ISI foiled an attempt by the French Ambassador to Pakistan, Le Gourrierce and his First Secretary, Jean Forlot who were on a surveillance mission to Kahuta nuclear complex on June 26, 1979. Both were intercepted and their cameras and other sensitive equipment were confiscated. Intercepted documents later on showed that the two were recruited by the CIA.

After the failure of Operation Eagle Claw, the U.S. media outlets such as Newsweek and Time reported that CIA agents stationed in Tehran had obtained information in regards to the location of the hostages, in-house information from a Pakistani cook who used to work for the U.S. Embassy. ISI successfully gathered evidence, and intercepted communication documents and showed it to the Iranian Chief of J-2 which cleared the cook. The Iranian chief of intelligence said, "We know, the Big Satan is a big liar."

ISI successfully intercepted two American private weapons dealers during the Soviet-Afghan war of the 1980's. One American diplomat (his name has not been de-classified) who lived in the F-7/4 sector of Islamabad was spotted by an ISI agent in a seedy part of Rawalpindi by his Car's diplomatic plates. He was bugged and trailed and was found to be in contact with various tribal groups supplying them with weapons for their fight with the Soviet Army in Afghanistan. Another was Eugene Clegg, a teacher in the American International School who also indulged in weapons trade. All of them were put out of business.

ISI had placed a mole in the Soviet Embassy in Islamabad. The mole reported that the Third Secretary in the Soviet Embassy was after information in regards to the Karakurum Highway and was obtaining it from a middle level employee, Mr. Ejaz, of the Northern Motor Transport Company. ISI contacted Mr. Ejaz who then confessed that a few months ago the Soviet diplomat approached him and threatened his family unless he divulged sensitive information in regards to the highway such as alignment of the road, location of bridges, the number of Chinese personnel working on the Highway, etc. The ISI instead of confronting the Soviet diplomat chose to feed him with false information. This continued until the Soviet diplomat was satisfied that Mr. Ejaz had been bled white of all the information and then dropped him as a source.

ISI was very worried that among the large influx of Afghan refugees that come into Pakistan due to the Soviet-Afghan war were members of KHAD (Afghan Intelligence). In order to gather information on these spies, the ISI successfully convinced Mansoor Ahmed who was the Charge-de-Affairs of the Afghan Embassy in Islamabad to turn his back on the Soviet backed Afghan government. He and his family were secretly escorted out of their residence and were given safe passage on a London bound British Airways flight in exchange for classified information in regards to Afghan agents in Pakistan. The Soviet and Afghan diplomats tried their best to find the family but were unsuccessful.

A routine background checks on various staff members working for the Indian embassy raised suspicions on an Indian woman who worked as a school teacher in an Indian School in Islamabad.

Her enthusiastic and too friendly attitude gave her up. She was in reality was an agent working for RAW. ISI monitored her movements to a hotel in Islamabad where she rendezvoused with a local Pakistani man who worked as an engineer for Pakistan Atomic Energy Commission. ISI then confronted her and were then able to turn her into a double agent spying on the Indian Embassy in Islamabad.

ISI became aware of a plot to assassinate the President of Pakistan, Zia-ul-Haq and then launch a bloody coup to depose the current government and install an extreme Islamic government in its place. The attempted assassination and coup was to occur on March 23, 1980 during the annual March 23 Pakistan day parade. The masterminds behind the coup were high ranking Military and Intelligence officers and were led by Major General Tajammal Hussain Malik, his son, Captain Naveed and his nephew Major Riaz, a former Military Intelligence officer. ISI decided against arresting these men outright because they did not know how deep this conspiracy went and kept these men under strict surveillance. As the date of the annual parade approached, ISI was satisfied that it had identified the major players in this conspiracy and then arrested these men along with quite a few high ranking military officers.

Ilam Din also known as Ilmo was an infamous Indian spy working from Pakistan. He had eluded being captured many times but on March 23 at 3 A.M., Ilmo and two other Indian spies were apprehended by Pakistani Rangers as they were illegally crossing into Pakistan from India. Their mission was to spy and report back on the new military equipment that Pakistan will be showing in their annual March 23 Pakistan day parade. Ilmo after being thoroughly interrogated was then forced by the ISI to send false information to his RAW handlers in India. This process continued and many more Indian spies in Pakistan were flushed out such as Roop Lal.

ISI uncovered a secret deal in which naval base facilities were granted by Indian Prime Minister Indira Gandhi to the USSR in Vizag and the Andaman & Nicobar Island and the alleged attachment of KGB advisers to the then Lieutenant General Sunderji who was the commander of Operation Bluestar in the Golden Temple in Amritsar in June 1984.

ISI, CIA and Mossad carried out a covert transfer of Soviet made PLO and Lebanese weapons captured by the Israelis during the Israeli invasion of Lebanon in June 1982 and their subsequent transfer to Pakistan and then into Afghanistan. All knowledge of this weapon transfer was kept secret and was only made public recently.

ISI played a central role in the U.S.-backed guerrilla war to oust the Soviet Army from Afghanistan in the 1980s. That Central Intelligence Agency (CIA)-backed effort flooded Pakistan with weapons and with Afghan, Pakistani and Arab "mujahideen", who were motivated to fight as a united force protecting fellow Muslims in Soviet occupied Afghanistan. The CIA relied on the ISI to train fighters, distribute arms, and channel money. The ISI trained about 83,000 Afghan mujahideen between 1983 and 1997, and dispatched them to Afghanistan.

CIA through the ISI promoted the smuggling of heroin into Afghanistan in order to turn the Soviet troops into heroin addicts and thus greatly reducing their fighting potential.

Major General Sultan Habib who was an operative of the ISI's Joint Intelligence Miscellaneous department successfully procured nuclear material while being posted as the Defense Attaché in the Pakistani Embassy in Moscow from 1991 to 1993 and concurrently obtaining other materials from Central Asian Republics, Poland and the former Czechoslovakia. After Moscow, Major General Habib then coordinated shipping of missiles from North Korea and the training of Pakistani experts in the missile production. These two acts greatly enhanced Pakistan's Nuclear weapons program and their missile delivery systems.

ISI engineered the takeover of Afghanistan by the hard-line Islamic Taliban regime after the fall of the Communist government in Kabul in 1992.

Altaf Hussain, was tasked by the ISI to start the political movement Muhajir Qaumi Movement, political party which represented the Muhajir (Immigrants from India during the partition of 1947) population in [[Karachi] to counter Pakistan Peoples Party. However, later MQM started a terror campaign by bombing, random murders and political assassinations to force the Pakistani government into creating an independent country for the Pakistan's Muhajir population. Hussain who had the backing of India and was living in exile in London, England and out of the reach of the Pakistani Justice but nevertheless, the ISI systematically dismantled his terror campaign and MQM has since supposedly renounced its militant ways.

ISI played a major role by informing British agencies in advance about terrorist plan to simultaneously blow up 10 airplanes over the Atlantic using liquid explosives in August 2006.

Failures

The 1965 war in Kashmir provoked a major crisis in intelligence. When the war started, there was a complete collapse of the operations of all the intelligence agencies, which had been largely devoted to domestic investigative work such as tapping telephone conversations and chasing political suspects. The ISI, after the commencement of the 1965 Indo-Pakistan war, was apparently unable to locate an Indian armored division due to its preoccupation with political affairs. Ayub Khan set up a committee headed by General Yahya Khan to examine the working of the agencies.

In 1981, a Libyan Security company called Al Murtaza Associates sends recruiters to Pakistan to entice former soldiers and servicemen for high paying security jobs in Libya. In reality, Libya was recruiting mercenaries to fight with Chad and Egypt as it had border disputes with both nations. Only later did the ISI become aware of the plot and the whole scheme was stopped, but nearly 2,700 Pakistanis had already left for those jobs.

The PAF Field Intelligence Unit at their base in Karachi in July 1980 captured an Indian agent. He was interrogated and revealed that a large network of Indian spies were functioning in Karachi. The agent claimed that these spies, in addition to espionage, had also assassinated a few armed personnel. He also said the leader of the spy ring was being headed by the food and beverages manager at the Intercontinental Hotel in Karachi and a number of serving Air Force officers and ratings were on his payroll. The ISI decided to survey the manager to see who he was in contact with, but then President of Pakistan Zia-ul Haq superseded and wanted the manager and anyone else involved in the case arrested immediately. It was later proven that the manager was completely innocent.

ISI failed to perform a proper background check on the British company which supplied the Pakistan Army with its Arctic-weather gear. When Pakistan attempted to secure the top of the Siachen Glacier in 1984, it placed a large order for Arctic-weather gear with the same company that also supplied the Indian Army with its gear. Indians were easily alerted to the large Pakistani purchase and deduced that this large purchase could be used to equip troops to capture the glacier. India then mounted an operation (Operation Meghdoot) and secured the top of the glacier before Pakistan.

ISI failed to calculate the international reaction to the Kargil operation in summer of 1999. Subsequent heavy pressure by foreign countries such as USA forced the Pakistani-backed forces to withdraw from Kargil.

ISI & FOMENTING OF GLOBAL TERROR

In the post 9/11 decade, ISI's involvement in fomenting terror modules in different parts of the world, using proxy outfits like the LeT or the HUJI has been exposed, be it through the arrest of Virgil Brigitte in Australia (2003) or the failed terror plots in the UK and the US in more recent times.

This global terrorist networks with linkages to ISI us shown in the diagram that follows. Outfits inside Pakistan which have had links with or were spawned by the ISI include the LeT, the Jaish e Mohd (JeM), Lashkar e Jhangvi (LeJ – more into sectarian terrorism), Harkat ul Mujahideen (HuM) which morphed into HUJI, and the Dawood underworld mafia. On the periphery ring are outfits with presence in countries like Bangladesh-the Ahle Hadis al Bangladesh (AHAB), HUJI-BD, Jamiyatul Mujahideen Bangladesh (JMB) and Jagrata Muslim Janata Bangladesh (JMJB). In recent years though, security agencies of the new government in Bangladesh havedone much to dismantle these outfits. Nevertheless, linkages persist between ISI and Pakistan based religious or ideologically motivated terrorism outfits like LeT, Jaish and HUJI in countries like Afghanistan. Modules have also been found in Europe or USA.

Decision makers in army/views and orientation of senior officers in Army/ISI on matters of geo-strategic import.

A career or a posting in the ISI has now emerged as a desirable option, with young officers of the rank of captain, major or colonel enjoying far greater power, perks and privileges in the ISI than many of their peers in more routine army field assignments. At any given time, the decision makers in the ISI are the army chief and the DG, ISI. At the second rung of ISI are major generals, one or the other of them could be personally close to the COAS, in which case they may be able influence policy decisions but this may be the exception than the rule. As in the army itself, a collegiate or consensus decision making pattern is usually the norm and prevails in decision making and operational initiatives undertaken by ISI.

Army/ISI & Politicization

With regard to military-civilian interaction, all ISI officers believe in the primacy of the army and its status as the vanguard institution of state. There is a general contempt for all manner of politicians and political parties. This is compounded by the fact that there are no politicians of individually high popularity or charismain Pakistan at present.

Though the lustre attaching to ISI was somewhat tarnished by the US sealsmission to take out Osama bin Laden in Abbotabad in Ma,2011, as well asthe opprobrium following the Saleem Shehzad murder post the attack on theMehran Naval Base. But by and large, all army officers, especially those in ISI,even at middle or relatively junior levels believe that the army's dominant rolein taking vital foreign policy decisions has only been good for the country andcannot be questioned. They would not readily countenance any erosion in thisdominance, unless the army chief himself and the collegiate leadership group of Corps Commanders acquiesce in such a role re-definition. This is not likely to happen in the foreseeable future.

FUTURE ENGAGEMENT WITH THE ISI

When interviewed about the relationship between the West and Pakistan and the ongoing conflict in Afghanistan, the bestselling author Steven Coll stated:

This could not be a more complicated war. If you think about it, the United States is essentially waging a war against its own ally. The Taliban are a proxy of the government of Pakistan [orchestrated by the ISI]. We are an ally of the government of Pakistan. We are fighting the Taliban. In the end, the Taliban will be defeated strategically when the government of Pakistan makes a strategic decision that its future does not lie in partnership with Islamic extremists. (2009)

Coll pinpoints the root of current and future problems in dealing with the ISI and their clandestine terrorist support networks. In 2009, the U.S. provided close to $6.5 billion dollars in aid to the Pakistani government; $300 million of that was dedicated to military spending (Mohammad). The West is figuratively caught between a rock and a hard place. It requires the assistance of Pakistan to successfully prosecute counter-terrorism campaigns in Southwest Asia. Yet, the ISI has infiltrated all ranks of Pakistan's military structure and leverages sympathizers and supporters throughout the Pakistani population. A large amount of that military aid is falling into the hands of the sponsors of the exact networks the West is attempting to defeat. On February 16, 2010 the Taliban's second in command, Mullah Baradar, was captured in a raid conducted jointly by the ISI and the U.S. Western leaders hoped that this would be a catalyst for strengthening the cooperation between the ISI and Western intelligence agencies and serve as an indication that the ISI would begin dismissing its historical involvement with militants. However, after a close examination into the raid, the New York Times provided: Relations between the intelligence services, [CIA and ISI], of the United States and Pakistan have long been marred by suspicions that Pakistan has sheltered the Afghan Taliban. The Pakistanis have long denied it. New details of the raid indicate that the arrest of the No. 2 Taliban leader was not necessarily the result of a new determination by Pakistan to go after the Taliban, or a bid to improve its strategic position in the region. Rather, it may be something more prosaic: "a lucky accident..." (Shane and Schmitt) Upon Baradar's capture, ISI officers delayed allowing U.S. intelligence officers to question him and were hesitant in sharing news and information about his detention with the Pakistani press (in fear of casting themselves in a pro-Western light).

The ISI will continue to act out of its own interest. It has grown in size from its inception and now forms a state within the Pakistani state. While it serves as an intelligence agency of the Pakistani government, the Pakistani government is largely unable to control its actions or relationships with terrorist organizations, both domestic and abroad. Ongoing operations to defeat extremists and terrorists places the ISI at a crossroads with Western intelligence agencies and irregular warfare personnel. Without a complete transformation of the ISI's motivations, allegiances, extremist slant, and structure, it will continue to exist as more of an enemy to the West than an ally.

Conclusion

The historic actions of the ISI in sponsoring organizations like al-Qaeda, JEM, LET and HUM, as well as their utilization of the Taliban as a proxy for foreign policy, signals that the ISI is a significant state sponsor of terrorism. "Since Pakistan has terrorism, nuclear weapons, religious extremism, economic instability, and political volatility, easy [foreign policy] answers provide little guidance in a dangerous, fluid environment. If, due to ISI sins of omission or commission, terrorists acquire Pakistani nuclear weapons and there is a nuclear incident or nuclear war, the consequences will be unthinkable" (Roberts 109). These variables set the ISI's sponsorship apart from other international sponsors and make it definitively the most dangerous.

A careful policy of continued engagement with the ISI and accountability of Western funding to Pakistan will be essential to secure future stability in the region.

The ISI will continue to be a clandestine sponsor of worldwide extremism and transnational terrorism. The fragile nature of Pakistani politics, the existence of deeply entrenched Islamic foundations, and insecurity surrounding the Pakistani nuclear arsenal make the ISI the foremost terrorist threat and non-state sponsor of terrorism in the international community. The ISI masquerades as a controllable tool of the Pakistani government while covertly supporting enemies of the international community – conclusively acting as a threat to international stability and as a fifth column within the Pakistani state.

ORIGINS OF A PAKISTANI SPY AGENCY

The Islamic Republic of Pakistan, or Pakistan, achieved its initial independence in 1947 when the British divided the colonized Indian sub-continent based on religious lines. Pakistan was centered on the religion of Islam, drawing geographically separated regions out of Muslim population centers in the West (West Pakistan) and the eastern portion of Bengal (East Pakistan).

The Indian state catered to the Hindu faith and resided between the two newly formed Pakistani provinces. The British divisions forced the relocation of millions of people on all sides, creating poverty, destruction, and casualties in its wake. "Partitions along ethnic lines usually result in The Pakistani Inter-Service Intelligence Directorate's Sponsorship of Terrorism mutually inflicted violence, but the politicians of that time had no understanding of the magnitude of what they had prepared" (Ali 30). After the dust and blood had settled, the world embraced a newly emerged Muslim state, drawn from loosely constructed boundaries and ethnic divisions.

A structural contradiction lay at the heart of the new country. "Religious affinity was the only rationale for uniting West Pakistan and its Muslim majority provinces – Punjab, Sind, Baluchistan, and North-West Frontier – with East Pakistan, which was the Muslim majority slice of Bengal". The new state was led initially by the Governor-General Mohammad Ali Jinnah and Prime Minister Liaquat Ali Khan, who sought cooperative relations between the newly divided Hindu and Muslim states, but was challenged over the contested territory of Kashmir. A poorly established border between India and Pakistan left Kashmir contested between both nations, as well as the Chinese. The disputes over the small region resulted in the 1947 Indo- Pakistani war and the birth of the modern day ISI. The ISI stemmed from the Pakistani desire to streamline intelligence collection and dissemination between its military branches in the time of conflict. After the 1947 Indo- Pakistani war over Kashmir, the ISI was created as a separate entity from the intelligence bureau (IB) to meet this function and expand Pakistan's collection capabilities. "The agency was initially charged with performing all intelligence tasks at home and abroad… its scope of operation extended to all areas related to national security" (Hussain 13). Originally, the role of the ISI was crafted to focus the efforts of the agency on foreign intelligence collection and the dissemination of national security concerns. However, in the 1970s, the ISI's responsibility took a new shape as it was given additional responsibilities including the oversight of domestic politics.

"Ironically, it was a civilian leader, Zulfikar Ali Bhutto who created the ISI's internal wing which played a critical role in the ousting of his government a few years later. [The ISI] was to cast a heavy shadow over the country's politics in later years" . Beginning with Bhutto's creation of the internal wing, set to monitor domestic security threats and political trends, the ISI began to take on the shape of a 'big brother' entity.

However, the seeds of militancy, religious fundamentalism, and clandestine terrorist support were planted when Bhutto appointed General Zia al-Haq as the army chief in 1976. General Zia was a devout Muslim, and Bhutto thought he would never betray his trust (Coll). "Once elevated to the top position, the General did not take much time to develop secret contacts with hard-line religious groups and conspired with them to overthrow his benefactor". In 1977, General Zia al-Haq took the seat of power from Bhutto, with strong support from the ISI and religious groups, and immediately began to instill Islamist fundamentalism and teachings throughout the Pakistani military. Jamaat-i-Islami (JI), the largest Islamic political party, gained strength and momentum and fostered extremist leadership within the military ranks under Zia's guidance. "The main objective of the JI was to penetrate the army and use it to seize state power. The practice introduced by General Zia of sending combat officers to universities in Pakistan, in which the JI often had pervasive influence facilitated the party's [Islamic] objective" (Hussain 20). The ISI began to take shape as a mediator, facilitator, representative, and liaison for militant Islam, extremism, and Pakistani covert action.

During the Cold War, Pakistan proved to be a strategic ally for the U.S. due to its geographic location and inherent rivalry with India which drove an automatic anti-Soviet stance. The ISI was leveraged by Western intelligence services, including the Central Intelligence Holt and Gray Agency (CIA), to undermine Soviet action in the region and provide an outlet for the sharing of intelligence between Pakistan and the U.S. When the Soviet Union invaded Afghanistan in the 1980s the CIA and ISI embarked on one of the largest covert campaigns in history: financing and arming the Mujahedin, comprised of Islamic extremists, for their efforts in Afghanistan. "Zia did not allow the CIA or any other foreign intelligence agency to aid the Mujahedin directly, enter Afghanistan, or plan the Mujahedin's battles and strategy. That became the prerogative of the ISI, which, with its newfound wealth and American patronage, had become a state within a state, employing thousands of officers in order to run what was now also Pakistan's Afghan war" (Rashid 10).

While increased funding and motivation from the West poured through the ranks of the ISI to bolster the capabilities of the Mujahedin in Afghanistan, Zia mandated strict Islamic and religious training and indoctrination for the military and agency. "The ISI's training of guerrillas was integrated with the teaching of Islam. The prominent theme was that Islam was a complete socio-political ideology under threat from atheistic communists. The Afghan war produced a new radical Islamic movement" (Hussain 17).

Simultaneously, Zia took steps to turn Pakistan into an Islamic state, obedient to a strict interpretation of Sharia law (Islamic law), and used the ISI as the face of enforcement and religious cultivation. [Military] units were required to take non-combatant mullahs with them to the front line. Soldiers were encouraged to attend 'Tablighi' [(Deobandi movement within Pakistan)] gatherings. The purpose was to indoctrinate cadets and young officers with an obscurantist interpretation of Islam. Many of those cadets later rose to positions of power and took control of sensitive institutions, including ISI.

The Afghan war created a leviathan and powerful intelligence agency in the ISI while Zia mandated Islamic fundamentalism and Deobandism (a strict interpretation of the Hanafi school of Sunni Islam) into their shadowy ranks. With aid from the U.S. and a pivotal and violent struggle against the Soviets in Afghanistan, the ISI cultivated a relationship with extremists from across the globe, including al-Qaeda. While being forced to adhere to fundamental Islam from the Pakistani state, the ISI itself became recognized in the international system and feared within domestic society. Throughout the 1990s, the ISI maintained its relationship with extremist networks and militants that it had established during the Afghan war to utilize in its campaign against Indian forces in Kashmir.

The ISI had become a state-mandated and Western-built sponsor of contemporary and fundamental terrorism.

An Unsavory Past

Many high-profile terrorist incidents, ranging from the September 11, 2001 attacks on New York and Washington to the July 7, 2004 subway bombings in London to the November 2008 assault on Mumbai, have had direct connections to individuals and groups operating in Pakistan (Ganguly and Kapur 47). The sponsorship and recruitment of terrorist and guerilla movements against the Soviets in Afghanistan is paramount when examining historic ties between terrorism and the ISI.

However, the agency also took part in, and was responsible for, numerous international operations and violent acts across the globe. The instilled radicalization from Zia and the campaigns in Afghanistan and Kashmir vetted and emboldened the ISI. Yet the of Terrorism agency's clandestine operations and sponsorship for violence and Islamic extremism abroad generated the attention of the international community.

The most notable and dangerous connection to transnational terrorism is the ISI's cooperation and support for al-Qaeda (AQ) and its leader, Osama bin-Laden. During the 1980s, militants poured into Pakistan from the Muslim world, including Palestinian teacher and preacher Abdullah Azzam, who had taught in Jordan and Saudi Arabia, preaching Muslims' duty to wage Jihad.

One of his students was Osama bin-Laden. Azzam created Maktab al-Khidmat (Services Office or MK) in Peshawar to recruit Arabs and raise funds. Bin Laden, with ISI ties, was a key MK organizer. Under bin Laden, MK transformed into al-Qaeda. ISI Directory General Akhtar Abdul Ramna personally met with him many times, providing money and intelligence. (Roberts 105)

AQ and the ISI enjoyed a close relationship in the 1980s when Muslims from across the globe shared bases of operations in the Northwest Frontier Province (NWFP) and Federally Administered Tribal Areas (FATA).

The tribal regions, governed strictly by Pashtun tribal codes, were considered a safe haven for militants, foreign fighters, and terrorists. Following the Afghan war, the U.S. essentially lost interest in the region, cutting ties with the Islamic militants who fought across the border and also losing influence over the large population of refugees created by the fighting. The refugee population was a virtual breeding ground for Islamic extremism, spearheaded by the ISI and its network of madrassas. "The Taliban (the word literally means 'students') were children of the Afghan refugees and poor Pathan families 'educated' in the madrassas in the 1980s" (Ali 136).

The same Taliban controlled and supported by the ISI harbored today's most wanted terrorist: Osama bin-Laden. Pakistani President Pervez Musharraf observed: We helped created [sic] the mujahedin, fired them with religious zeal in seminaries, armed them, paid them, fed them, and sent them to Jihad against the Soviet Union in Afghanistan. We did not stop to think how we would divert them to productive life after the Jihad was won. This mistake cost Afghanistan and Pakistan more dearly than any other country. Neither did the United States realize what a rich, educated person like Osama bin Laden might later do with the organization that we all had enabled him to establish. (Roberts 106) Leading up to the attacks of September 11, the ISI had a working relationship with Osama bin-Laden and his militant network and had a supportive and controlling relationship with the Taliban, which was then firmly in control of Afghanistan. "In 1996, Osama bin Laden settled in Afghanistan. He met an ISI representative, who proposed an alliance between bin- Laden's network and the Taliban, which won the Afghan civil war in 1996, achieving ISI's aim of a sympathetic government in Kabul" (106). Following the Afghan war, the ISI directly sponsored, controlled, and orchestrated the Taliban's movement into Afghanistan. They brokered a relationship between al-Qaeda, Osama bin-Laden, and the Taliban and sponsored the terrorist state which had been established. "In 1997, the ISI asked Saudi intelligence for permission to sponsor bin-Laden"...only four short years before the deadliest terrorist attack the international community had ever experienced.

Aside from the strong influence and sponsorship of terrorism exemplified in Afghanistan, the Taliban, and al-Qaeda, the ISI has also focused a great deal of effort on fostering terrorist organizations in the Kashmir region. Kashmir sits at the top of Pakistan, bordering both India and China. All three nations dispute the territory as falling under their sovereign control. Historically, the region has been a catalyst for three wars and repeated military exchanges involving guerilla action, artillery fire, and high-altitude fighting.

The ISI has actively sought to enhance, finance, and promote terrorist organizations which serve to undermine the Indian influence in Kashmir. "In 1990, ISI operated 30 training camps for Kashmiri militants. By 2002, there were 128 ISI-sponsored camps training militants to fight in Kashmir. Approximately, 1,000 members of Harakat-ul-Mujahideen [(HUM)], Jaishe- Muhammad (JEM), and Lashkar-e-Taiba (LET) received training each year" . The lessons learned by the ISI, including its strategy of low-intensity conflict in Afghanistan were applied in the Kashmiri campaign. The ISI served as Pakistan's liaison and training force for HUM, JEM, and LET, equipping and planning operations against Indian targets. Aside from attempting to seed Islamic extremism into the Kashmiri movement, the ISI also sought to preoccupy Indian forces in Kashmir, limiting India's ability to utilize them elsewhere and undermining their control of the military (Weaver). The ISI enabled HUM, JEM, and LET, hardline Islamic groups, to lead the terrorist action in Kashmir, and change the complexion of the struggle (Hussain 25).

Many of those Islamic groups expanded their terrorist operations outside of Kashmir and into neighboring India. In 2008, the city of Mumbai fell under siege at the hands of heavilyarmed LET militants. Using assault rifles and explosives, a handful of LET terrorists killed almost 200 people on Indian soil. "Indian officials implicated the ISI [for the attack]. India's foreign ministry said the ISI had links to the planners of the attacks, the banned militant group [LET], which New Delhi [blamed] for the assault" (Bajoria 2009). The men were later found to be controlled by operators within Pakistan using cellular phones. While Pakistan has denied all of the Indian allegations that the ISI was involved, it is likely that the ISI's connection with LET remains strong, even following the attacks in Mumbai.

Outside of the Southwest Asian sphere of influence the ISI, has maintained an active influence over the operations of terrorist organizations and guerilla movements, most notably with the expansion of ISI operations and sponsorship overseas under the leadership of General Javid Nasir. "A member of the proselytizing Tablighi Jamaat, Nasir had become a devout Muslim with a flowing white beard. And he had no intelligence background" (Nawaz 452). After his appointment to lead the ISI, Nasir oversaw covert action across the international community.

The ISI's involvement was not limited to India, however. Under General Nasir's instructions, the ISI violated the UN embargo on supplying arms to the warring parties in Bosnia-Herzegovina and airlifted heavy weapons and missiles for the Bosnian Muslims. In 1993, several Arab countries, including Egypt, Tunisia, and Algeria, had complained about General Nasir extending support to radical Islamic movements in their countries. (Hussain 27) After Zia's extremist indoctrination and Nasir's expansion of the ISI, the agency continued to expand its influence across borders and among terrorist organizations worldwide. The ISI's track record for sponsorship of terrorist organizations is extensive and stretched far beyond the conflicts in Afghanistan and Kashmir. The links it established to al-Qaeda and other global Islamic movements during the Soviet-Afghan war enabled its actions in other nation states. "At least two former ISI chiefs, General Hamid Gul and General Javid Nasir, remained actively involved with Islamic radical movements. Both promoted pan-Islamism and strove for an Islamic revolution that would free Pakistan from perceived western, and particularly American, cultural and political influences" . Those relationships and motivations within the ISI remain strong today and continue to threaten the stability and counter terrorist goals of the international community.

PAKISTAN'S UNHOLY ALLIANCE THE MILITANTS

The heavily guarded, high-walled concrete structure right in the heart of Islamabad has no signboard. But everyone in the capital knows that the sprawling compound surrounded by barbed wire houses the Directorate for Inter-Services Intelligence (ISI). The spy agency has been the country's big brother. It is powerful, ubiquitous and has functioned with so much autonomy from the central government that it has almost become a state within a state. It is not only responsible for intelligence gathering, but also acts as a determinant of Pakistan's foreign policy and a vehicle for its implementation. For every civilian and military government, control of the ISI was seen as crucial to maintaining a firm grip on power. The agency had been so powerful for so long that it played by its own rules. Its various heads had contrasting profiles, but emerged among the most powerful figures in the country's establishment. For years they ran semi-independent operations in Afghanistan and Kashmir and helped to form and topple civilian governments.

For more than two decades the ISI had sponsored Islamic militancy to carry out its secret wars. It was a crucial partner in the CIA's biggest covert operation ever, one that forced the Soviet

Union to pull out of Afghanistan and served as a catalyst to the disintegration of the communist superpower. In Afghanistan, as well as Kashmir, the agency discovered the effectiveness of covert warfare as a method of bleeding a stronger adversary, while maintaining the element of plausible deniability.

The ISI falls directly within Pakistan's military chain of command and had also served as an instrument for promoting the military's domestic political agenda and the guardian of its self-professed 'ideological frontiers' of the country. Almost all ISI officers are regular military personnel, who are rotated in and out for a fixed tenure. However, there have been some exceptions.

The export of jihad sponsored by the ISI had its blowback. It had allowed the Islamists a huge space for their activities. State patronage, in the form of an 'unholy alliance' between the military and the mullahs, resulted in an unprecedented rise of radical Islam.

The ISI had helped to create much of the Islamic militancy and religious extremism that Musharraf was confronted with. That unholy alliance had been a major factor in the country's drift to Islamic fundamentalism. Founded in 1948 by a British army officer, Major-General R. Cawthome, then Deputy Chief of Army Staff in Pakistan, the agency was initially charged with performing all intelligence tasks at home and abroad. Its scope of operation extended to all areas related to national security. Until the 1960s, the ISI largely remained an obscure organization that confined itself to playing its specified role. But in the mid 1970s its scope was expanded to domestic politics. Ironically, it was a civilian leader, Zulfikar Ali Bhutto who created the ISI's internal wing which played a critical role in the ousting of his government a few years later. It was to cast its heavy shadow over the country's politics in later years.

A charismatic and populist leader, Bhutto took over a humiliated military and a brutally truncated Pakistan in search of a new identity, following the Indian-supported secession of East Pakistan (now Bangladesh), in 1971. The country had been dismembered by civil war and Indian military action. It was no longer the country created by Mohammed Ali Jinnah. The Pakistan that emerged from the ashes of defeat required a different geopolitical orientation. A revolt by young Turks in the army in the aftermath of a humiliating defeat in the war had forced the military ruler, General Yahya Khan, 3 to hand over power to Bhutto. His legitimacy was rooted in the country's first democratically held elections in 1970. Bhutto's socialist Pakistan People's Party had swept the fateful polls in the western wing of then-united Pakistan, trouncing the right-wing Islamic parties.

The scion of a feudal family of Sindh and a former foreign minister, Bhutto was seen as the savior of the new Pakistan. He successfully negotiated with India the release of 90,000 troops taken prisoner by Indian forces. He had come to power with the largest support base of any Pakistani leader since the inception of the country in 1947.

But he failed to sustain the confidence of the nation. Bhutto was ideally placed to put into practice the objective of social democracy and develop secular ideas and institutions. But it did not happen. Bhutto's strategy was to bring the disparate elements of this divided society together through a kind of Islamic nationalism, which was then supposed to create the cohesion and stability necessary for socialist economic reforms, but unfortunately all Bhutto succeeded in doing was to rehabilitate religious extremism. Under pressure from the religious parties whose cooperation they were courting, Bhutto's government increased the religious content in school syllabuses and, succumbing to pressure from Saudi Arabia as well as to the demands of religious parties, declared the Ahmedis, an Islamic sect, to be non-Muslim. This apparently minor action had long-term implications for the country as it fuelled Islamic zealotry and sharpened the sectarian divide. Bhutto's attempt to co-opt religious elements merely emboldened them, and eventually the clergy joined hands with their traditional ally, the military, to plot the overthrow of his government. Bhutto's attempt to establish an authoritarian rule led him to rely more and more on the coercive apparatus of the state and the intelligence agencies.

Bhutto did little to strengthen democratic institutions and to make the process of democratic reform irreversible. Instead, his entire effort was aimed at promoting a personalized rule. He did not trust anyone. Given his overwhelming paranoia and insecurity, Bhutto geared up the ISI to keep surveillance not only on his opponents, but also on his own party men and cabinet ministers. The agency kept dossiers on politicians, bureaucrats, judges and anyone else considered important.

The collapse of democratic institutions and the Constitution's loss of sanctity created a vacuum of authority that provided a favourable condition for the Bonapartist generals. Bhutto's use of the army to crush the uprising in Pakistan's western province of Balochistan provided an opportunity to the military to reassert itself in the country's politics. Bhutto's politics of expediency and attempts to appease the country's religious lobby allowed the Islamists, who were routed in the 1971 elections, to revive themselves. A nationwide agitation, led by right wing Islamic parties in the aftermath of the controversial elections in 1977, shook his government. In a desperate attempt to appease the Islamists, Bhutto prohibited the sale and use of alcoholic beverages, banned gambling and closed down nightclubs. But the die had already been cast.

Bhutto had handpicked General Zia ul-Haq, a lesser-known officer, for the post of army chief in 1976 over the heads of half a dozen senior officers, believing he did not have any personal ambitions. General Zia was a devout Muslim and Bhutto thought he would never betray his trust. Once elevated to the top position, the General did not take much time to develop secret contacts with hardline religious groups and conspired with them to overthrow his benefactor. On 5 July 1977, a bloodless military coup brought an end to Bhutto's six-and-a-half-year civilian rule. There was a complete convergence of interests between the Islamists and the military leadership which had ousted the Bhutto government. Several accounts of Bhutto's last days in power revealed that Major-General Ghulam Jilani, Bhutto's handpicked chief of the ISI, played a key role in the coup plan. Two years later, in April 1979, Bhutto was hanged after a dubious trial on charges of murdering a political rival. A secularist, elected with an overwhelming mandate in 1970, Bhutto probably had the best chance of any leader of taking on the Islamists and winning. His inglorious demise can only fill Pakistan's current leader, attempting a similar task, with foreboding.

Bhutto's usurper, General Zia, came from a humble lowermiddle-class background. His father, a religious man, held a clerical government post during British rule in India. Despite his poverty, he provided his son with a decent education. Zia was educated at Delhi's most prestigious St Stephen's College before getting a commission in the Royal Indian Army in 1942. He was a captain at the time of the creation of Pakistan in 1947. He was a hard-working officer, but lacked brilliance. Many of his colleagues believed he was lucky to be promoted beyond Colonel. From a young age, Zia was actively involved with the popular religious movement, Tablighi Jamaat, 6 one of the most influential grassroots Islamic movements in the South Asian subcontinent, which had hardline traditionalist views on the role of Islam in modern society.

A short man with a thick moustache, Zia bore a strong resemblance to the British comedian, Terry-Thomas. But he was by no means a fool. He was shrewd enough to know how to make his way up. He convinced Bhutto of his absolute loyalty and more importantly of his incapacity to be otherwise. Zia was not only an authoritarian; he also aspired to turn Pakistan into an ideological state ruled by strict Islamic sharia laws. He was an unpopular and controversial leader, whose survival in power largely owed to the external factors that emerged after the invasion by Soviet forces of Pakistan's northern neighbour, Afghanistan, in 1979. Pakistan became a frontline state and a bulwark in the West's war against communism.

General Zia brought in his close confidant, Lt.-General Akhter Abdur Rehman, to head the ISI in 1979, as the spy agency became a crucial cog in the resistance against the Soviet forces. Its tentacles started to spread far and wide. An artillery officer, General Rehman 'had a cold, reserved personality, almost inscrutable, always secretive, with no intimates except his family.' His officers remembered him as a hard man to serve due to his brusque manner and reputation as a strict disciplinarian. 'That made him an ideal man for the job,' said Brigadier Mohammed Yousuf, a former ISI officer who served under him. General Rehman ran the organization until 1987. He was not a radical Islamist, but a staunch Muslim nationalist. Under General Rehman, the ISI, in partnership with the CIA, conducted the biggest covert operation in modern history. The two organizations had secretly collaborated for years, yet General Zia was not prepared to give a free hand to the CIA. He laid down strict rules to ensure that the ISI would maintain control over contacts with Afghan mujahidin groups. No CIA operatives would be allowed to cross the border into Afghanistan. Distribution of weapons to the Afghan commanders would be handled only by the ISI. All training of mujahidin would be the sole responsibility of the ISI. While the CIA supplied money and weapons, it was the ISI that moved them into Afghanistan. The Americans relied almost entirely on the Pakistani service to allocate weapons to the mujahidin groups. The framework provided the Pakistani spy agency with almost total control over the covert operation inside Afghanistan. The decade-long secret war raised the organization's profile and gave it huge clout. With the active help of the CIA and Saudi Arabia, the ISI turned the Afghan resistance into Islam's holy war.

The decade-long conflict in Afghanistan gave the Islamic extremists a rallying point and a training field. Young Muslims around the world flocked to Afghanistan to fight against a foreign invader. Some 35,000 holy warriors joined the Afghan war from 1979 to 1989. The largest number came from the Middle East. Some were Saudis, among whom was a young man called Osama bin Laden.

The 23-year-old son of a wealthy construction magnate said he arrived in Peshawar for the first time in 1980. He was a very shy person who had no experience of war and, as a fresh graduate from the King Abdul Aziz University, bin Laden had left the luxury of his home to help the mujahidin fighting jihad in Afghanistan. It was the beginning of his long association with Afghan and Pakistani Islamic radicals. By 1984 he was spending most of his time in Peshawar, sometimes with Abdullah Azzam, a Palestinian Islamic scholar and an ideologue who inspired the rush of foreign Muslims to fight in Afghanistan. It was also during this period that he developed links with the ISI, which had become the main conduit for arms and training for the Islamic warriors. The Afghan war placed enormous resources at the agency's disposal. Weapons provided by the CIA were channelled to Afghan fighters through the ISI. By the mid 1980s, every dollar given by the CIA was matched by another from Saudi Arabia. The funds, running into several million dollars a year, were transferred by the CIA to the ISI's special accounts in Pakistan. The backing of the CIA and the funnelling of massive amounts of US military aid helped the ISI develop into 'a parallel structure wielding enormous power over all aspects of government.' It became all-pervasive and there was an unprecedented expansion in the surveillance of political opponents.

Even those in the army were not spared. According to a former senior intelligence officer, part of the ISI's function was to keep a careful watch on the generals and ensure their loyalty to the regime. In the words of Brigadier Yousaf, 'So powerful had the ISI become that apprehension, even fear, of what the ISI could do, was real.' The Afghan war provided the agency with the public profile that it did not have before. Former ISI officials point out that the general expansion the agency underwent as a consequence of its Afghan role had a bearing on its overall functioning. While its role in supervising a successful covert operation in Afghanistan won the ISI international acclaim, at home it was a dreaded name.

The Afghan resistance was projected as part of the global jihad against communism. The ISI's training of guerrillas was integrated with the teaching of Islam. The prominent theme was that Islam was a complete socio-political ideology under threat from atheistic communists. The Afghan war produced a new radical Islamic movement. Besides the holy warriors from Islamic countries, thousands more joined madrasas set up with funding from Saudi Arabia and some other Muslim countries. More than 100,000 foreign Muslim radicals were directly influenced by the Afghan jihad. The military's involvement in the politics of religion, however, had started long before the Afghan jihad. General Zia not only ushered Pakistan into its longest period of military rule, but also tried to turn the country into an ideological state. He extended the army's role in domestic politics much further than defined by earlier military rulers. Previously, the military was seen as the ultimate guarantor of the country's territorial integrity and internal security. But Zia expanded its role as the defender of Pakistan's ideological frontiers as well.

Addressing army officers, Zia argued that, as Pakistan was created on the basis of the two-nation theory and Islamic ideology, it was the duty of the 'soldiers of Islam to safeguard its security, integrity and sovereignty at all costs, both from internal turmoil and external aggression'.

He claimed the state was created exclusively to provide its people with the opportunity to follow 'the Islamic way of life.' Preservation of the country's Islamic character was seen to be as important as the security of the country's geographical frontiers. Zia's military rule differed by its very serious attempt to create an ideological basis for all areas of activities of the state and society. General Zia cleverly used Islam to consolidate his power and legitimize his military rule. The Islamization process became the most important feature of his eleven- year rule and its raison d'e^tre. For General Zia, Pakistan was an Islamic ideological state and therefore politics could not be separated from religion. He believed that he had a divine obligation to establish an Islamic society ruled in accordance with the Qur'an and sharia. Afraid to face a free electorate and having no mandate to govern, the General turned to Allah. He introduced a rigid interpretation of Islamic sharia, thus empowering the clergy. The move to Islamize the state found ready allies among the religious parties, many of which already had close ties with the military. The Jamaat-i-Islami and other Islamic groups were co-opted by the government. For the first time in Pakistan's history, the Islamists occupied important government positions. Being in power helped Jamaat-i-Islami, the most influential and organized mainstream religious party, penetrate state institutions. Thousands of party activists and sympathizers were given jobs in the judiciary, the civil service and educational institutions. These appointments strengthened the hold of the Islamists on crucial state apparatuses for many years to come.

The process of the Islamization of the state and society took place on two levels. Firstly, changes were instituted in the legal system. Sharia courts were established to try cases under Islamic laws. For the first time, the government assumed the role of the collector of religious taxes. Secondly, Islamization was promoted through the print media, radio, television and mosques. Through a series of religious decrees, the government moved to Islamize the civil service, the armed forces and the education system. School textbooks were overhauled to ensure their ideological purity. Books deemed un-Islamic were removed from syllabuses and university libraries. It was made compulsory for civil servants to pray five times a day. Confidential reports of government officials included a section in which the staff were given marks for regularly attending prayers and for having a good knowledge of Islam. General Zia's move to Islamize the army carried the most critical implications. Pakistan's army, carved out of the British Indian army, inherited British traditions and remained a secular organization until General Zia tried to give it a new Islamic orientation. Islam was incorporated into the army's organizational fabric. For the first time Islamic teachings were introduced into the Pakistan Military Academy.

Islamic training and philosophy were made a part of the curriculum at the Command and Staff College. A Directorate of Religious Instruction was instituted to educate the officer corps on Islam. Islamic education also became a part of the promotion exams. The officers were required to read The Quranic Concept of War, a book written by a serving officer, Brigadier S. K. Malik. The officers were taught to be not just professional soldiers, but also soldiers of Islam.

In his foreword to the book, General Zia wrote: 'The professional soldier in a Muslim army, pursuing the goals of a Muslim State, cannot become "professional" if in all his activities he does not take on "the colour of Allah".' To gain promotion an officer was required to be a devout Muslim. Scores of highly professional and secular officers were sidelined for not meeting the criterion of a 'good Muslim'. As a consequence of this policy, many conservative officers reached the senior command level. Radical Islamist ideology permeated the army with the free flow of religious political literature in the armed forces training institutions. Friday prayers at regimental mosques, a matter of individual choice in the past, became obligatory. Mullahs belonging to the Deobandi sect were appointed to work among the troops.

They were supposed to be the bridge for officers between the westernized profession and the faith. Units were required to take noncombatant mullahs with them to the front line. Soldiers were encouraged to attend 'Tablighi' gatherings. The purpose was to indoctrinate cadets and young officers with an obscurantist interpretation of Islam. Many of those cadets later rose to positions of power and took control of sensitive institutions, including the ISI. The change in the social composition of the officer corps also led to the ideological reorientation of Pakistan's army in the 1980s. The army officer corps, till the 1970s, was elitist in character and composition.

But the trend changed. In the past, members of the upper class or the rural aristocracy had largely dominated the army ranks; now the new officers mostly came from the lower and middle social strata. The rank and file of junior officers since the 1970s had come, not from prosperous central Punjab, but from the impoverished and relatively backward northern districts where a fundamentalist religious ethos prevailed. Unlike their predecessors, the new officers did not come from elite English-language schools, but were the product of modest state-run educational institutions. The spirit of liberalism, common in the 'old' army, was practically unknown to them. They were products of a social class that, by its very nature, was conservative and easily influenced by Islamic fundamentalism. They were distinctively less westernized.

Their narrow nationalist orientation and education, professional training and culture made them very receptive to the influence of Islamic groups, particularly to the Jamaat-i-Islami (JI), which freely carried out propaganda work among the officers and circulated Islamic literature. Most importantly, the JI's propaganda among vast numbers of troops was officially sanctioned by commanding officers on the battalion level and above. That led to the evolution of a long-lasting alliance between the military and the mosque. The main objective of the JI was to penetrate the army and use it to seize state power. The practice introduced by General Zia of sending combat officers to universities in Pakistan, in which the JI often had pervasive influence, facilitated the party's objective. The influence of the JI was particularly visible among officers from rural and semi-urban backgrounds. They had a high level of religious intolerance and held extremist views regarding 'external enemies' and the threat to Islam.

The number of officers sporting beards for religious reasons had visibly risen. These young officers constituted the main base for General Zia's regime. According to a retired general, 25 to 30 per cent of the officers had Islamic fundamentalist leanings. Many of them regularly attended 'Tablighi' groups that propagated the faith. They would take time off to join missionary bands preaching a return to purist Islamic values and recruiting other Muslim men to join them. Thousands of soldiers and army officers would join the annual gathering of the TJ at Raiwind on the outskirts of Lahore. More than one million faithful from across the country and abroad attend this Muslim congregation, the largest after the Haj in Mecca. Even the liberals adopted the philosophy on issues like jihad and support for militancy in Kashmir. The humiliating military defeat by the Indian army in the 1971 war, coupled with the disintegration of the country, also had a very deep impact on the psyche of army officers. Many young officers turned to religion for solace and became born-again Muslims. Given this situation, it was not surprising that radical Islamic officers made unsuccessful coup attempts in the mid 1980s. They wanted to bring about an Islamic revolution and establish a theocratic state. The fact that the attempts were crushed and the rebel officers were charged with treason indicated that, notwithstanding its Islamization, the state was not prepared to tolerate a theocratic rule.

The situation in Afghanistan provided inspiration to a whole generation of Pakistani Islamic radicals who considered it their religious duty to fight the oppression of Muslims anywhere in the world. It gave a new dimension to the idea of jihad, which till then had only been employed by the Pakistani state in the context of mobilizing the population against the arch rival – India. The Afghan war saw the privatization of the concept of jihad. Militant groups emerged from the ranks of traditional religious movements, who took the path of an armed struggle for the cause of Islam. The ISI's active role in the Afghan jihad brought Pakistani army officers into direct contact with the radical Islamists.

The handling of jihad also indoctrinated the military and intelligence officers. At least two former ISI chiefs – General Hamid Gul and General Javed Nasir – remained actively involved with Islamic radical movements. Both promoted pan-Islamism and strove for an Islamic revolution that would free Pakistan from perceived western, and particularly American, cultural and political influences. General Gul, who liked to call himself a 'Muslim visionary', succeeded General Rehman in 1987 when the Afghan resistance had entered its most critical juncture.

The most charismatic of the ISI chiefs, he openly aligned himself with the hardline Afghan mujahidin leader, Gulbuddin Hekmatyar, and right-wing Pakistani Islamic parties. He would later take credit for dismantling the Soviet Union. General Gul had worked closely with the CIA, but turned anti-American after the Geneva Accord in 1987, which paved the way for the withdrawal of Soviet forces from Afghanistan. The Accord was signed by the Pakistani civilian government led by Prime Minister Mohammed Khan Junejo against the wishes of President Zia, who believed it deprived the Afghan mujahidin of the opportunity to take over Kabul. Resentment among the military and ISI officers deepened in 1990, just one year after the Soviets pulled out of Afghanistan and the US administration imposed sanctions on Pakistan for its nuclear programme. The CIA ended its support for the Afghan rebels and its links with the ISI went cold. It was a sudden end to the strong link between the two agencies. The military leadership accused the United States of dumping Pakistan after the collapse of the Soviet Union. Long before the Afghan war was over, General Gul had started organizing a new jihad front in Kashmir. 'It is the years of our work that has realized the armed uprising against the Indian forces in Kashmir,' he told me in early 1990 when he was commanding the country's elite armoured corps.

The death of General Zia ul-Haq in a mysterious air crash in August 1988 brought an end to Pakistan's longest-serving military government. It left the generals with the choice of either imposing martial law again or holding elections and transferring power to a democratically elected civilian government. They went for the second option, realizing that a perpetuation of military rule might provoke public resistance and exacerbate the turmoil in an already highly polarised society.

However, the generals were not prepared to pull out completely and leave the political field solely to the politicians, particularly to the daughter of Zulfikar Ali Bhutto, Benazir Bhutto, who now led the Pakistan People's Party, which was certain to sweep the polls. To contain Benazir, the military cobbled together the Islamic Democratic Alliance (IDA), uniting all the right-wing parties under the leadership of Nawaz Sharif. General Aslam Beg, then Chief of Army Staff, and General Gul justified the move by saying it was necessary for the viable functioning of a democratic system.

The main objective, however, was to ensure the military's continued role in the new system, overseen by the generals.

By creating a counterbalance in the form of the IDA, the generals constrained the new government of a political party that had led the resistance against military hegemony for ten years. The military-sponsored alliance comprised a mix of traditional power brokers, religious parties and politicians who had emerged on the scene during the 1980s under military patronage.

General Zia's regime, needing a measure of legitimacy and a social base of support, had co-opted segments of Punjab's dominant socio-economic strata: influential landlords, industrialists and emerging commercial groups. The new leadership of the Pakistan Muslim League thus largely consisted of politicians who owed their political rise to the military's backing. The other important components of the alliance were the right-wing Islamic groups, including the Jamaat-i-Islami, which had been involved in the Afghan jihad against the Soviet forces and the separatist war in Indian-controlled Kashmir.

While the IDA, which carried General Zia's legacy, could not achieve any significant electoral gains in the 1988 elections in the three smaller provinces, it did relatively well in Punjab and prevented the PPP from winning an absolute majority in the

National Assembly. The military reluctantly handed over power to Benazir at the centre, but prevented her party from forming the government in Punjab, the biggest and most important of Pakistan's four provinces, which was being ruled by Nawaz Sharif.

Political manipulation by the ISI helped Sharif retain power in the province with the support of independent members. Benazir Bhutto's assumption of power, touted at the time as the dawn of a new democratic era, was in fact a transition from direct to indirect military rule. The formal restoration of civilian rule in 1988 did not reduce the ISI's clout. A return to the barracks did not mean that the military's structure of control and manipulation had been dismantled. The ISI still kept a close watch on civilian rulers. The strains in civil and military relationships remained the biggest obstacle to democracy taking root in Pakistan.

The Chief of Army Staff remained the power behind the scenes in alliance with the new President, Ghulam Ishaq Khan, who held sweeping powers under the Eighth Amendment in the constitution introduced by General Zia.

For the army, the new political situation offered power without responsibility. The military continued to oversee Pakistan's policies on Afghanistan and India, managing relations with the USA and controlling the country's nuclear weapons programme.

The army high command's decision to rest content with dominance, rather than direct intervention, was based on a careful calculation of the advantages and disadvantages of playing arbiter in Pakistan's highly polarized and conflict-ridden political scene. A hamstrung Benazir Bhutto found herself directly clashing with the army when she removed General Gul from the ISI. The General, who was the architect of the IDA, had never reconciled himself to even restricted civilian rule. Benazir was never trusted by the establishment and many generals made it a point not to salute her. It was in February 1990 when I met General Gul in Multan, where he was posted as the commander of Pakistan's main strike corps, after being sacked from the ISI. It was the period when the army had just concluded a major war exercise called 'Zarb-i-Momin'. The General accused Prime Minister Benazir of trying to make peace with India and questioned her patriotism. 'By conducting the exercise we have blocked her designs to undermine Pakistan's defence,' he said.

It was apparent that the generals were looking for an opportune moment to remove Benazir from power. The clash came to a head when the Prime Minister tried to retire the Chairman of the Joint Chiefs of Staff Committee, Admiral Iftikhar Ahmed Sarohi, and gave a year's extension in service to Lt.-General Alam Jan Mehsud, a senior general believed to be close to her government.

The army top brass saw this as blatant interference in the army's internal affairs. Eventually, on 6 August 1990, President Ghulam Ishaq Khan dismissed her government on charges of corruption and dissolved the National Assembly. President Khan, a former top bureaucrat, was the central pillar of General Zia's military rule and represented his legacy. Benazir's party met a humiliating defeat in the following elections, losing the government even in her home province and political stronghold, Sindh.

The military leadership did not want to take any chances that time. To ensure the IDA's electoral victory, the ISI financed the election campaign of many top Alliance leaders. The list, which was published in national newspapers, contained the names of some leading politicians, including Nawaz Sharif.

Most of them later held important posts in the new government. In 1988, the long-simmering political discontent in Kashmir exploded into a popular uprising against Indian control. Thousands of young Kashmiris crossed over to the Pakistani side of the Line of Control to receive guerrilla training as the Indian authorities tried to crush the insurgency by brute force. Essentially an indigenous rebellion, it soon turned into an armed struggle against Indian forces. Thousands of Kashmiri youths joined the separatist struggle, which was initially led by the independent nationalist organization, Jammu and Kashmir Liberation Front (JKLF)

The ISI used the extensive intelligence and militant network that it had built up during the Afghan war to support a new jihad against the Indian forces in Kashmir. In Afghanistan in the 1980s, jihadist cadres came from the ranks of motivated Islamists across the Muslim world who were prepared to die for the cause, as well as kill the 'communists'. The spirit saw its continuation in Kashmir, which became one of the world's hottest 'Islamic jihad' spots. The ISI's involvement increased further in the early 1990s when, in an attempt to sideline the JKLF, it started supporting the pro-Pakistani Hezb-ul Mujahideen. The move divided the Kashmiri struggle and led to internecine battles. The mid 1990s saw the increasing role of Pakistani-based militant groups. That was when Harkat-ul-Mujahideen (HuM), Lashkar-e-Taiba (LeT) and later Jaish-e-Mohammed (JeM) emerged as the main guerrilla forces in the disputed state. Those hardline Islamic groups changed the complexion of the struggle.

8

Second Sunrise of Indian Jihad

"You who have ruled India for eight hundred years, you who lit the flame of the one true God in the darkness of polytheism: how can you remain in your slumber when the Muslims of the world are awakening?" the al-Qaeda ideologue Asim Umar asked India's Muslims last summer. "If the youth of the Muslim world have joined the battlefields with the slogan 'Shari'a or Martyrdom,' and put their lives at stake to establish the Caliphate, how can you lag behind them? Why is there no storm in your ocean," Mr. Umar demanded to know.

Last week's arrests of key Indian Mujahideen operatives have led to speculation that India's most feared terror group — responsible for savage serial bombings in major cities, including the 2006 attacks on Mumbai's suburban train system — may be disintegrating. Tehseen Akhtar, its key recruiter, is now in prison; so is Muhammad Zarar Siddibapa, its operation chief.

For investigators though, these breakthroughs have brought forth disturbing new evidence that Mr. Umar, and other propagandists like him, are succeeding in calling a new army into being — an army born in Indian towns and cities scarred by communal warfare and hardened in the battlefields of Pakistan's north-west. The dusk that shrouds the Indian Mujahideen heralds, the evidence suggests, the coming of its second sunrise.

THE NEW JIHADIS

Karachi residents Muhammad Fahim and Muhammad Abdul

Walid, held by the Uttar Pradesh police last week, told investigators that they had first been recruited by the Lashkar-e-Taiba, and then broke with it to make their way to a Taliban training camp in Afghanistan's southern Helmand district. Then, they were led by the fugitive Pune *jihadist*, Mohin Chaudhury to the Indian Mujahideen's Karachi-based chief, Riyaz Shahbandri. Faisalabad-based bombmaker Zia-ur-Rahman, Mr. Akhtar's recently arrested deputy, served with Taliban groups in Pakistan's Punjab before volunteering to serve with the Indian Mujahideen fighting across the border.

Meanwhile, new *jihadist* cells have sprung up within India. The recruits include young people, their minds fired by Internet Islamism, as well as veterans once linked to the proscribed Students Islamic Movement of India (SIMI). Fugitive Ranchi resident Haider Ali, the National Investigation Agency (NIA) says, raised volunteers from both these groups for the bombing of the revered Buddhist shrine at Bodh Gaya last year, as an act of vengeance for communal violence against Myanmar's Rohingya Muslim minority.

Mr. Ali's cell, only loosely connected through him to the Indian Mujahideen, followed up that attack with an attempt to assassinate Gujarat Chief Minister Narendra Modi at a rally in Patna, surprising the organisation's leadership in Karachi.

In Tamil Nadu, volunteers at a Chennai college even signed up to serve with *jihadists* in Syria — recruited by local Islamists, and financed by a Singapore-based executive.

Key commanders of the Indian Mujahideen, meanwhile, remain active in Karachi, most important of them being Riyaz Shahbandri, his brother Iqbal Shahbandri and Abdul Subhan Qureshi. There are a host of second-rung leaders still at large, like Mirza Shadab Beg, Shahnawaz Alam, Muhammad "Bada" Sajid, Alamzeb Afridi, Zulfikar Fayyaz "Kagazi," Rahil Sheikh and Ariz Khan. The man who financed them all, ganglord Amir Raza Khan, is also at large.

The western storm

From Internet chats between Mr. Shahbandri and Mr. Siddibapa, recovered by the NIA, we know that several of those men have sought combat training with *jihadists* in Pakistan's north-west, and in Afghanistan, developing skills the Indian Mujahideen's cadre never had.

It has long been evident that the gathering storm of violent Islamism in Pakistan would lash India, too. In 2010, al-Qaeda released a posthumous audio message from Egyptian *jihadi* Said al-Masri, claiming responsibility for the bombing of the German Bakery in Pune. "The person who carried out this operation was a heroic soldier from the Soldiers of the Sacrifice Brigade, which is one of the brigades of Qaedat al-Jihad [the al-Qaeda's formal name] in Kashmir, under the command of Commander Illyas Kashmiri, may Allah preserve him."

Mr. al-Masri's message was wrong on several details of the operation, but for investigators, news that elements of al-Qaeda had developed links with *jihadi* groups acting against India did not surprise anyone.

David Headley, the Pakistani-American Lashkar operative now serving a life term for his role in the 26/11 attacks, had told the NIA of an anti-India "Karachi project" linked to global *jihadi* groups.

Driven by communal events

Following Pakistani military ruler General Pervez Musharraf's 2007 siege of jihadists holed up inside Islamabad's Lal Masjid, Mr. Headley told the NIA, that an ideological war broke out among Pakistan's*jihadis*. In spite of efforts by Pakistan's Inter-Services Intelligence, he said, the "aggression and commitment shown to *Jihad* by the several splinter groups influenced many committed fighters to leave Kashmir-centric outfits and join the Taliban."

In turn, al-Qaeda became increasingly interested in India, as a means of competing for influence and legitimacy with traditional *jihadi* groups like the Lashkar, which were supportive of the Pakistani state. In the wake of 26/11, al-Masri himself released a statement warning India of attacks if it struck against Pakistan.

The renewal of a *jihadist* constituency within India shouldn't be a surprise: the rise of Mr. Modi, and the Hindu nationalist tendencies he represents, has unleashed existential anxieties among large numbers of Indian Muslims. Though the numbers of jihadi recruits are minuscule, the members of the new cells are also true to a familiar pattern. The earliest Indian *jihadist* formation, the Tanzim Islahul Muslimeen, was formed to protect Muslims against communal violence, and carried out its first strike, the 1993 bombings of inter-city express trains, to avenge the demolition of the Babri Masjid.

In interrogations, Indian *Jihad* volunteers have repeatedly said they acted to avenge the Gujarat carnage of 2002. Feroze Ghaswala told police he had volunteered to join *Jihad* training after witnessing the mass burial of 40 Gujarat riot victims.

Peedical Abdul Shibly and Yahya Kamakutty, both successful computer professionals, are alleged to have prepared to carry out attacks in Bangalore. Men from Kerala trained in the mountains of Jammu and Kashmir with the Lashkar-e-Taiba. Zabiuddin Ansari, from Maharashtra, famously ended up in the 26/11 control room.

Founded in April 1977, SIMI, the fountainhead of the modern Indian *jihadist* movement, was itself driven by the forces of communal violence.

From the outset, scholar Yoginder Sikand has said "that Islam alone was the solution to the problems of not just the Muslims of India, but of all Indians and, indeed, of the whole world." It drew thousands disillusioned with traditional politics, Dr. Sikand has recorded, providing supporters "a sense of power and agency which they were denied in their actual lives."

From December 1992, following the demolition of the Babri Masjid, SIMI's language became increasingly aggressive. In a statement in 1996, it declared that since democracy and secularism had failed to protect Muslims, the sole option was to struggle for the caliphate. Soon after, it put up posters calling on Muslims to follow the path of Mahmood Ghaznavi, the 11th century warlord. In 2001, after the 9/11 attacks, SIMI activists organised demonstrations hailing Osama bin-Laden as a "true mujahid."

Early in the summer of 2004, a group of young men fed up with SIMI's inability to act on its own talk gathered in the small coastal town of Bhatkal in Mangalore — and founded what we now call the Indian Mujahideen.

THE JIHADI TRADITION

To understand the durability of the *Jihad* within India, it is important to remember that its cadre are inheritors of a long political tradition. In a manifesto sent to the media after their September 2008 bombings in New Delhi, the group said the attacks were carried out "in the memory of two most eminent Mujahids of India: Sayyed Ahmed Shaheed and Shah Ismail Shaheed (may Allah bestow His Mercy upon them) who had raised the glorious banner of Jihad against the disbelievers." The historian Ayesha Jalal has shown that the notion of *Jihad* was an important theme in both pre-colonial and colonial India. Syed Ahmad and Shah Ismail were killed battling Sikh troops in a failed *Jihad* involving the tribes of Pakistan's north-west.

Historian Stephen Dale has observed that these ideas stretched to the south of India, noting the work of the Sixteenth Century author, Zayn al-Din al-Ma'bari, who chronicled the *Jihad* against Portugal's intrusions into the Indian Ocean, hoping to "inspire the Faithful to undertake a *Jihad* against the worshippers of the cross."

Each bombing the Indian Mujahideen carries out is a medium for a political message enmeshed with India's dystopic communal landscape: that democratic politics cannot defend India's Muslims. India's intelligence and police services deserve credit for the long war they have fought, but it is time for politicians to act to heal our fractured nation.

THE MUMBAI BLASTS AND THE INDIAN MUJAHIDEEN

On Wednesday evening, bombs tore through three separate parts of Mumbai over a 15 minute period. They spanned Dadar West, Zaveri Bazaar, and Opera House. Early estimates of the injury and death toll suggest that this is more lethal than the February 2010 bombing of a bakery in Pune, which killed 14, but much less severe than the November 2008 commando-style raids that killed nearly 170.

Mumbai, as the commercial capital of India, has long been a target of foreign and domestic jihadi groups. For residents, these explosions will trigger terrible memories of a series of blasts in

1993 that killed 250. Those attacks were the first acts of mass casualty terrorism on Indian soil, and the first jihadi (as opposed to, say, separatist) attacks against India outside Kashmir. After a lengthy gap, a pair of CAR bombs killed 50 in 2003, and seven bombs against trains killed 209 in 2006. Since 1993, roughly 700 people have been killed in Mumbai.

THE INDIAN MUJAHIDEEN

Indian sources have indicated, though tentatively, that the Indian Mujahideen (IM) may be responsible. This is an opaque group about which relatively little is known. It first claimed responsibility for serial bombings in multiple north Indian cities in 2007, and came to prominence after attacks in Ahmedabad in 2008. It has also claimed responsibility for numerous other attacks, including those in Jaipur, Bangalore, and Delhi.

Indian TELEVISION channel NDTV noted in 2008 that "investigators say the Indian Mujhadeen is a front for groups operating out of Pakistan most likely the [Pakistan-based group] Lashkar-e-Taiba [LET]". This is almost certainly a severe oversimplification of the group's origins.

The IM is principally the product of the Student's Islamic Movement of India (SIMI). SIMI formed in 1977 within India itself, as a student wing of the Jamaat-e-Islami-i-Hind (though the latter has condemned terrorist attacks, including the 2008 Mumbai attacks). In 1986 SIMI called for the 'liberation' of India's Muslims and, at some point in the 1990s, evolved into a militant organisation with (ongoing) ties to LET.

SIMI then evolved into IM from 2001 after increasing numbers of the group acquired a violent pan-Islamic, but India-focused, agenda (many other members wished to remain non-violent). Praveen Swami, an Indian journalist and expert on Indian jihadi groups, describes IM as 'a loose cluster of semi-autonomous SIMI-linked cells' rather than an independent and separate organisation.

Indian intelligence also claims that elements of the pan-Islamic Harkat ul-Jihad-e-Islami (HUJI, whose operational commander, Ilyas Kashmiri, was recently killed in Pakistan) and a separate criminal-jihadi network led by Aftab Ansari contributed to the formation of IM.

Home-grown terrorism

SIMI's (and, thereafter, IM's) distinguishing characteristic was that it was, essentially, home-grown. Its activists and leaders are virtually all Indian. It recruited lower and middle class Indian Muslims, as well as a smaller number of educated professionals.

Key members of the network were motivated by the 2002 anti-Muslim pogroms in the Indian state of Gujarat; that horrific event proved a boon for wider recruitment too. IM's training was reportedly in places like Kerala and Gujarat, not primarily on Pakistani soil. Core leaders hailed from the Indian state of Uttar Pradesh (UP).

This is quite unlike that GENERATION of groups who cut their teeth on the anti-Soviet Jihad, later shifted to Kashmir with the assistance of the ISI, and today form ad hoc groupings of inter-operable or cooperative networks across Pakistan.

This is crucially important, because it greatly lessens the likelihood that these attacks will precipitate an India-Pakistan crisis, as with the major standoff that occurred during 2001-2.

INDIAN MUHAJIDEEN AND LASHKAR-E-TAIBA

This is not to say that Pakistani intelligence plays no role. SIMI and IM have extensive ties to Pakistan-based groups like LET and HUJI. The general secretary of SIMI, Safdar Nagori, after his arrest in 2008, claimed that the ISI had provided FUNDS to the group. Captured members of LET have also described a broad funding, training, and operational interface between that group and IM.

Indeed, far from being a self-contained group, 'LET serves as a provider of logistical and ideological infrastructure to the regional jihadist movement'-including IM. Christine Fair, a professor at Georgetown, notes that 'SIMI/IM appears to be an important vector of LET infiltration and cultivation of Indian leaders and cadres'.

Interrogations of David Coleman Headley, the Pakistani-American member of LET with a major role in the 2008 Mumbai attacks, pointed to the existence of a 'Karachi Project'. This was a scheme, overseen by the ISI, to mobilise Indian Muslims for attacks on Indian urban targets, moving them to Pakistan via third countries like Bangladesh or Nepal.

Vikram Sood, the former head of India's foreign intelligence service, argues that this heralds 'a new phase of terrorism within India, where international terrorist groups like LET and HUJI (and through them Al Qaeda), are likely to exert influence on a small and diffused group of individuals to take up arms against the state in the name of religion'.

The devastating 2006 attack on multiple Mumbai targets was, according to some ACCOUNTS, a LET operation implemented through SIMI or IM. This indicates the depth and strength of ties between these ostensibly discrete groups. In turn, LET is closely connected to the ISI.

Although THE DEGREE of granular ISI control over LET operations is contested, most authoritative accounts are in agreement that, at the very least, the state determines the parameters in which the group can operate. Christine Fair, for instance, notes simply that 'for Pakistan, LET is an existential asset in the same way that it is an existential enemy for countries like India and even the United States'.

Although the semi-indigenous character of IM undercuts repeated Indian claims that Indian Muslims are not a meaningful part of jihadi terrorism, this should not be understood as diminishing the major problem of Pakistani state sponsorship and de facto protection of militant organisations. Although it is important to remember that SIMI and IM would not vanish were Pakistan to become cooperative, their operational capabilities and underlying strength would suffer serious damage.

Implications for the India-Pakistan relationship

But SIMI and IM, unlike LET or Jaish-e-Mohammed or other such groups, are perceived to be outside the direct control or immediate influence of the Pakistani state. One officer involved with the investigation at Zaveri Bazaar did observe that this "attack is very different from the one we had in 2008... here there is no

Pakistani involvement it is very clear from the early evidence we have collected."

This will limit not just Indian demands for retaliation against Pakistan, but also persuade influential states, and the US in particular, that Indian action would not be warranted. Moreover, the use of explosives rather than *fedayeen* (commando) tactics lessens the prolongation of the attack and therefore the theatrical effect. This, too, lessens the prospect of a forceful response.

Indian investigators have not yet made any conclusions about responsibility. The absence of an email claiming responsibility, the usual practice of IM hitherto, is strange. Moreover, a series of arrests by Indian security officials since 2008 had weakened the group's operational capability. In December 2010, Indian authorities claimed that four LET members had entered Mumbai with the intention of carrying out an attack.

It remains possible that these attacks were carried out by (1) LET, under the supervision of the ISI (perhaps to deflect attention from the Pakistani military's travails at home); (2) LET, without the supervision but with the cognizance of the ISI; (3) LET, with neither the supervision nor cognizance of the ISI; (4) a separate but affiliated Pakistan-based group; (5) by IM, acting in close concert with Pakistani affiliates; (6) IM, acting in relative isolation.

These (non-exhaustive) possibilities are not all equally likely. Prior attacks suggest that scenario (5) is the most plausible, though it is crucially important to stress that this assessment is purely speculative. The Indian authorities' praiseworthy reticence in apportioning blame indicates that the evidence is still ambiguous.

If IM turns out to have been at the front-line of the attack, this is almost certainly enough to guarantee that India-Pakistan relations will remain stable. India's prime minister, Manmohan Singh, is suffering serious domestic political difficulties. He has staked large amounts of political capital on the resumed dialogue with Pakistan, which was scheduled to convene later this month, and has been perceived as relatively successful by both parties.

If, however, LET's role is prominent, then the situation is far more unpredictable-options will quickly appear. In the longer-term, it is imperative to understand *both* the domestic factors enabling the consolidation of SIMI and IM *and* the thicket of cross-border links on which they rely for their operational potency; ignoring either of these will simply allow the stream of such killings to continue apace.

JIHADIST DISCOURSE INCREASINGLY TARGETING INDIA'S MUSLIM POPULATION

Islamist militants, including Al-Qaeda, have recently released a number of appeals to India's Muslim population to join them in Jihad. Animesh Roul reports from Delhi on these latest attempts and examines whether they may prove to be more successful than previously.

Transnational militant Islamist groups such as Al-Qaeda and its affiliates seem to be desperately attempting to attract India's sizeable Muslim population to global Jihad. Some recent developments in regard to such attempts to entice Indian Muslims have necessitated renewed attention and an assessment of whether groups like Al-Qaeda could succeed or if the call to Jihad will falter, as previously.

In June 2013, a Pakistan-based veteran jihadist ideologue, Maulana Asim Umar, released a video message exhorting Indian Muslims to join the global jihadist movement. Entitled "Tere darya me tofaan quyon nahi hai" (Urdu for "Why is there no storm in your ocean?"), Umar lamented the lack of jihadist spirit among India's Muslim community whose "forefathers had descended into the battlefields of Jihad". To remind Indian Muslims about the historical glory of Muslim rule over the Indian subcontinent, citing Muslim kings of long ago such as Tipu Sultan and Emperor Aurangzeb, the message prodded Indian Muslims to take inspiration from the ongoing militant Islamist insurgencies in Afghanistan, Iraq, or Yemen. Invoking the concept of the Ummah (the global Islamic community), Umar urged India's Muslim population to wage Jihad in India and elsewhere, assuring them that Islamic fighters from Egypt, Libya, Palestinian Territories, Saudi Arabia, Syria, and beyond would come to help.

On 15 January, Al-Qaeda leader Ayman al-Zawahiri released a video directly addressing "our brothers and our people in Kashmir, Gujarat, Assam, and Ahmedabad who are living under the dark shade of Hindu occupation". The places mentioned were a specific reference to episodes of inter-communal violence between India's Hindus and Muslims, and Zawahiri expressed the hope that such events would "expose the extent of deception and falsity of the nationalist democratic way, which calls for your participation, side-by-side with the Hindus, in a national democratic system that brings together Hindus and Muslims". He added, "Perhaps you would have realised by now that this system brings Muslims and Hindus together only to present the Muslims as an easy prey for the Hindus."

Earlier, in October 2013, a previously unknown group, identifying itself as Ansar-ut-Tawheed fi Bilad al-Hind, which in Arabic and Urdu means the 'Partisans of Monotheism in the Land of India', released a video message on Islamist forums vowing to avenge "atrocities" committed against Muslims in the country. The video, which was released by Ansar-ut-Tawheed's media wing, Al-Isabah Media, and was entitled "Usood al-Hind", or the 'Lions of India' in Urdu, called for Indian Muslims to participate in global Jihad.

Ansar-ut-Tawheed released a second video in November, entitled "Kandahar Se Dehli Ki Taraf", or 'From Kandahar to Delhi' in Urdu, which exhorted Indian Muslims to take revenge against the Hindu population in retaliation for instances of heavy inter-communal violence in the country, such as in Gujarat in 2002, and more recently in Assam, Andhra Pradesh, and Uttar Pradesh states-the same incidents referenced by Zawahiri in January 2014. The video contains still images of communal violence, followed by a statement by group leader Maulana Abdul Rahman al-Hindi, flanked by seven militants.

TARGET INDIA

Ansar-ut-Tawheed's videos pay homage to and eulogise those Islamist militants who have perpetrated punitive attacks in India since the early 1990s. Terming all dead Islamist militants as martyrs, the videos are dedicated to all mujahideen of Indian origin who are fighting on jihadist battlefields in different parts of the world.

Ansar-ut-Tawheed's two messages and Umar's video have the same Islamic references, citing verses from the Quran and jihadist mythology depicting the "black flag of the Khurasan [a historic reference to parts of Afghanistan and areas of Central Asia]" piercing the heart of India, seemingly indicating that this new anti-India jihadist wave is originating from Afghanistan and Pakistan. The mythology cites an army from Khurasan waging the Ghazwat-ul-Hind (meaning the 'Battle of India' in Arabic)-also cited as Ghazwa-e-Hind in Urdu-for the re-establishment of the khilafa (the Islamic caliphate).

However, there is a slight difference in the messages from the two different sources. Although Umar's video tries to exhort Indian Muslims to join militant Islamist groups either in Syria or elsewhere to fight Western forces, Ansar-ut-Tawheed's messages sound a war cry against India, calling its Muslim population to join in the group's battle to overthrow the Hindu supremacy and to facilitate the establishment of an Islamic state under sharia (Islamic law).

An important aspect of the above-mentioned messages is the use of Urdu-along with verses in Arabic and subtitles written in Devanagari script (Hindi)-that is widely prevalent, both written and spoken, within the Muslim communities in northern India. Jihadist media have been translated into Hindi and Urdu on earlier occasions in order to appeal to the Muslim population of India. For example, in September 2012, a message by Al-Qaeda in the Arabian Peninsula (AQAP) ideologue Sheikh Harith bin Ghaazi Al-Nadhaari, entitled "Who will Fight America? For it has offended Allah and His messenger", was translated into Hindi by Deen Al-Haqq media. The latter has subsequently released further translations of jihadist statements into Hindi and Urdu via Islamist forums.

There are several reasons for India being such a prime jihadist target. India, which is a Hindu dominated country, has the largest Muslim population in the world after Indonesia and Pakistan. Arguably, this is the prime motive for transnational militant Islamist groups such as Al-Qaeda to attract a segment of alienated and disgruntled young Muslims in the country, which could be considered to be a major future recruitment ground for global Jihad. Among the other notable factors that continually draw jihadist attention are the perceived atrocities committed by authorities in the Muslim-dominated state of Jammu and Kashmir, the long-running animosity with Pakistan, and India's pursuit of its strategic interests in Afghanistan.

United jihadist front?

Jihadist discourse regarding India frequently cites a hadith (a report of the deeds and sayings of the Prophet Muhammad), stating, "Allah has saved two groups of the Ummah from hellfire; the group that will invade Al-Hind [India] and the group that will be with Isa Ibn-e-Maryam [Jesus] in Damascus." This seems to be one of the key doctrinal factors behind the renewed jihadist surge against India.

Proponents of a unified global ummah have long perceived that India, as a geographical and demographical entity, should be part of the khilafa, and Al-Qaeda and other affiliated jihadist organisations fully endorse this view and the Ghazwat ul-Hind concept. The concept is surprisingly unifying when considered across the relevant spectrum of Islamist militant groups in Pakistan and Afghanistan, from transnational jihadists such as Al-Qaeda to nationalist Islamist actors such as the Taliban, Pakistani sectarian groups such as Lashkar-e-Jhangvi (LeJ), and Kashmir-centric jihadists such as Jaish-e-Mohammed (JeM).

In a March 2010 edition of JeM's Urdu-language weekly publication Al-Qalam, Pakistani cleric Mufti Asghar Khan Kashmiri claimed that the ongoing Ghazwat ul-Hind (referring to the Kashmiri insurgency) was a continuation of a series of battles begun by the Prophet Muhammad. Senior Harakat-ul-Jihad-ul-Islami (HUJI) commander Ilyas Kashmiri vowed in October 2009 to wage Ghazwat ul-Hind against India, before his reported death in an unmanned aerial vehicle (UAV) missile strike in Pakistan's Federally Administered Tribal Areas (FATA) in June 2011. Similarly, in a February 2011 speech, Lashkar-e-Tayyiba (LeT) leader Hafiz Muhammad Saeed threatened, "If freedom is not given to the Kashmiris, then we will occupy the whole of India including

Kashmir. We will launch Ghazwa-e-Hind." The Tehrik-e-Taliban Pakistan (TTP) has also released a number of statements threatening India. In January 2013, then TTP commander Wali-ur-Rehman Mehsud warned that once the group had established an Islamic state under sharia in Pakistan, its focus would turn to India and the establishment of an Islamic state therein. One month later, TTP commander Asmatullah Muawiya threatened that Kashmir would become the next battlefield for militants following the scheduled US withdrawal from Afghanistan in 2014.

India has also featured in Al-Qaeda's propaganda on a number of occasions since late 2001. In April 2006, Zawahiri-then serving as deputy leader-for the first time appeared in a video in which he praised the jihadist movements fighting the Indian state in Jammu and Kashmir. In August 2007, US national and Al-Qaeda propagandist Adam Yahya Gadahn (alias Azzam al-Amriki) stated in a video message that US and Indian interests and their diplomatic missions were Al-Qaeda's "legitimate targets". Al-Qaeda's first direct message to India came in February 2009 when senior commander Mustafa Abu al-Yazid (alias Saeed al-Masri) warned the country of violent consequences if it attacked neighbouring Pakistan. In September 2012, Al-Qaeda's Urdu-language spokesperson, Ahmad Farooq, warned the Indian government that the group would launch attacks in retaliation for alleged atrocities perpetrated against Muslims in the northeast Indian state of Assam.

Indigenisation of Jihad

These increasing references to India and calls to its Muslim population have raised many questions within Indian security establishments, particularly whether elements of the indigenous Muslim population-especially those disenchanted, alienated, and vulnerable to radicalisation-will prove to be susceptible to the jihadist rhetoric and discourse.

To date, Al-Qaeda's influence on Indian Muslims has been largely limited, and its jihadist ideology has failed to affect their psyche. To a certain degree this is due to the fact that the indigenous Muslim population largely adheres to the moderate Sufi form of Islam, and that the community is largely well integrated into

India's societal structures-despite periodic instances of inter-communal violence.

Nonetheless, there have been several well-documented occurrences of Muslims of Indian origin involved in, or arrested on suspicion of, terrorist plots internationally that have served to challenge the potential complacency of the Indian authorities over the country's cohesive social structures. A cursory examination of the cases of four such individuals seemingly indicates that each individual was at least under the influence of Al-Qaeda ideology, if not under direction from the group itself.

Dhiren Barot (alias Abu Musa al-Hindi) was a UK national of Indian origin who scouted targets for Al-Qaeda in New York ahead of the 11 September 2001 attacks and was arrested in 2004 by UK authorities. Subsequently, he pleaded guilty to plotting to attack the New York Stock Exchange (NYSE), the International Monetary Fund (IMF) office, and the World Bank office in New York on behalf of Al-Qaeda. He was sentenced to life in prison in November 2006 but this was reduced to 30 years in prison on appeal in May 2007.

Like Barot, Haroon Rashid Aswat was also a UK national of Indian origin. He was arrested in the United Kingdom in 2005 on a US arrest warrant on suspicion of participation in attempting to establish an Al-Qaeda training camp in the US state of Oregon in 1999. The US government requested his extradition to face these charges, but in April 2013, the European Court of Human Rights ruled that this extradition would breach Aswat's rights-a decision that the UK government appealed five months later with no success.

Kafeel Ahmed was an Indian national who worked and studied in the UK in the early-to-mid 2000s. He was one of two militants involved in the June 2007 attack at Glasgow International Airport in the UK, when a vehicle filled with propane tanks was driven into the airport terminal building and set alight. The attack did not cause any serious injury, apart from to Ahmed himself, who died in hospital over a month later. A subsequent investigation into Ahmed revealed that he possessed significant militant Islamist materials, including Osama bin Laden's speeches, indicating that he was at least motivated by militant Islamist ideology, if not specifically by Al-Qaeda.

Finally, Mohammed Niaz Rashid, an Indian national, was arrested in the French capital Paris in May 2011 on arrival from Algeria, on suspicion of plotting terrorist acts. In October 2013, he was jailed for eight years by a French court in Paris. Indian officials also alleged that Rashid was a member of an organisation affiliated with indigenous militant Islamist group the Students Islamic Movement of India (SIMI).

Domestic jihadists

Although these four cases are largely isolated and mostly involve the Indian Muslim diaspora, the alleged link with SIMI in at least one case is noteworthy. The SIMI leaders and fellow indigenous militant Islamist group Indian Mujahideen have been vocal in their support of Al-Qaeda and its ideology. For example, both organisations are committed to propagating a fundamentalist interpretation of Islam, the creation of a global ummah, waging Jihad, and establishing an Islamic state in accordance with Quranic tenets.

The Indian Mujahideen was formed from a small core of the most violent wing of SIMI, and the two groups have maintained a symbiotic relationship. In the mid-to-late 2000s, the Indian Mujahideen increased the intensity of its armed campaign and carried out a series of high-profile improvised explosive device (IED) attacks in India's urban centres. The first attack, for which the Indian Mujahideen claimed responsibility, was the detonation of six IEDs across three cities in Uttar Pradesh state in November 2007-although the group had also claimed responsibility for an earlier double-IED attack in Hyderabad, Andhra Pradesh, in August 2007, which killed almost 50 people. Indian authorities subsequently linked the group to the July 2006 IED attacks in Mumbai that left over 200 people dead.

Over the following year, the Indian Mujahideen took responsibility for a series of bombings in major cities, such as Jaipur (May 2008), Ahmedabad (July 2008), Bangalore (July 2008), and in the national capital New Delhi (September 2008), killing at least 166 people. After an operational lull of over a year, an Indian Mujahideen IED attack in the city of Pune in February 2010 left 17 people dead. Thereafter, the group has launched intermittent IED attacks across India, primarily focusing on religious and court buildings, crowded market places, and business centres. Security forces have also alleged that the Indian Mujahideen was responsible for multiple IED attacks in the Indian state of Bihar: at the Bodh Gaya temple and at a political rally in Patna, in July and October 2013 respectively. However, the group released no claim of responsibility at the time.

Although Indian Mujahideen elements have additionally worked as a support network for foreign militant groups operating in India, such as HUJI and LeT, there is also increasing evidence that the group has been influencing and motivating young Muslims with stories about the plight of fellow Muslims in Afghanistan, Chechnya, Iraq, and elsewhere. The Indian Mujahideen has also appealed for greater international support for its cause. Although it is yet to release any specific video messages, the group's propaganda manifestos contain Quranic verses and invoke the ummah for help in its Jihad against India. For example, following the May 2008 Jaipur attacks, the group emailed a statement claiming responsibility entitled "Declaration of open war against India", which linked the attacks to the broader global Jihad and warned the US and UK in particular that "Muslims are one across the globe". It added that Western visitors to India "will be welcomed by our suicide attackers". Similarly, the Indian Mujahideen's September 2010 manifesto, called "As we bleed, so you will seep", makes an appeal, saying, "O Muslim umma! Awake from deep slumber, these Hindus are recklessly killing your brothers and sisters." A December 2010 manifesto, entitled "Let's feel the pain together", urges all Muslim countries to voice concern at the perceived suppression and injustice towards Muslims in India, calling the country an "empire of falsehood and tyranny".

Ongoing struggle

The potential threat posed by indigenous groups that are successfully linking up with foreign militant groups in order to launch attacks was underlined in mid-to-late 2013 following the capture of alleged senior Indian Mujahideen commander Muhammad Ahmad Zarar Siddibappa (alias Yasin Bhatkal) in August in an operation along the Indo-Nepali border. In a series of statements over the following months, Bhatkal allegedly revealed to his interrogators at the counter-terrorism National Investigation Agency (NIA) in November that the group was planning to join with Al-Qaeda to launch attacks in India. The statement that Bhatkal provided for the NIA also allegedly revealed that the group's senior commanders in Pakistan maintained a relationship, based on funding and logistical support, with Pakistan's Directorate for Inter-Services Intelligence (ISI). However, none of this information could be independently substantiated, and Pakistan has denied any such allegations.

Nonetheless, India's Intelligence Bureau (IB) reported in early 2010 that information had emerged that Al-Qaeda was seeking to collaborate with indigenous groups similar to SIMI and the Indian Mujahedeen to establish militant networks across India. That said, Bhatkal's alleged revelations about the efforts undertaken by two of the Indian Mujahideen's senior Pakistan-based commanders, identified as Mohammed Riyaz Shabandri (alias Riyaz Bhatkal) and Mirza Shadab Baig, to meet with Zawahiri on an undisclosed date speak volumes. Bhatkal claimed that the two were unable to see Zawahiri, but instead met with an aide to discuss possible collaboration. Through such meetings, Bhatkal allegedly revealed that Al-Qaeda had tasked the Indian Mujahideen with targeting foreign nationals, including Jews, in India.

However, no such attacks have occurred, and the providence and veracity of the reports remain difficult to prove. Nevertheless, the developing of such links would make a lot of sense tactically, if not strategically, for Islamist militant groups that are looking to either operate directly in India or generate and support recruits there. The statements by actors such as Ansar-ut-Tawheed and Asim Umar indicate that there is a growing recognition of the importance of India's Muslim population in this regard, with Zawahiri admitting in his latest messages that the "struggle is a long one", and "Jihad is in need of consistent support in terms of men, finances, and expertise". As such, Al-Qaeda and other groups may be increasingly forced to develop so far untouched areas for recruits, funding, and support, with India seemingly being a prime candidate. However, it remains to be seen whether they will prove to be capable of successfully or sufficiently subverting India's integrationist, liberal form of Islam.

"THE FUTURE OF INDIAN INTERNAL SECURITY"

India is a cyclopean nation with myriad languages, a veritable babel of tongues, and a plethora of religions and faiths. Unity in diversity is our heritage, and respect for all faiths and religions has been our innate strength and a source of survival against all odds and obduracy.

The colourful assortment of Indian festivals and fairs, as diverse as its land, is an eternal expression of the spirit of celebration. Observed with enthusiasm and gaiety, festivals are like gems ornamenting the crown of Indian Culture. India is a mosaic in which different pieces retain their identity while contributing to a colourful collage. From the eternal snows of the Himalayas to the cultivated peninsula of far South, from the deserts of the West to the humid deltas of the East, Indian lifestyles clearly glorify its geography.

Post Independence, India has emerged as a strong nation in all aspects, viz. technological, economic, defense, education, sports, tourism and the likes. India has embarked upon a high growth trajectory in economic development. It cropped up as a great economy, with a healthy growth rate of 6.7 %, amid the economic mishap that engulfed almost the entire world, with the World Economy dipping by 0.3 % in 2009-10.

Its poverty alleviation is making slow and steady, if not a spectacular progress. It is a Nuclear and Missile power. Indian Army is third largest in the world, equipping its 'Jawans' with the requisite skills at 15 state-of-the-heart Training centers. Some of the leading names in Indian arsenal are INS Viraat, Vikrant & Shakti, Prithvi, Agni, Akash, Brahmos, Tejas & MBT-Arjun. The recent Nuclear Deal has given a new dimension to Indian Defense power. It is coming to be accepted as a major global player and one of the balancers in the global balance of power system.

While India has established itself in the global arena and registered a phenomenal growth, specter of security threats is haunting the nation. The menace of threats has been increasing over the years. The multi-facet, pernicious consequences of terrorism and security threats need be known to the world so as to facilitate the formulation of effective plans to ridicule it. The entire growth process will come to a screeching halt if security concerns are not timely and adequately addressed. Through this essay, an attempt has been made to bring out the various security concerns India is facing from both inside as well as outside the country, which of them are more severe and what measures can be employed to eliminate them.

Security Threats – the two facets

National security refers to the security of a nation that includes protection of its territorial integrity, sovereignty and advancement of vital national interests. And, a declaration of an intention or determination to inflict national security is called a threat. Threats are a matter of perception. Their assessments take into account capacities, not so much intentions, of a potential adversary. There can be two types of threat – external and internal.

The two sources of security threats to India's stability are gravely impinging on her internal law and order situation. Manifestations of threat range from communal/sectarian violence to Jihadi terrorism, separatist insurgencies in northeast and Naxalite extremist militancy. A new report from US has revealed that besides persistent and significant external threats from groups like Pakistan's Lashkar-e-Taeba and Jaish-e-Mohammad and Bangladesh's Harakat-ul-Jihad-i-Islami-Bangladesh, India faces numerous attacks from domestic terror outfits. The report also said that over 1000 people have died from terrorist attacks in India in 2009.

The nexus

In the changing security scenario, it is becoming increasingly difficult to separate internal and external threats to security. Both of these are posing challenges before India to maintain the stability and security conditions in the country. However, it should be maintained that internal cohesion and strength bolsters a nations' overall strength, deters its adversaries, enhances the morale of its citizens and safeguards its national security. No nation can be secured unless its internal security is also ensured. A nation in chaos cannot be secured from external threats. Internal strife and disorder can damage national interests, endanger the lives of citizens, lead to breakdown of law and order, make enforcement of laws difficult & the country more vulnerable to external threats. In such a state, society cannot progress smoothly nor can citizens feel secured.

Also, in the Arthashastra, Kautilya wrote that a state could be at risk from four types of threats-internal, external, externally-aided internal and internally-aided external. He advised that of these four types, internal threats should be taken care of immediately, which are far more serious than external threats. The most dangerous enemy is the enemy within.

India's story of economic growth, its official entry into the nuclear club with the NSG waiver and an overall growing global clout justifies its third stand, with eight percent of global power, in the list of the World's most powerful nations, as per the Global Governance Report 2025 issued by National Intelligence Council and EU's Institute for Security Studies. On the same toll, it should also be realized how the Indian Prime Minister defined the largest challenges facing India at the beginning of 2010 – "Terrorism, Naxalism, Communalism, Corruption and Regionalism", which can also be attributed as the various internal threats haunting the country. India is experiencing internal security problems due to insurgency movements, ethnic conflicts, religious fundamentalism or cussed political polarization.

So, let's now unpack and explore the various kinds of internal security threats India is facing, reasons that lead to these security concerns, and form a better opinion as to why internal security is a vital element to national security.

Naxalite Insurgency

Naxalism, synonymous with Left Wing Extremism, has come to pose the single biggest threat to India's internal security.

Revolutionary Left Wing violence, which has persisted for a long time now, has assumed serious and threatening proportions. In fact, it has emerged as India's security blind spot. Today, the Security Experts describe the Naxal Groups as a direct challenge to the might of India. In words of Mr. Ajit Dovel, the former Director of Bureau of Indian Intelligence, "Naxalism is now a bigger threat to the country than the Islamic Militancy in Kashmir or the Separatist Militancy in the North – East."

The Naxalite problem has grown exponentially over the last few years. The recent attacks on security personnel and civilians have shown how violent and barbaric the Naxalities have become. They have stopped being rebels protesting against the government machinery, and become domestic terrorists/militants. One can never forget the biggest Maoist attack in April 2010, when at least 70 CRPF Jawans were killed & several injured in the ambush in Dantewada District in Chhattisgarh. What started as a purely agrarian dispute in a small place called Naxalbari in West Bengal has today transformed into the biggest armed insurrection that the State has witnessed since its inception over sixty years ago.

Naxalism, in the light of its violent nature and pre-defined aims, is a 'political ideology', and 'not a socio – economic movement dedicated to uplift the poor'. Naxals believe in Marxist – Leninist as well as Moist methodologies. These twin ideologies extol the Naxal violence as means to "seize political power". Naxals do not believe in parliamentary democracy and consider state as an agent of aberration of the elite class, which does not cater to the interests of the lower strata of society.

There is what is known in India as a "Red Corridor" in which the Maoist are particularly present, which stretches for 2000 km along the entire length of India's east coast from the city of Sikkim in the north to the outer edge of the southern state of Tamil Nadu. The States most strongly affected by militant Maoist activity are West Bengal, Jharkhand, Orissa, Andhra Pradesh, Chhattisgarh, Bihar, Karnataka, Madhya Pradesh, Maharashtra, and Uttar Pradesh. The primary reason for the "success" of the Maoist movement is to be found in the severe poverty and consequent dissatisfaction of the rural populations. The region comprising backward rural areas and dense forests is ideally suited for Maoists to carry out the Guerilla Warfare strategies and trainings.

Till recently, Naxalism has been considered more as a Law and Order problem of the States, and less as an issue to be dealt with by the Central Government. The States have used inadequately armed, equipped, trained and motivated police forces and other resources in a 'switch on' and 'switch off' mode. There has been a lack of lucid analysis and consistency in formulating and implementing a viable strategy. However, the Central Government has woken up to the problem now. In late January 2010, the Union government began a renewed offensive strategy to curb the escalating Naxal pressure – "Operation Green Hunt". The aim was to restore the Rule of Law in the Red Corridor region. A total of 42 battalions of the Central Reserve Police Force (CRPF) and the Indo-Tibetan Border Police (ITBP) are involved in the action, over 60,000 armed forces.

Maoist volcano erupted in Nepal and its lava is spilling over vast Indian territories. In recent months, the rebels have succeeded in extending the radius of their actions considerably and in exploiting the social grievances of the local population. However, the Naxalite problem is not just about the violence, it is also about the State's failure to adequately provide for the tribals. The Central and State Governments should ensure that the fruits of development should reach those backward areas as well. Only then we can lay down a strong foundation for an equitable, stable and peaceful society.

Religious Fundamentalism and Ethnic Conflicts

A plethora of communal riots have plagued the nation since independence. The earlier communal discord was adopted by the British through their 'Divide and Rule' policy, which has now been scooped by the terrorists. Communalists of various shades and categories have consistently harped on the differences and encouraged divisive trends. This has been especially noticeable in the highly sensitive and vulnerable regions where the timber has only to be ignited by a match stick, the embers remain hot. Even a minor and apparently innocuous incident is sufficed to arouse communal passions and provoke rioting.

Islamist fundamentalist organizations rooted in religious obscurantism have long been prone to sudden bursts of irrational violence at the slightest provocation. The Kashmir conflict and upsurge of the groups like Student Islamic Movement of India (SIMI), Harkat-ul-Jihad-ul-Islami Bangladesh (HUJBI), Jama'at-ul-Mujahideen Bangladesh (JMB), and Jama'at-e-Islami Bangladesh (JIB) is a glaring representation of a similar 'fundamentalist religious empowerment'. Such communal conflicts have resulted in tragic traumas and an intolerant atmosphere of hostility and hatred created by the terrorists, who bluff themselves as Jihadi – in the name of almighty Allah.

Communal terrorism poses yet another grave threat to India's sovereignty and integrity. It subverts the fundamental rule of law, denies basic rights to citizens, endangers the social fabric, and threatens political and economic stability. The crying need of the hour demands an introspective and corrective action at different levels to curb the concern that the Indian might may falter and succumb before the evil designs of caste and communal politics.

Drug Trafficking

With the 'Golden Crescent' and the 'Golden Triangle' in Indian neighbourhood, drug trafficking poses yet another threat to our internal security. Drug syndicates are generating huge funds, a part of which is being used to give financial support to some of the subversive terrorist groups. The intelligence agencies like the ISI are recruiting a number of 'carriers' in drug trafficking as their agents. These agencies provide legal immunity for their criminal activities in their own country in addition to giving them financial and logistical support. The serious internal security problem, if not checked effectively can develop an external dimension.

Political Polarization

The success of organized crime within the country is linked up with the nature of governance. Indian politics has attained a bad odour and generally implies unfair underhand dealings, exploitation of poor and the ignorant, and seizure of power by all available methods. Politics is often characterized by the dominance of the politician – bureaucracy – crime nexus. Most of the politicians building their careers on the basis of linguistic, caste, communal and ethnic bases are less interested in overall national security considerations than in the parochial one of getting money for their politics, thereby leading to caste wars and ethnic conflicts. The pernicious implications of Vote-Bank Politics lead to numerous socio-economic and religious conflicts within Indian society, and forging unity and security in a diverse society, especially where conflicts generate violence, is no mean task.

Corruption

It is the mother of all evils. Corruption – an act done with intent to gain an undue advantage; a behavior deviating from ethics, morality, tradition and law; lack of integrity & abuse of power in decision making process. Taken simply, corruption is the use of public office for private gain. It is a global phenomenon which has progressively increased over time, and is no rampant in all societies across the globe. It is a by-product of the close nexus between bureaucrats, criminals and politicians. As rightly said by John Acton,

"Power tends to corrupt, and absolute power corrupts absolutely."

Corruption is a vicious circle which has engulfed almost all the sections of the society under its shackles, and is continually escalating. From Tehelka Scandal to Share Paper Scam to Cash for Votes Scam to Commonwealth trauma, the imprints of corruption can clearly be visualized. Pelf, power and prestige, no matter what means are adopted and how many emotions are crushed, have become the obsessive growth stairs, facilitating corruption. In nations like India, the Government will have to call on the patriotism of citizens to fight against the evils of corruption to rejuvenate their minds and stir their sullen sole. The golden message by Rabindranath Tagore – 'Kicks raise dust, not crops' – has to be instilled in their minds to ensure National Security.

EFFECTIVE POLICING FOR NATIONAL SECURITY

It is apparent that the existing security policies and the primary instruments for tackling law and order and internal security have not been able to cope with these growing challenges. The history of last sixty years proves that the most difficult problem in addressing to our internal security concerns is not our capability to deal with them in terms of men and material, but our inability to organize our national security planning and management framework in an effective manner to anticipate threats in time. If that is efficiently addressed with foresight, half the task of managing the threat would be done. So, this section attempts to propose some suggestions that, if effectively employed, could bolster the country's security and national integration.

Strengthening the Indian Police

A very basic pre-requisite of any internal security system is an adequate number of well – trained policemen. The problems of inadequate number of policemen and deficiency in their training methods have been underlined time and again. Unfortunately, there has not been adequate progress in these areas. The present dwindling state of Indian Police provides a fertile soil for imperialists to hatch their plans for secessionist agitations. We have to adopt certain prudent measures to turn the situation around, and some of these are mentioned as under.

The Police force should be insulated from political interference and politicization so as to provide them an independent stature to work towards achieving the eminently desired goals for national integration. Secondly, Police training and capacity building should be given special emphasis.

Particular attention should be laid upon sensitizing them in regard to human rights. Community oriented Police should be encouraged. Thirdly, the service conditions of constables and lower ranking officials should be improved so as to assure them economic and social stability, & arouse their passion towards the Police and the country.

Finally, the proposed measures by the Central Government should be implemented as soon as possible, such as Crime and Criminal Tracking Network System (CCTNS) to facilitate the collection, storage, retrieval, analysis, transfer and sharing of data among police stations; National Database Grid (NATGRID) to network 21 sets of databases to achieve quick, seamless and secured access to desired information; and establishment of Unified National Counter Terrorism Centre (NCTC).

Role of Intelligence

Intelligence is a key to make the police effective, particularly in preventing or dealing with naxalism and terrorism, insurgency, communal riots, mass migrations and other internal security threats. One cannot deny the fact that India is not among laggards since it has established strong measures to tackle counter-terrorism and counter-intelligence, and one such instance is the Multi Agency Centre. MAC shares the intelligence with other agencies, including those of the State Governments and Union Territories on a continuous and real time basis. Reciprocally, the other agencies are also obliged to share intelligence with the Multi Agency Centre.

However, India's track record on internal security and counter-terrorism makes it obvious that the Intelligence establishment in the country at various levels requires revamping. The intelligence agencies are yet to develop new tradecraft and techniques for the penetration of non-state actors through human and technical moles, for the collection of intelligence, greater expertise in collation, analysis, and better coordination between intelligence and law enforcement agencies. This effort is underway now and should produce better results in the future.

Centre – State coordination

The Union – State nexus has always been a matter of controversy. The episodes of this bitter relationship have been repeated numerous times since independence, the basic reason being hunger for political power. But, this complex and sensitive situation is adversely affecting the nation. The need of the hour is to synergize the Centre – State strategies and doctrines to deal with different aspects of internal security. These could cover the law and order-related reforms, better coordination as well as the broad-based domains of national and state policies like accelerated economic development and social justice, security and media policies in affected areas. The States, in collaboration with the Centre, can create Special Intervention Units to enhance the speed and decisiveness of the Quick Response Teams. The States can also develop specialized commando forces which could be deployed to act as a deterrent to security attacks.

Conclusion

The present essay clearly reflect that internal cohesion and strength bolsters a nations' overall strength, enhances the morale of its citizens and safeguards its national security. No nation can be secured unless its internal security is also ensured. A nation in chaos cannot be secured from external threats, and destabilizing such a country through internal imbalances is more economical and less objectionable. Internal strife and disorder can damage national interests, endanger the lives of citizens, lead to breakdown of law and order, make enforcement of laws difficult & the country more vulnerable to external threats. In such a state, society cannot progress smoothly nor can citizens feel secured.

In the light of various facts and instances, which have embarked upon the current scenario of internal security in India, it can prudently be concluded that if the proposed suggestions could not be implemented by the Government in time, "The nation will face serious security threats from inside the country".

THE HISTORY OF KASHMIRI JIHAD

More than half a century after Partition, the vexed Kashmir issue continues to fester, threatening to plunge India and Pakistan into the throes of nuclear war. Meanwhile, an estimated 80,000 Kashmiris have lost their lives in the on-going civil war in the area, leaving thousands more raped, orphaned and permanently maimed for life. Religion plays a central role in defining the very way in which the Kashmir issue is seen, by the Kashmiris themselves, and by both India and Pakistan. As a Muslim majority state, albeit with a significant Hindu minority, Pakistan insists that the very logic of the 'two-nation' theory on which it is founded demands that Kashmir should be a part of it. India, on the other hand, claims that the Kashmiris had thrown in their lot with it in 1947, thus forcefully challenging the legitimacy of the theory of Hindus and Muslims being two separate and antagonistic nations. For many

Kashmiri themselves, religion per se is not at the root of the problem, which is seen as essentially political, a quest for self-determination of their own political future. A considerable section of the Kashmiris themselves would seem to support the idea of an independent Kashmir. Indeed, the Kashmiri nationalists who launched the militant struggle in the region in the late 1980s aimed at setting up a sovereign, democratic state, with equal rights for all its citizens, irrespective of religion. From the early 1990s, however, owing particularly to growing Pakistani involvement, Islam emerged as a central issue defining the way in which the Kashmiri struggle came to be framed. For a new breed of Islamist militants, their struggle against India was seen as an Islamic jihad, fired by an irrepressible zeal against the 'enemies' of the faith. This so-called jihad is now being sought to be taken further into India, with attacks by Islamist suicide squads on temples, government buildings and other sensitive locations in various parts of the country.

Muslim militancy in Kashmir and Hindu militancy in India feed on each other, with Hindu chauvinist outfits portraying the conflict in Kashmir as a defence of the indivisible 'Hindu' motherland from marauding Islamic hordes. The events in Kashmir have led to a complete breakdown of inter-faith relations in the state of Jammu and Kashmir, with most of the Hindus of the Kashmir valley having fled their homes, and scores of Hindus and Muslims having lost their lives in internecine violence. Elsewhere in India, the Kashmir imbroglio has contributed to a general heightening of Hindu-Muslim strife and conflict, as well as a rapid deterioration of relations between India and Pakistan, setting off fears of a nuclear catastrophe in the region.

This article looks at how the terms of discourse of the Kashmiri struggle have been transformed over time, and how the secular, nationalist Kashmiri movement has been overtaken by radical Islamists pursuing a very different political project, as represented by the Jama'at-i Islami of Jammu and Kashmir and the Lashkar-i Tayyeba. It focuses, in particular, with the issue of how Islam has been understood by Islamists to legitimize their involvement in the current struggle in the region as a jihad, looking at what this means for relations between Kashmiri Muslims and the Kashmiri Hindus and for the ways in which the former are expected to relate to the Indian state. It seeks to grapple with the crucial question of the shifting identities of the Kashmiri Muslims, faced with the might of the Indian state, increasingly defined by an aggressively militant Hindu agenda, on the one hand, and with the increasing salience of Islamist organizations, on the other.

Roots of Revolt

The early Kashmiri independence movement, whose roots go back to the uprising against the Hindu Dogra regime in the 1930s, saw itself principally as a nationalist struggle. From the 1930s till 1947, the Kashmiri movement, under the charismatic Shaikh Muhammad 'Abdullah, aimed at challenging the autocratic rule of the Dogras, demanding proper representation for the Kashmiri Muslims in the administration of the state. In 1947, most of Kashmir came under Indian rule, and from then onwards, a sizeable section of the Muslims of Kashmir carried on, largely through peaceful agitation, a movement for the establishment of an independent state. As 'Abdullah's charisma's gradually declined, with the failure of his National Conference to meet the aspirations of the people and to preserve the autonomy of Kashmir, a new breed of Kashmiri nationalists emerged, disillusioned with what they saw as 'Abdullah's complicity with the Indian state. The leadership of the movement was provided by young Kashmiri Muslims who had received a modern education in the colleges that began to be set up in the region after 1947. Their principal demand was that India should fulfil its commitments to the United Nations and allow a plebiscite to be held in the territory to enable the people to decide their own political future. Challenging the legitimacy of Indian rule, these Kashmiri nationalists advocated an independent, secular democratic Jammu and Kashmir. The ideology informing their nationalist project was that of Kashmiriyat or 'Kashmiri identity', which they saw as a unique amalgam of traditions drawing upon local Muslim, Hindu and other sources. The Kashmiri nationalist project was spearheaded by several organizations and parties, the foremost being the JKLF, established in 1964. The JKLF demanded that the state of Jammu and Kashmir as it existed prior to 1947 be united as 'one fully independent and truly democratic State'. It advocated 'equal political, economic, religious and social rights' for all citizens in the proposed state, 'irrespective of race, religion, region, culture and sex'.

Parallel to the rise of the Kashmiri nationalists, Kashmir in the late 1930s also witnessed the emergence of an Islamist movement. The roots of the Islamist emergence can be traced to the reformist efforts of the Ahl-i Hadith ('People of the Prophetic Tradition'), established in Kashmir in 1925. The Ahl-i Hadith saw themselves as inheritors of the legacy of the Prophet and his Companions, crusading against popular Sufism, the dominant form of Islamic expression in Kashmir, branding it as un-Islamic. Given the deep-rootedness of the Sufi tradition in Kashmir, the Ahl-i Hadith singularly failed to develop a mass following. Rather, it remained, as it does even today, a largely elitist phenomenon, with its core support base among a limited section of the urban middle classes. Ahl-i Hadith-style reformism did, however, provide fertile ground for the emergence of other Islamist trends from the 1930s onwards. Islamism in Kashmir found its most vocal champion in the Jama'at-i Islami, established in 1941 by Sayyed Abul 'Ala Maududi, and organised as an independent organisation and political party in Kashmir in 1952.

The Jama'at-i Islami of Jammu Kashmir (JIJK) remained, at least at the political level, a marginal force in Kashmir till the 1980s, but with the launching of the armed struggle in 1989 it came to play a central role in Kashmiri politics. It forcefully sought to present the armed struggle as a jihad between Islam and disbelief (kufr), thereby challenging the Kashmiri nationalists' definition of the struggle as one between the Kashmiri nation and the Indian state. The Jama'at sees the struggle as a war between Muslims and the 'enemies' of the faith, and is bitterly critical of the notion of a separate Kashmiri national identity. Rather, it insists that the Kashmiris are simply a part of the worldwide Muslim ummah, not a nation by themselves, for, according to it, Islam and nationalism are incompatible with each other. Hence, it argues, the mission of the Kashmiri struggle is not to set up an independent state, which is what the nationalists' project is all about, but, rather, to make Kashmir a part of Muslim Pakistan.

The JIJK's efforts at restructuring the framework of discourse within which the Kashmiri struggle sought to express itself has, from the early 1990s, been given further impetus by the growing intervention in Kashmir of Islamist groups based in Pakistan. These groups tend to see the Kashmiri struggle not simply as a jihad between the Muslims of Kashmir and the Indian state, but in far wider terms: as a 'holy war' between the Muslims of the world, on the one hand, and the Hindus as an entire community, in league with other 'disbelieving' 'enemies of Islam', on the other. In this grand battle, all national and geographical barriers are completely demolished—all Muslims, wherever they may be, are seen as being responsible for contributing in some way or the other in this jihad. On the other hand, Hindus are seen as complicit in the oppression of the Kashmiri Muslims, and hence, considered as enemies. Interestingly, the Hindus are regarded as being hand in glove with other 'enemies' of the Muslim ummah—the Jews and the Christian West—against whom, too, a jihad needs to be waged.

The JIJK and the Kashmiri Jihad

The JIJK was established as an independent organization in 1952, although from the late 1930s a growing number of Kashmiri Muslims had come under the influence of the founder of the Jama'at, Maulana Maududi, principally through his powerful writings. The JIJK presented itself as committed to establishing an Islamic state in Kashmir based on the shari'ah, but using democratic means of peaceful persuasion for attaining its goals. This was stressed in its Constitution, adopted in 1953. Article 2 [b] of its Constitution states that, The Jama'at shall not employ ways and means against ethics, truthfulness and honesty or which may contribute to strife on earth.

Article 2 [c] of its Constitution lays down that the Jama'at shall use democratic and constitutional methods, while working for the reform and righteous revolution. Till the late 1960s, the JIJK sought to cultivate a constituency for itself through publishing and distributing literature, establishing reading rooms and discussion groups, setting up a network of schools all over the state, and through public lectures. In 1969, for the first time, the JIJK decided to enter the electoral fray, by sponsoring a number of candidates for the local level (panchayati) elections which were held on a non-party basis. Apparently, it was felt that by remaining outside the sphere of electoral politics it was being rendered increasingly ineffective. It was thought, therefore, that elections were 'the best platform to popularize the message of the movement'. Later, the JIJK went on to participate in successive provincial as well as general elections as an independent political party. It failed, however, to win an impressive number of seats in any election, owing both to widespread rigging engineered by the Indian authorities as well as a definite lack of enthusiasm for the JIJK's agenda on the part of the electorate.

The last time that the JIJK participated in the electoral field was in the 1987 elections, as part of the eleven-party alliance, the Muslim Muttahida Mahaz (Muslim United Front or MUF), a group of several Kashmiri parties championing the right to political self-determination of the Kashmiri people. It was widely expected that the MUF would do well in the elections and might even be able to win a majority. However, these elections, like all the others previously held in Kashmir, were marked by massive rigging by the Indian authorities, as a result of which only four MUF candidates were officially declared elected. The election results met with an upsurge of rage and opposition, with mass demonstrations being held against the Indian state for subverting the democratic process. Then, in 1988, having tired of the democratic path of seeking to win the right to self-determination, an armed struggle for the liberation of Kashmir from Indian rule was launched. On 31 July 1989, two massive bomb blasts in the heart of Srinagar, the capital of the state, heralded the launching of the armed struggle. The JKLF claimed responsibility for the act.

The armed struggle launched by the JKLF for the independence of Kashmir found mass support among the Kashmiri Muslims, disillusioned as they were with Indian rule and with the subversion of democratic institutions in Kashmir. The MUF initially hesitated in joining the armed struggle, directing its four representatives within the state assembly, including Sayyed 'Ali Gilani, chief ideologue of the JIJK, to retain their seats so as to be able to air the grievances of the people. However, the rising tide of the JKLF-led struggle soon proved too much for the MUF high command to ignore, and in 1989, it instructed its members in the state assembly to resign and to join the struggle. The JIJK now decided to fully immerse itself in the militant movement, and in 1990 it set up its own militant wing, the Hizb ul-Mujahidin ('The Army of the Holy Warriors', HM).

Given the JKLF's immense popularity among the Kashmiri Muslims, and the mass support for its goal of an independent, democratic and secular Jammu and Kashmir, the JIJK and the HM had to struggle against great odds in putting forward their own agenda of making Kashmir part of Pakistan and establishing an Islamic state in the region. One of the major hurdles that the JIJK had to face in expanding its base beyond a narrow circle of middle class sympathizers was its perceived attitude towards popular Sufi traditions. The JIJK, rooted as it was in a fierce opposition to popular Sufism, was seen by many Kashmiris as opposed to the Sufi saints as such, whom they held in great respect, and despite its efforts to convince people that this was not the case, the JIJK was unable to dispel the notion. Since Sufism is still a dominant form of Islamic expression in Kashmir, this was seen by many as hostility towards Islam itself. Making the JIJK's project more difficult for itself was the fact that although most Kashmiri Muslims were certainly disillusioned with India, it is unlikely that a majority of them would have preferred to join Pakistan instead or to be ruled under a strict Islamist regime, as the JIJK and the HM advocated. To make matters even more difficult for the Islamists was the widespread abuses of human rights by the Indian armed forces, resulting in the killings of many Kashmiri Muslims, among whom were several known Islamist activists and sympathizers.

Despite the immense odds that the Islamists had to contend with, from both the Kashmiri nationalists as well as the Indian armed forces, they strove, through publications, mass meetings, public rallies and the work of their activists, to convince the Kashmiris that the solution to the crisis lay in the project that they were advocating, a counter to both Indian rule and demands for independent nationhood. In this manner, a shift was sought to be made in the terms within which the liberation struggle was being waged. Islam, not Kashmiriyat, and accession to Pakistan, not an independent Kashmir, were presented as the solutions to the Kashmir problem.

Such arguments now began to exercise a broader appeal, especially with the rise of militant anti-Muslim Hindu groups in India, and the subsequent large-scale killings of Muslims in the wake of the destruction of the Babri mosque in 1992. Indeed, the growing popularity of the Islamists in Kashmir and the consequent marginalization of the Kashmiri nationalists has much to do with the rapid spread of the radical Hindu Right in India.

The very real dangers that the rise of Hindutva posed to Muslim lives and identity in India, and to the Muslims of Kashmir as well, made the argument more convincing that the struggle being waged in Kashmir was one between kufr and Islam.

The Islamist reworking of the discursive framework in which the Kashmiri struggle has sought to express itself is well illustrated in the case of the writings of Sayyed 'Ali Shah Gilani.

Gilani has held many top positions in the JIJK, and was for long the chief political spokesman of the party, besides holding the post of chairman of the All-Parties' Hurriyat Conference, an alliance of thirty-four Kashmiri Muslim parties and organizations fighting for Kashmir's freedom from Indian control. He is one of the most senior present-day Kashmiri political leaders and also has the distinction of being the most prolific writer among them all.

Gilani's major writings all date to the 1990s, a period when the JIJK had already immersed itself in the armed struggle, in which Gilani himself played a key role, and for which he was forced to spend several years in various jails.

Not surprisingly, Gilani's writings focus almost solely on the issue of Kashmir's freedom from Indian control. He devotes little attention in his writings to Islamic law, theology and doctrines, for being an ideologue of the JIJK, he takes Maududi's voluminous writings on these subjects as authoritative. Gilani's concern is to place the Kashmiri struggle within the Islamist discursive framework. Thus, the struggle is depicted as a jihad, the goal of which is the merger of Kashmir with Pakistan and the establishing of an Islamic state in the region. As we shall see, however, Gilani's understanding of the struggle differs at some crucial points with the views of the Pakistan-based jihadist outfits, being considerably less radical and uncompromising, at least in some crucial aspects.

Three features are of particular importance in Gilani's description of what he calls the Kashmiri jihad. Firstly, the jihad is seen as directed against the Indian state and its agents, and not against Hindus or Indians as such. Secondly, the jihad has the limited goal of freeing Kashmir from Indian control. Thirdly, the mujihadin have no intention of intervening in Indian internal affairs after the liberation of Kashmir. Once the Kashmir issue is solved by freeing the territory from Indian control and merging it with Pakistan, India and Pakistan, Gilani writes, will be able to establish peaceful and cordial relations with each other, for the root cause of the tensions between the two countries is the dispute over the issue of Kashmir.

Gilani sees the armed struggle being waged in Kashmir not as a war of national liberation, but as a jihad between Islam, on the one hand, and the forces of kufr or disbelief, on the other. He argues that a combination of various developments—India's denial to the Kashmiris of their right to self-determination, its brutal suppression of the Kashmiri struggle which has resulted in the deaths of many thousand Kashmiris, and the rapid rise in India of anti-Muslim Hindu chauvinism—have necessitated the launching of a jihad against India.

He writes that the Indian state has, by its actions, 'proved its extreme hostility towards the religious and moral sensibilities [of the Muslims] and the tenets of Islam'. 'Wherever and whenever the laws of Islam are held out for insult and the religious rights [of the Muslims] are trampled upon', he declares, 'jihad becomes a binding obligation (farz) for all Muslims'.

Such a situation, he says, prevails in Kashmir, and hence the need for a jihad to be waged there. This jihad, he stresses, calls for the participation of all Muslims, not just Kashmiris alone. In a telephonic interview in 1992 with a Lahore-based journalist soon after his release from a long spell in prison, Gilani declared: It has now become incumbent, in the light of the teachings of the Holy Qur'an, upon all the people of Pakistan to participate in the [Kashmir] jihad. They should now stand up determinedly and assist their Kashmiri brethren in the practical jihad. This jihad is a religious duty binding not only on the people of Pakistan, but, in fact, on the entire Muslim ummah [...] The extreme oppression that the Kashmiri Muslims are having to face is an open challenge for the entire Muslim ummah. All Muslims must now move ahead, help the oppressed Muslims [of Kashmir] and stop the hands of the oppressors.

While declaring the armed struggle a jihad, Gilani makes it clear, however, that the armed struggle is directed against the Indian state and not against Hindus or Indian citizens per se.

He makes a clear distinction between the Indian state, on the one hand, and ordinary Indians and Hindus, on the other. Thus, in an appeal to the Kashmiri militants in April 1992 Gilani asserted that, 'The mujahidin have just two enemies: the Indian state and its agents. To waste the power of our youth on targets other than these two is like pouring salt on the wounds of our oppressed people'.

Gilani has, on numerous occasions, appealed for communal harmony between Hindus and Muslims in Kashmir. He stresses that Hindu-Muslim relations in the state have traditionally always been cordial, and that in the past the Valley has never known the wild bloodletting between Hindus and Muslims that has erupted periodically, and now on a menacingly increasing scale, in India. Defending the armed struggle from charges of being anti-Hindu, he asserts that the mass exodus of the Kashmiri Pandits in the early 1990s was actually instigated by the Indian authorities in order to project the Kashmiri struggle as an 'Islamic terrorist' movement, so as to discredit it in the eyes of the West.

Gilani has issued several appeals to the Kashmiri Pandits who have fled from their homes to return and join their Muslim brethren in the struggle. He has also warned the mujahidin that they should desist from any actions 'which will give their opponents a chance to brand them as terrorists'.

Gilani's opposition to the Indian state is limited insofar as his prime objective is to liberate Kashmir from Indian control. The jihad against India, in other words, is circumscribed by the limited objective of freeing Kashmir from Indian rule. Thus, he asserts that after Kashmir is freed from Indian occupation, the JIJK would 'like to see India as free, prosperous and peaceful'. Criticizing certain un-named Kashmiri militant groups for spreading anti-India hatred, he says:

Emotional slogans such as 'Crush India!' are neither realistic nor do they reflect the spirit of Islam. At root, Islam is based on invitation to prosperity, witness to the truth, salvation in the Hereafter, protection of the truth, the ending of every form of oppression and creating understanding between all children of Adam. This, indeed, is the message of the life of the Prophet Muhammad (may peace be upon him). Even when the people of Ta'if unleashed a wave of unlimited oppression on the Prophet of Islam (may peace be upon him), he did not pray to God that they should be destroyed but, rather, that He should guide them [to the right path]. This is why I believe our struggle should be geared only to gaining our rights [...] The slogan of Islam is not one of destruction but of invitation [to the Truth], prosperity, peace and truth.

The legitimacy of the category of the 'Kashmiri nation' that forms the subject of Kashmiri nationalist discourse is vehemently denied by Gilani, this being a logical outcome of his own Islamist position that sees Islam and nationalism as being in complete contradiction to each other.

Here, of course, Gilani seeks to question the very basis of the political agenda of the major rivals of the JIJK, the various Kashmiri nationalist groups such as the JKLF. Gilani argues that nationalism is a 'poisonous philosophy' which the 'enemies of Islam', foremost being 'various Western philosophies', have deliberately sought to infect Muslims with so as to divide and weaken them so that they can be kept under their control.

He insists that the Muslim world-wide ummah is one, monolithic ideological community, cemented together on the basis of 'common belief and faith', which sees no differences of colour, race, language, caste, tribe or family.

He asserts that 'whenever Muslims have ignored the principles of Islam, which sees no boundaries of region, they have lost their power and have become like any other community'. Territorial nationalism, he writes, has proved to be the bane of the Muslims, for it has divided them into different states and, thereby, has deflected them from the task of 'changing the conditions of the entire human race'.

Islam, says Gilani, makes a clear distinction between 'love for their country' (watan dosti), which it allows, and territorial nationalism or 'nation worship' (watan parasti), which it clearly forbids.

'Nation worship', based on the principle of 'my nation, right or wrong', Gilani writes, leads to group prejudice, a quality of the period of the pre-Islamic period of jahiliya, an age of utter darkness. He lays much of the blame for strife, war and bloodshed that characterizes the world today on territorial nationalism. 'Nationalism is the slogan of the jahiliya', he argues, because the nation has usurped from Islam the 'right to decide the criterion for what is right and what is wrong'.

Because of this, large states, such as India, prey on smaller, weaker states, causing endless suffering and misery, 'with millions of people being sacrificed at the altar of nationalism'—in the Kashmiri case, 'at the hands of the priests of Mother India'. However, he asserts, by denying the narrow boundaries that 'nation worship' has inscribed, Islam has 'destroyed into smithereens the idol of nationalism until the Day of Resurrection'.

All Muslims being considered as one nation, Muslims and Hindus in India, and Kashmir as well, are considered to be members of two different nations despite living in the same territory. This, Gilani says, is 'an undeniable truth' (na qabil-i tardid haqiqat).

He writes, conveniently glossing over the remarkable degree to which Muslims in India and Kashmir share a common culture with the Hindus, that not just in matters of faith, beliefs and customs do the two differ, but that they are also distinct and sharply set apart from each other in such matters as food, clothing and lifestyles. For Muslims to stay among Hindus or in an environment which is very different from their own is said to be as difficult as it is 'for a fish to stay alive in a desert'. Muslims, he says, cannot live harmoniously with a Hindu majority without their own religion and traditions coming under a grave threat, one major factor being Hinduism's capacity to absorb other religions and communities into its fold. Hence, for Islam to be preserved and promoted in Kashmir, he insists, it is necessary for Kashmir to be separated from India. Curiously enough, he is silent on the fate of the over 150 million Muslims living in the rest of India.

If all Muslims form one nation and nationalism is antithetical to Islam, then, Gilani implicitly argues, the Kashmiri nationalist project of groups such as the JKLF is itself 'un-Islamic'. From this it follows that the 'Islamic' solution to the Kashmir question is not the establishment of an independent Kashmiri nation-state but, rather, the incorporation of Kashmir into an already-existing existing Muslim state, Pakistan. This is seen as the first step towards the eventual unity of all Muslims. In a pamphlet titled Masla Ka Hal ('The Solution to the Problem'), issued in 1992, Gilani expressed this view thus:

To advocate that one Muslim group (qaum) be kept apart from the rest would be against the very definition of a people (millat), whose communal identity is based only on one pure creed (kalima tayyiba), especially so when that group shares common ideological, cultural and communal relations with a neighbouring [Muslim] group as well as a common border [...] For such a group to maintain a separate political identity of its own is against the broader interests of the entire Muslim millat.

The JIJK has, in fact, been among the most vocal champions of the merger of Jammu and Kashmir with Pakistan. In a letter to Nawaz Sharif, the then Prime Minister of Pakistan, in June 1993, Gilani commented that in Kashmir the JIJK and the HM 'were the most reliable groups supporting the ideology of Pakistan', and declared that the final goal of the JIJK was Kashmir's accession to that country. In the Kashmir jihad, therefore, the Pakistanis state is seen as having a central role to play, in addition, of course, to the Pakistani people, who are asked to assist the jihad. Thus, in his letter Gilani appealed to the Pakistani Prime Minister for further assistance, but bitterly criticized Pakistan's alleged policy of 'taking everyone together', by which he meant Pakistani support for Kashmiri nationalist groups, in addition to the Islamists. Gilani complained that such a policy was not only 'un-Islamic'; it also is against the very interests of Pakistan itself. He labeled the nationalists as 'enemies of the jihad', and foes of Pakistan, and cautioned that assistance to such groups as advocate secular nationalism posed a grave threat 'to Pakistan's stability and existence'.

Bibliography

Ahmad, R.S. : *Al-Harakat Al-Islamiyya.* Cairo: Sina Linasr. Allport, G. 1958.

Allana, G.: *Pakistan Movement: Historic Documents,* Karachi, Department of International Relations, University of Karachi, 1967.

Allison, Graham: *Nuclear Terrorism: The Ultimate Preventable Catastrophe,* New York: Times Books, 2004.

Arif. S.M.: *Islamic Fundamentalism and Jihad,* MD Pub, Delhi, 2010.

Ayesha Siddiqa-Agha: *Military Inc.: Inside Pakistan's Military Economy,* London: Pluto, 2007.

Daniel Pipes : *In the Path of God: Islam and Political Power,* New York: Basic Books Inc., 1983.

Das. P.K.: *Jihad : Terrorist Strategies Against the West,* Sumit Enterprises, Delhi, 2009.

Dekmejian, R. Hrair : *Islamic Revolution: Fundamentalism in the Arab World* Syracuse, New York: Syracuse University Press, 1995.

Dilip H. Mohite : *Rise of Islamic Fundamentalism and the Grand American Strategy* : Kalinga, Delhi, 2002.

Fox, Lisa L. : *Management Strategies for Disaster Preparedness,* Chicago, American Library Association, 1989.

Gupta, J.B. Das : *Islamic Fundamentalism and India* : Hope India Publications, Delhi, 2002.

Hasan Askari Rizvi: *Military, State, and Society in Pakistan,* New York: St. Martin's Press, 2000.

Hassan, Lt Gen Gul, *Memoirs of Lt Gen Gul Hassan,* Oxford University Press, 1993.

Hiro, Dilip : *Holy Wars: The Rise of Islamic Fundamentalism* New York: Routledge, Chapman and Hall, Inc., 1989.

Hoffman, Bruce, *Inside Terrorism,* New York: Columbia University Press, 1998.

John O. Voll : *Islam: Continuity and Change in the Modern World,* Syracuse, New York: Syracuse University Press, 1994.

Khan, Major General Sher Ali: *The Story of Soldiering and Politics in India and Pakistan,* Wajidalis, 1978.

Kusum Lata Chadda: *Islamic Fundamentalism, Pakistan and the Muslim World* : Kanishka, Delhi, 2009.

Laquer, Walter, *The New Terrorism: Fanaticism and the Arms of Mass Destruction,* Oxford: Oxford University Press, 1999.

Multani, R K P : *Islamic Fundamentalism in South Asia* : Sumit Enterprises, Delhi, 2007.

Noorani, A.G.: *Islam and Jihad,* Leftword, Delhi, 2002.

Riedel, Bruce: *Deadly Embrace : Pakistan America and the Future of the Global Jihad,* HarperCollins, Delhi, 2011.

Rizvi, Hassan Askari: *The Military and Politics in Pakistan: 1947 - 86,* Progressive Publishers 1986.

Roxanne L. Euben, *Enemy in the Mirror : Islamic Fundamentalism and the Limits of Modern Rationalism : A Work of Comparative Political Theory* : Oxford University Press, 2001.

Shahid Javed: *Pakistan: The Continuing Search for Nationhood,* Westview Press, 1991.

Sharma, Rajeev: *Global Jihad : Current Patterns and Future Trends,* Kaveri Books, Delhi, 2006.

Shuja Nawaz: *Crossed Swords: Pakistan, Its Army, and the Wars Within,* Karachi: Oxford University Press, 2008.

Stephen P. Cohen: *The Idea of Pakistan,* Washington, DC: Brookings Institution Press, 2004.

Thomas Arnold: *The Spread of Islam in the World, A History of Peaceful Preaching,* Goodword Books, 2001.

Thomas R. Metcalf : *A Concise History of India and Pakistan,* New York: Cambridge University Press, 2002).

William R. Thompson: *The Grievances of Military Coup-makers,* Beverly Hills: Sage Publications, 1973.

Index

A

Al-Qaeda, 41, 42, 43, 44, 45, 46, 47, 48, 49, 115, 116, 129, 140, 141, 153, 155, 156, 199, 201, 203, 206, 207, 208, 209, 211, 219, 253, 277, 283, 284, 286, 287, 288, 289, 291, 292.
Allegations, 113.

C

Counter Terrorism, 64, 278.
Counter Violent Extremism, 152.

D

Domestic Jihadists, 99, 101, 267.

G

Global Threat, 118, 119, 120, 144.
Global Venture, 152, 154, 155.
Global War, 54, 55, 60.
Government Machinery, 74, 273.

H

Hadith, 10, 20, 113, 123, 125, 131, 187, 188, 192, 264, 282.

I

Inter-Services Intelligence, 54, 68, 100, 197, 203, 206, 208, 209, 217, 236, 254, 269.
Internal Security, 59, 76, 205, 243, 272, 275, 276, 277, 278, 279.
Investigation, 5, 10, 12, 13, 26, 30, 49, 64, 66, 79, 108, 109, 111, 112, 208, 216, 253, 259, 266, 269.
Islam, 2, 3, 4, 14, 19, 20, 21, 68, 88, 90, 91, 92, 94, 113, 116, 120, 121, 122, 123, 124, 126, 127, 128, 129, 130, 131, 132, 135, 136, 137, 138, 139, 142, 144, 145, 147, 148, 149, 150, 151, 153, 154, 175, 179, 181, 185, 186, 187, 188, 189, 190, 191, 192, 193, 194, 195, 214, 237, 240, 242, 243, 244, 245, 246, 247, 255, 265, 267, 270, 280, 282, 285, 286, 287, 289, 290, 291.
Islamic Doctrine, 187.
Islamic Terror Networks, 205.

J

Jehadi Terrorism, 76, 78.
Jihadi Threat, 67.
Jihadi Tradition, 256.

K

Kashmiri Jihad, 279, 283.

L

Lashkar-e-Taiba, 67, 72, 106, 200, 251, 253, 255, 257, 258.
Leadership, 3, 14, 20, 27, 30, 33, 35, 47, 62, 67, 68, 71, 76, 81, 83, 87, 94, 98, 100, 101, 102, 115, 138, 155, 160, 168, 169, 192, 213, 263, 278, 288, 291, 292.

M

Mumbai Attacks, 13, 72, 257, 258.

N

National Security, 25, 27, 32, 58, 63, 81, 82, 83, 118, 201, 213, 237, 271, 272, 276, 277, 279.
Naxalite Insurgency, 272.

O

Organisation, 2, 3, 4, 6, 10, 12, 14, 21, 23, 106, 113, 116, 174, 175, 177, 178, 179, 213, 215, 216, 257, 267, 282.

P

Policy, 41, 44, 45, 61, 63, 80, 81, 82, 83, 86, 87, 96, 97, 105, 109, 118, 119, 142, 158, 162, 165, 178, 193, 207, 228, 237, 244, 245, 254, 283, 292.
Political Polarization, 275.
Press Confusion, 107.

S

Security, 1, 2, 10, 11, 25, 27, 30, 32, 51, 54, 58, 59, 63, 66, 67, 75, 76, 78, 81, 82, 83, 85, 87, 96, 98, 107, 110, 113, 116, 118, 119, 120, 146, 149, 151, 152, 200, 201, 202, 205, 207, 213, 224, 226, 237, 243, 260, 265, 268, 270, 271, 272, 273, 275, 276, 277, 278, 279.
Sharia, 104, 113, 130, 131, 132, 139, 187, 193, 195, 196, 240, 243, 244, 263, 265.
Sphere of Influence, 116.
Students Islamic Movement of India, 2, 3, 49, 67, 68, 91, 98, 106, 203, 208, 213, 216, 217, 253, 267.

T

Terror Incidents, 6.
Terror Networks, 205.
Terror Tentacles, 69.
Terrorist Group, 17, 47, 51, 67, 79, 207.
Terrorist Groups, 29, 41, 43, 44, 55, 56, 58, 61, 63, 68, 75, 204, 206, 217, 219, 260, 289.
Transnational Islamism, 179.

❑❑❑